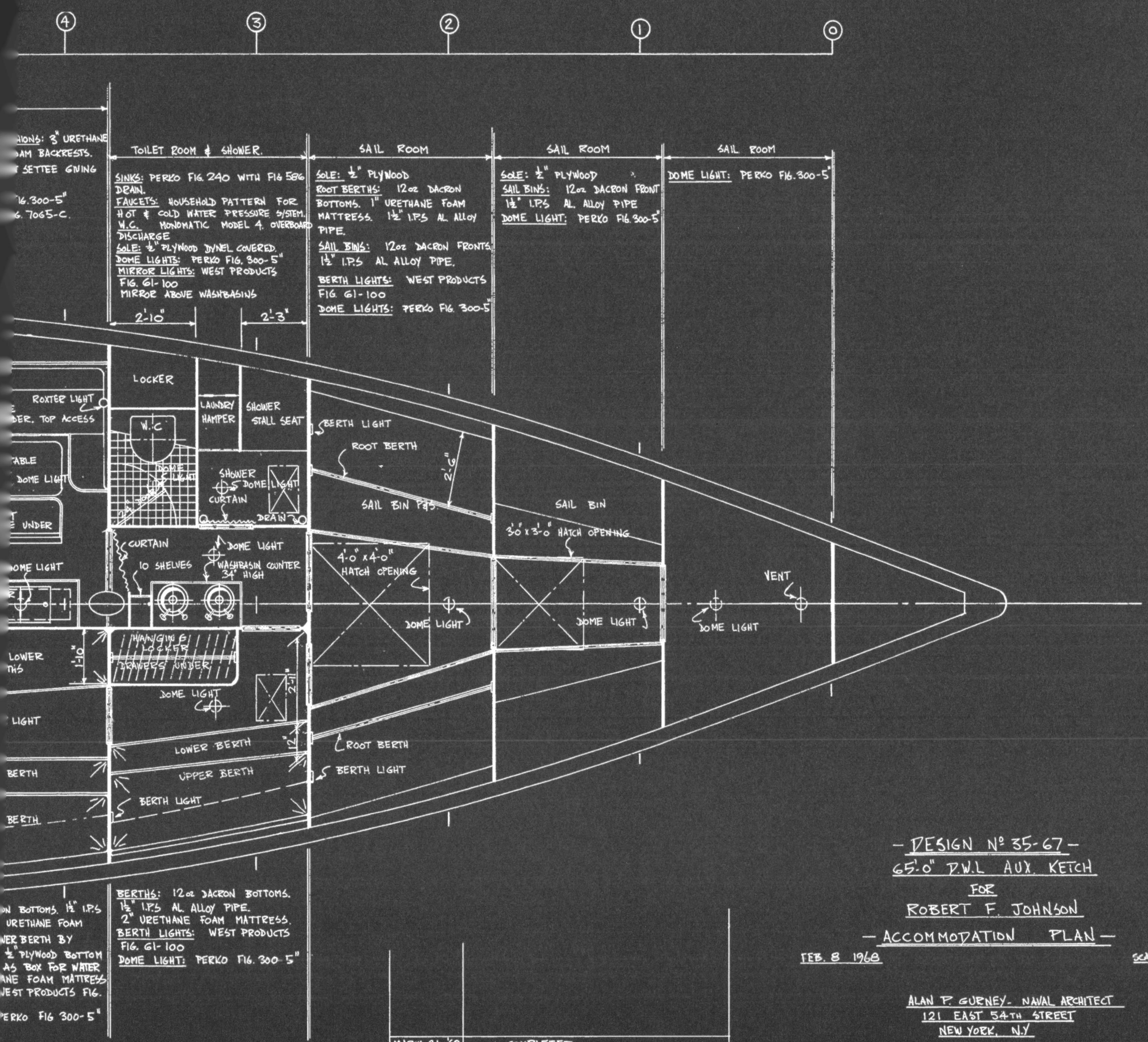

– DESIGN Nº 35-67 –
65'-0" D.W.L AUX. KETCH
FOR
ROBERT F. JOHNSON
– ACCOMMODATION PLAN –

FEB. 8 1968 SCALE: ½" = 1'-0"

ALAN P. GURNEY - NAVAL ARCHITECT
121 EAST 54TH STREET
NEW YORK, N.Y

DATE	ISSUE DATA & REVISIONS
MARCH 21 '68	COMPLETED
FEB. 8 '68	FIRST INCOMPLETE ISSUE

DWG. Nº 7A-35

WINDWARD PASSAGE

WINDWARD PASSAGE

A MAXI YACHT IN HER SIXTH DECADE

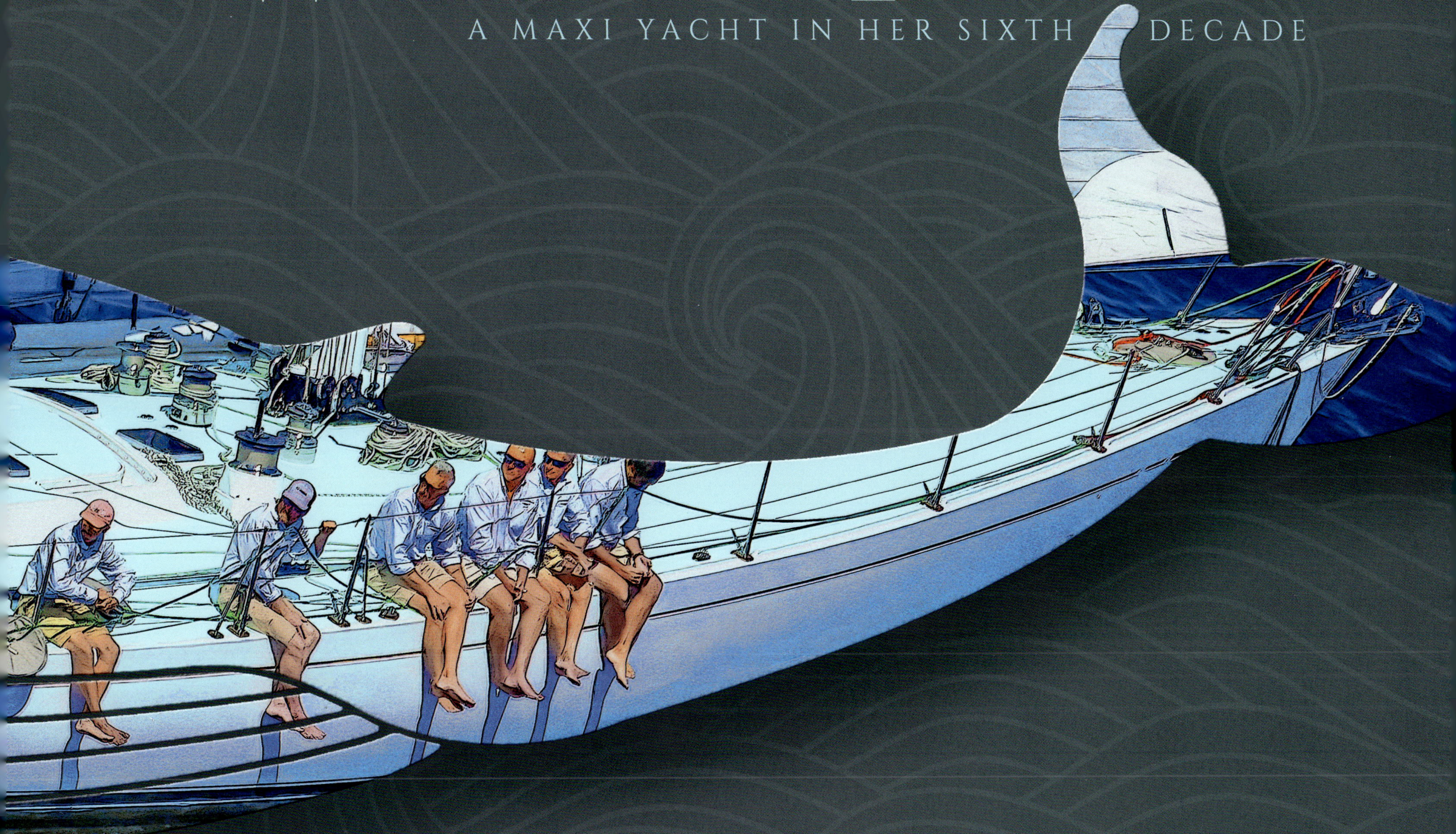

RANDALL PEFFER TEXT
STEVE JOST PHOTOGRAPHY
RONALD GEISMAN DESIGN

WoodenBoat

Contemporary photography is by photographer Steve Jost.
Photo-illustration is by designer Ronald Geisman.

Printed in Italy | Verona Libri

ISBN 978-1-934-98226-6

Windward Passage *off Newport Beach, California, 2021*

Table of Contents

Introduction

MATTHEW P. MURPHY

CHIEF CONTENT OFFICER, *WOODENBOAT* MAGAZINE

The May/June 2021 issue of *WoodenBoat* magazine (No. 280) carried an article by Randall "Randy" Peffer on the legendary maxi yacht *Windward Passage.* That story, delivered in just 4,000 words, was as vivid as the image that graced the issue's cover. That photograph, shot by Australian Richard Bennett, shows "*Passage*," as she is affectionately known to her crews and fans, trucking downwind propelled by a spinnaker and blooper. Elements of the scene—the obsolete blooper, sartorial nuances, the cut and construction of the mainsail—suggest that it took place some time ago. It was stunning nonetheless to realize that nearly a half century has passed since that moment, which shows *Passage* at the start of the 1975 Sydney Hobart Race.

The cover struck a nerve. As any editor does, I had wondered, even worried, about how the readership would receive that cover. Would they find it dated? Would the image quality meet today's standards? I need not have fretted. The response to the image was superlative, in the truest sense of the word. "Best cover, ever!" said at least a few readers. In addition to that cover, we were treated, in the article itself, to a visual feast in which the brilliant veteran yachting photographer Steve Jost shared some of his photographs of *Passage*.

Steve, it turns, out, was just getting started with his coverage of *Passage*—as was Randy. This duo, over the years, have been something of a writer-photographer dream team for *WoodenBoat*, working together on several southern California topics. If I do say so myself, Randy's article for *WoodenBoat* was magnificent—poetic in its distillation of a story that warranted a book-length telling. And Steve's photographs likewise represented the boat in its post-refit glory. But he had not yet had the opportunity to chase her in a variety of wind condition, and from a number of angles.

The opportunity for Steve and Randy to collaborate on a book about *Windward Passage* arrived soon after publication of the *WoodenBoat* article, and they applied their respective and considerable talents to the project for many months to follow. The result of that effort, which you hold in your hands, is a comprehensive, Technicolor treatment, elegantly rendered by designer Ron Geisman, of the unlikely conception, construction, and career—and ongoing stewardship—of one of the most influential wooden ocean racers ever to roam the planet.

Matthew P. Murphy
WoodenBoat magazine
Brooklin, Maine

Owner's Acknowledgments

CLIFFORD R. RONNENBERG

There are great boats, and then there are exceptionally great boats. Those are the ones whose names, when mentioned, evoke emotions, images, and memories, conversations filled with amazing stories and enough adventures to fill volumes. *Windward Passage* is one such boat.

My first sailboat, *Alina*, was docked next to the legendary *Windward Passage* for a number of years, and as many do, I also admired her beauty and appreciated her abilities, and historical accomplishments. One day, I was delightfully surprised to receive a phone call that *Windward Passage* was for sale. Without a moment's hesitation, a sale took place, with credit going to Kevin Jaffé and to the brokers at Ardell Yacht Brokerage, for making the process seamless. For over twenty-three years it has been both a great pleasure and honor to be her owner and caretaker.

As you will read, "*Passage*," as she is often referred to, has undergone significant changes, from a purely racing vessel to her life now as a luxury yacht, albeit high-performance. My wife and I have had the opportunity to enjoy making memories with countless friends, our children, grandchildren, and extended family members. Some of our favorite times include being under sail on a brisk, windy day with spray coming up over the bow, or sailing into Santa Catalina Island's Moonstone Cove at sunset. Amazing memories have been made by countless others over the decades. Each adds to the legend that is *Windward Passage*.

It was during one of these glorious sails, about five years ago, that the idea for this book was born. We had recently met and invited Mark and Dotty Johnson and their family aboard for a sail. It seemed the perfect time to do this project, and we could include so many owners and crew that were still living, willing, and able to share their personal stories and so much of her history. This book is meant to be a tribute to Mark's father Bob Johnson, the man who envisioned, created, and carried out his dream to build and race *Windward Passage*. Mark and Dotty have been extremely hospitable and generous with their time, knowledge, and memorabilia.

The production of this book has been a labor of love for everyone involved. There has been an outpouring of encouragement from the sailing community around the world, and an incredibly generous sharing of stories, photos, news, and magazine articles. We are very grateful and want to thank the former owners as well as the former captains and the many wonderful crewmembers.

It takes time, talent, and dedication to produce a book like this, and we greatly appreciate writer Randy Peffer, photographer Steve Jost, and designer Ron Geisman, and the expertise they brought to this project.

For over twenty-eight years, Captain David "Halfdeck" Johnson has had the responsibility and honor of commanding the helm of *Windward Passage*. As captain, he has been instrumental in overseeing her care, improvements, and maintenance over the years. Halfdeck has also been the project manager on this book. He has spearheaded and coordinated meetings, interviews, photography sessions, and collecting and organizing data for this book.

Additionally, I would like to acknowledge and thank my wife Janet for her constant encouragement, support, and her valuable assistance in helping me with this book. We hope that you will enjoy reading about *Windward Passage's* wonderful fifty-plus-year history.

Clifford R. Ronnenberg
Newport Beach, California

From the Captain

For the last twenty-eight years I have had the pleasure of being the curator of one the most significant sailing vessels ever built and under the tutelages of both Kevin Jaffé and Cliff Ronnenberg. Kevin taught me that "perfect" is a term to strive for.

As the project manager on this book, I would personally like to thank the individuals who helped to put this history together. In addition to thanking Randy, Ron, and Steve, I want to acknowledge the other integral members of our core team. Matt Murphy, the Chief Content Officer of *WoodenBoat* magazine, guided us as co-publisher. Jane Crosen was our careful copy editor, proofreader, and indexer. The printing firm of Verona Libri turned our dreams into this elegant volume. I had no idea how to put a book together and learned quite a bit from these professionals.

Thank you to all the people who shared their experiences of building, sailing, and modifying *Passage* to what she is today. A special shout out to Mark and Dotty Johnson for their gracious hosting of Randy and me at their home at the very start of this project. A happenstance meeting several years ago with their niece Kate Murphy Malouf led to meeting the Johnsons and the beginning of our new friendship.

Finally, thank you, Captain Carson Jefferson. Your manual for the boat saved me more than once, especially in the early years.

Please enjoy!

Cheers,
Captain David "Halfdeck" Johnson
Newport Beach, California

US-7099

Career Highlights

St. Petersburg–Venice Race (SORC), first to finish	1969
St. Petersburg–Fort Lauderdale Race (SORC) first to finish, record time	1969
Fort Lauderdale–Palm Beach (SORC), first to finish	1969
Lipton Cup (SORC), first to finish, first in Class A	1969
Miami–Nassau Race, first to finish, first in Class A, record time	1969
Miami–Montego Bay Race, first to finish	1969
Transpac Race, first to finish, record time (penalized after protest)	1969
Long Beach–La Paz Race, first to finish, first in Class A, record time	1969
St. Petersburg–Venice Race (SORC), first to finish	1970
St. Petersburg–Fort Lauderdale Race (SORC), first to finish	1970
Newport Bermuda Race, first to finish	1970
Miami–Montego Bay Race, first to finish, record time	1971
Transpac Race, first to finish, first in Class A first overall, record time	1971
San Francisco Big Boat Series, first place	1971
Cal-Coastal Race, first to finish, first in class	1972
Long Beach Yacht Club match race, first	1972
San Diego–Acapulco Race, first to finish	1972
Transpac, second to finish, beat previous record time	1973
San Francisco Big Boat Series, first place	1973
Southern Cross Series/Sydney Hobart Race second place, beat previous record time	1975
Tasman Sea Race, first to finish	1975
Southern Cross Series/Sydney Hobart Race, second place	1977
Hong Kong to Manila, second place	1978
Swiftsure Race, first to finish, record time	1978
San Francisco Big Boat Series, first place	1978
Pan Am Clipper Cup, first in class	1980
San Francisco Big Boat Series, first place	1980
SORC series, first in class	1982
Pan Am Clipper Cup, first in Molokai Race	1982
SORC series, second in class	1983
Royal Norwegian Yacht Club Centennial Regatta 1983, second in class	1983
SORC series, second in class	1984
Sydney to Mooloolaba, first to finish	1986
Brisbane to Gladstone, first to finish, record time	1986
Gladstone to Hamilton, first to finish	1986
Hamilton Race Week, first place	1986
Kenwood Cup, second place	1986
Southern Cross Series/Sydney Hobart Race first in class, second on elapsed time	1986
Sydney–Newcastle Race, first in class, second on elapsed time first overall, first all-women's maxi racing crew	1989

◀ *Tough beating to windward, Pan Am Clipper Cup, 1982 —©Phil Uhl*

▼ Windward Passage *with her iconic whale resting comfortably in her slip in Newport Beach, California*

D PASSAGE
RT BEACH

Freeport Harbour | Grand Bahama Island

1

The Legend Begins

There was surely a moment on that star-strewn Bahamas night in the late fall of 1968—as *Windward Passage* leaned over with her big jib humming, put her shoulder into the Gulf Stream chop, and started to charge—when her owner, "Big Bob" Johnson, wanted to shout for pure joy, "What a boat!" Every one of the twelve or so young sailors—like John Rumsey, Alistair McIntosh, and Rex Banks—sitting on her windward rail would have joined in.

It was the 73-foot maxi yacht's first real sail. And this felt like a moment of both revelation and vindication. The boat still wasn't much more than a bare hull, a rig, and secondhand sails off the L. Francis Herreshoff ketch *Ticonderoga*. This was the shakedown run. *Windward Passage* was on her way from the Bahamas to Florida to document the boat in the United States and complete her fitting-out at the Spencer Boat Corporation. Very soon she aimed to test her mettle against the fastest and most famous yachts racing in the Southern Ocean Racing Conference (SORC) series.

Up to this sail, she had been little more than a curiosity for the citizens and tourists of Freeport, Grand Bahama Island. In the last nine months Johnson, his thirty-year-old designer Alan Gurney, builder Carl "Chappy" Chapman, and their band of sun-bronzed sailorboys had raised her from a pile of spruce in a lot of crushed coral next to Freeport Harbour. She had been the source of more than a few wry comments about a "beached wooden whale," and "Big Bob's Folly." People who thought they knew something about boats wondered why anyone in this day and age would build a new racing boat out of wood when you could use "modern" materials like fiberglass or aluminum.

But tonight . . . tonight Bob Johnson, Chappy, and their *wunderkind* designer Gurney felt fire in their bones. This boat, built of cold-molded spruce veneers and epoxy like an aircraft wing, was the phantom

◀ *. . . and so it all begins.*

▲ *Bob Johnson took pride in taking his own noon sights. He even wrote a light-hearted book about it.*

each of them had been trying to scratch loose from his psyche all his life. She was a huge surfboard. Under sail, she had the sleek beauty of a fighter jet. And she would be a champion among champions. As Preben Nyeland writes in his book *Maxi: The Ultimate Racing Experience,* "No maxi ever built can match *Windward Passage I* for pure glamour." He would go on to call her (along with her near sister Chay Blyth's *Great Britain II*) one of "the undisputed grandparents of the modern IOR maxis."

"She set a high standard to measure up to," says naval architect Ron Holland who drew some of *Windward Passage*'s fiercest rivals, "I spent ten years trying to design a boat that could beat her." Sometimes.

"She was everybody's favorite," says designer Bill Lee, whose *Merlin* went nose-to-nose with *Windward Passage* in multiple Transpacs, the Swiftsure Race, and the San Francisco's Big Boat Series. "I think it was because of her story. And she is very good-looking."

In his memoir *Stars & Spaghetti* Bob Johnson described himself as a logger, surveyor, sawyer, contractor, aircraft pilot, plywood manufacturer, and amateur tennis champion. But his heart and mind had a special place that nurtured his passion for sailboats. He liked to tell a story about a time in his twenties when he built his first sailboat in a garage in Toledo, Oregon. When he was finished, the boat was too big to fit out the garage door. He had to tear down the garage to get the boat free. It seemed to him a ruined garage was a small price to pay for a dream.

Racing sailboats played a big role in Johnson's dreams. He enjoyed the glory that goes with crossing the finish line first, for sure, but he truly relished the adventure that comes inevitably with offshore racing under sail. By the late 1950s Johnson had already sailed in more than a half-dozen ocean races sponsored by the Transpacific Yacht Club, including multiple Los Angeles-to-Honolulu "Transpacs."

Big Bob had caught racing fever in 1957 when he bought *Groote Beer*. It was a 52-foot Dutch *botter*, which had once been the personal yacht of Hermann Goering, commander-in-chief of the Nazi's *Luftwaffe*. Johnson entered his Third Reich relic into the Los Angeles–Honolulu Transpac. They came in nearly last in a fleet of forty yachts. For the next Transpac two years later, Johnson upped his game. He had the 73-foot, double-ended, Bill Garden–designed *Zia* built. She did better than *Groote Beer* in the 1959 and '61 sprints to Hawaii. But the L. Francis Herreshoff–designed 72-foot ketch *Ticonderoga* (built in 1936) humbled *Zia* and the rest of the fleet.

By the early 1960s Robert F. Johnson was the controlling shareholder of the highly successful Georgia-Pacific lumber behemoth and looking for new challenges. He wanted to set ocean-racing records, and he thought *Ticonderoga* was his ticket to scoring "line honors," like the Transpac's Barn Door Trophy, in major Pacific, Atlantic, Caribbean, and Southern Ocean regattas.

"It was all about being the first boat to finish," says *Passage*'s professional skipper since 1997, Dave "Halfdeck" Johnson.

It didn't take Big Bob long to make a deal to charter the Herreshoff ketch for the '63 Transpac. Exhilarated in mid-race, and with his typically cavalier enthusiasm, he radioed *Ticonderoga*'s owner, offered to buy her "as is, where is." When Johnson and *Ticonderoga* crossed the finish line at Diamond Head, she was first to finish and he was the owner/skipper of record.

Bob Johnson and his oldest son Mark aboard Groote Beer *sailing through the Windward Passage. Bob remarked to Mark, "This is the most beautiful place I have ever seen, and someday we will have a boat that will be worthy of calling it* Windward Passage*."*
—image courtesy of Dotty Johnson

Bob Johnson first won the "First to Finish" trophy with Ticonderoga.
—©Phil Uhl

S.W. BOAT CORP

Once he owned the boat, he flew to Marblehead, Massachusetts, to spend a week with her designer, L. Francis Herreshoff, discussing his plans for lightening the boat. Over the next two years Big Bob spent over $100,000 to reinvigorate the nearly thirty-year-old ketch for the 1965 dash to Hawaii. That year she took home the Barn Door Trophy again and set an elapsed-time record for the race—9 days,13 hours, 51 minutes, 2 seconds. Waterfront wags and the yachting press began calling Big Bob's ketch "Big Ti."

Bob Johnson aboard Ticonderoga

"Big Ti" from an earlier time in for repair in Southwest Harbor, Maine —image by W.H. Ballard, courtesy of Southwest Harbor Public Library

1370

2

A Singular Fantasy

By 1966 Bob Johnson could see Big Ti's 119-ton displacement would be a handicap when racing against a new generation of boats like designer Bill Lapworth's Cal-40s. Sooner or later an ocean racer with unlimited financial resources would build a big boat with the light displacement, fin keel, and spade rudder of the Cal-40 and its cousins.

Among these new racing rockets, Johnson admired *Guinevere*, a 48-foot aluminum yawl. She won the SORC series in 1966 and came from the drafting board of a young Englishman, a former draftsman in the New York office of naval architect Bill Tripp. His name was Alan Gurney.

One night Gurney and Johnson met to discuss sailboat designs over drinks at the New York Yacht Club on 44th Street in Manhattan. Gurney grabbed a cocktail napkin and started sketching on it with a pen. He said he had a concept in mind for a boat design.

Before Gurney could make his pitch, Johnson grabbed a napkin and pen as well and started drawing his own fantasy boat.

"This is what I want, Alan." Big Bob shoved his napkin across the table to Gurney. "I want a boat to break the record in the Transpac." He pictured a ketch the length of *Ticonderoga*, but with only about half of Big Ti's displacement, a modern fin keel, and a spade rudder. Gurney looked at Big Bob's sketch and smiled. His drawing and Big Bob's were nearly twins. By the time the night ended, the men had a deal.

In his eulogy to Gurney in 2012, the yachting writer and boat broker the late Ted Jones, paints a picture of his friend:

> Alan Gurney designed boats the old-fashioned way with drafting pencil on vellum, using splines and ducks (weights), a planimeter, and a seaman's eye. He thought like the water through which he had sailed, in England, transatlantic,

◀ Guinevere—©*Phil Uhl*

Alan Gurney in his design studio in New York City

the USA, both polar regions, and much of what lay in between. As a young lad, he would make boats out of toilet tissue (which at that time had characteristics of waxed paper) and float them in his bath . . . .

The design that emerged from Gurney's basement studio on East 54th Street in Manhattan would introduce a style of ocean racer that would become known as a "maxi" because these large sailing yachts were the maximum length (73 feet) allowed by the Cruising Club of America (CCA), the primary arbiter of ocean racing rules in the late 1960s for events like the Transpac, SORC, and the Newport Bermuda Race.

"I have always admired *Windward Passage*," says yacht designer Ron Holland. He admits that when he visits Newport Beach these days, he generally takes a walk along the harbor to see her. "Alan just designed a simple, fast dinghy. It stands the test of time."

Big Bob donated *Ticonderoga* to a Florida university and never looked back. Even before Gurney had finished the drawings for the new boat, Johnson and his older son Mark knew her name. Years earlier they had what Mark remembers as a "wild ride across the Windward Passage" in *Groote Beer* between Cuba and Hispanola. Father and son told each other they couldn't imagine a better name for a new boat. She would be a force of nature.

With Gurney's plans in hand, Johnson headed for the Palmer Johnson Yard in Sturgeon Bay, Wisconsin. The yard was well known for quality, light, aluminum construction popular with race boats of the era like *Guinevere*. But after an analysis of weight and cost calculations for an aluminum yacht, Johnson decided he could build his new boat lighter, faster, and cheaper in wood. Instead of plank-on-frame construction, Johnson would find someone to build *Windward Passage*, using aerospace

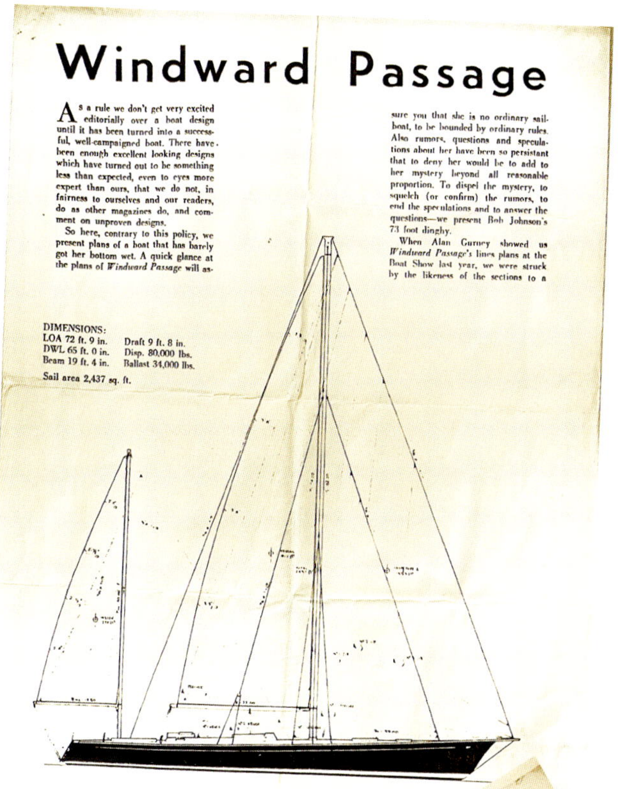

Windward Passage

As a rule we don't get very excited editorially over a boat design until it has been turned into a successful, well-campaigned boat. There have been enough excellent looking designs which have turned out to be something less than expected, even to eyes more expert than ours, that we do not, in fairness to ourselves and our readers, do as other magazines do, and comment on unproven designs.

So here, contrary to this policy, we present plans of a boat that has barely got her bottom wet. A quick glance at the plans of *Windward Passage* will assure you that she is no ordinary sailboat, to be bounded by ordinary rules. Also rumors, questions and speculations about her have been so persistant that to deny her would be to add to her mystery beyond all reasonable proportion. To dispel the mystery, to squelch (or confirm) the rumors, to end the speculations and to answer the questions—we present Bob Johnson's 73 foot dinghy.

When Alan Gurney showed us *Windward Passage*'s lines plans at the Boat Show last year, we were struck by the likeness of the sections to a

DIMENSIONS:
LOA 72 ft. 9 in. Draft 9 ft. 8 in.
DWL 65 ft. 0 in. Disp. 80,000 lbs.
Beam 19 ft. 4 in. Ballast 34,000 lbs.
Sail area 2,437 sq. ft.

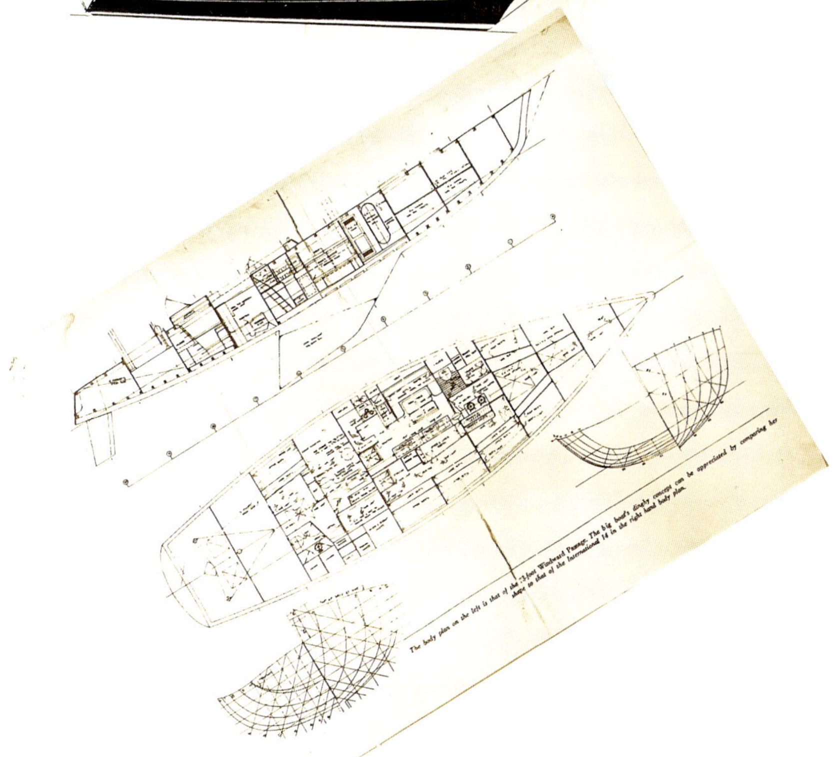

From Day 1, Gurney's design captivated the yachting world.

technology. As a lumberman and plywood manufacturer, Big Bob knew wood, and he could source the very best timber.

"Why not build a cold-molded hull of thin-ply veneers glued and nailed together into a monocoque structure the same way aviation pioneer Howard Hughes built his H-4 *Spruce Goose*?" he thought.

Gurney agreed. The development of epoxy glues offered the ability of creating durable and more long-lived wooden structures than the resorcinol adhesives used in plywood at the time. Gurney and Johnson decided to go with a ketch rig more or less the same size as *Ticonderoga*'s. To them, the ketch rig, with its two masts, seemed the best choice for flying all manner of large, downwind kites like spinnakers, bloopers, mizzen spinnakers, and mizzen staysails on the sleigh ride from Los Angeles to Honolulu.

Big Bob knew exactly who he wanted to build his boat. After years of racing boats out of Newport Beach, California, he had come to respect and admire the work of Carl Chapman whose shop and yard were in the adjacent town of Costa Mesa. Well-known for building light, non-traditional hulls like the Lapworth 36, Chapman and his partner Roley Kalayjian were part of a revolution in boat construction. In the 1960s Southern California boatbuilding and surfboard design (particularly around Costa Mesa) was evolving quickly, spurred on by the local aerospace industry's development and application of space-age adhesives, resins, and fabrics.

After plying Chappy with cocktails one night, Johnson persuaded the boatbuilder to drop everything in Costa Mesa and move 2,500 miles east to Grand Bahama to oversee the building of a "really big dinghy" with a gang of young sailors recruited from the crew of Big Ti and other race boats.

Game on.

While this looks like Passage *under construction, this is actually a model of the 1940s construction of the* Spruce Goose *at the Evergreen Aviation Museum. It used the same technique used later by Bob Johnson.*

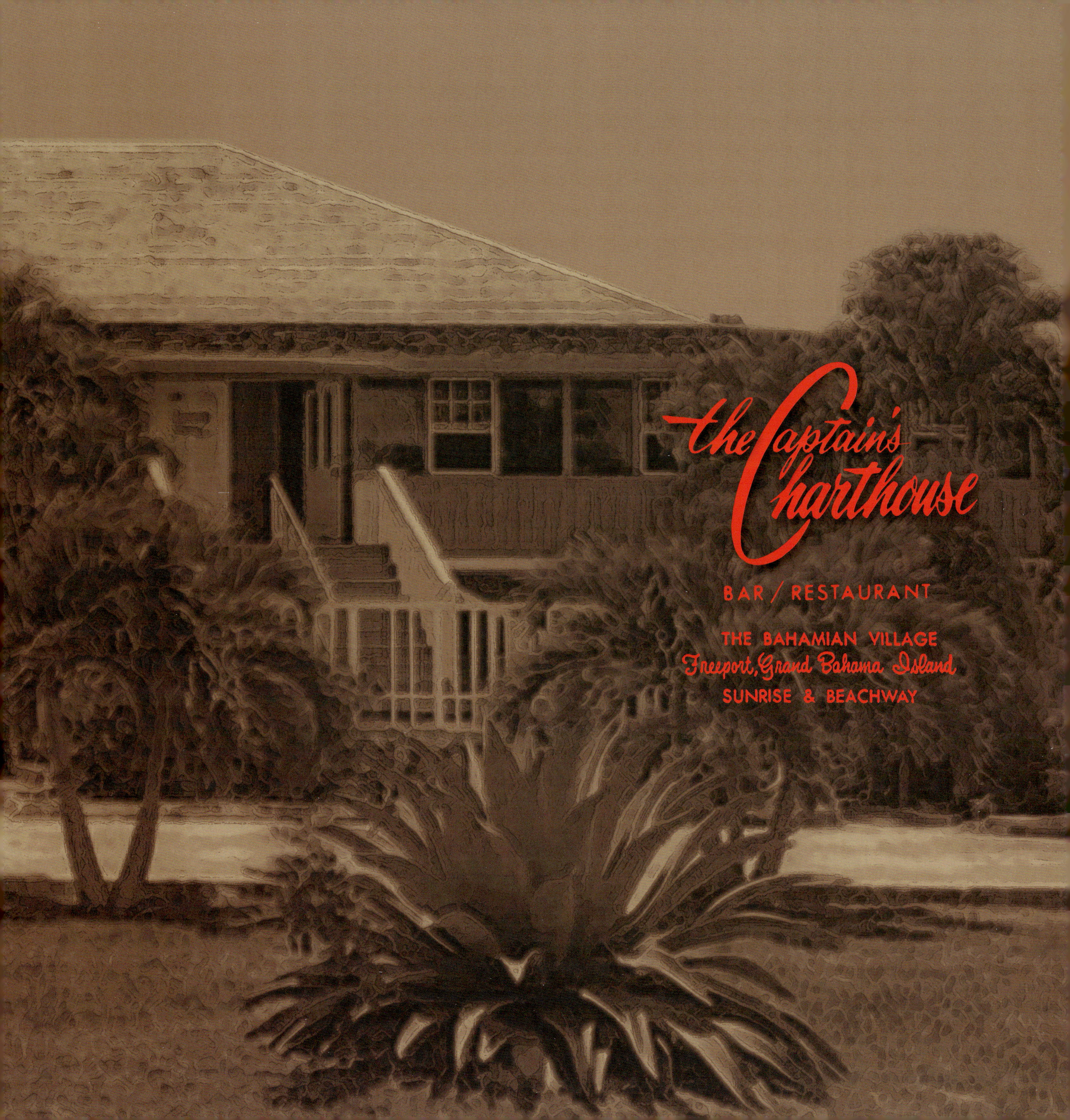
the Captain's
Charthouse
BAR / RESTAURANT
THE BAHAMIAN VILLAGE
Freeport, Grand Bahama Island
SUNRISE & BEACHWAY

3

In the Tropical Breeze

In keeping with his love of adventure, Bob Johnson had decided on an unconventional site to build his racing yacht. For some years he had been maintaining a residence and citizenship in the Bahamas for tax purposes. An admirer of the U.S. Charthouse restaurant chain, Big Bob built what he called the Captain's Charthouse restaurant as well as a cabana village in Freeport on Grand Bahama Island. It was as much a compound for family and friends as a business. He had some land nearby where he could build his new boat.

Bob's son Mark (age thirty) and Mark's wife Dotty had been living on Grand Bahama since 1964, growing hydroponic tomatoes. During the fall of 1967, Johnson brought together Chappy and a gang of about a dozen young men from *Ticonderoga*'s racing crew and headed to the Bahamas where Mark and Dotty were waiting. There they met a barge loaded with several trailers of tools and wood.

"It was the clearest Sitka spruce and Douglas-fir you could ever imagine," according to a young Scottish boatbuilder named Alistair "Tosh" McIntosh. He was a water-skiing champion who had come to Grand Bahama for a competition and discovered Big Bob's crew starting in on building *Passage*. Tosh ditched the water-skiing circuit and signed on to give Chappy and his mates a hand.

John Rumsey was also one of the *Windward Passage* gang. He had been a Star Class racer, working for North Sails out of San Diego in the early 1960s. Inevitably he ran into the fun-loving man everyone called "Big Bob," then in his early fifties, and joined his crew on Big Ti. The scuttlebutt in ocean-racing circles of the day was that "This kid Rumsey was born to drive, and Big Bob was blessed to have him at the helm, especially for the start of races."

Today Rumsey shrugs off the hype and prefers to turn the spotlight on Big Bob whom he calls "a great navigator and cook." A savvy competitor, Johnson left the details of sailing his yachts to a team of seasoned racers.

Dotty Murphy Johnson, Mark's wife, stood out among the Bahamas crew. She worked on *Windward Passage* in 1967–68 between giving birth to two children. Most of the crew thought of Dotty as their den mother who did her best to keep the gang of testosterone-soaked young boatbuilders and sailors from too many late-night encounters with the Royal Bahamas Police or young ladies on their Bahamas vacations.

"I grew up with four brothers," says Dotty. "None of what these guys were up to was news to me. We had a lot of fun."

Sometimes Dotty tended the bar at the Charthouse. Many of the guys were moonlighting as waiters and bartenders as well, and after they got off their evening shifts the party started.

"It was the best of times," remembers Rumsey, who at some point acquired the nickname "Rumdum."

Hijinks often ensued. One day Tosh coerced his mates to tow him with an Austin Minimoc. It zoomed alongside a canal while he carved slalom trails through the waterway and the Bahamians looked on in amusement. There was another time when Chappy told the guys they had to work on a Bahamian holiday. That was when someone epoxied all the locks shut on the tool chests during the night. The next morning there was nothing to be done but to head for the beach and crack open a few cases of "greenies" with the Bahamians.

Meanwhile, Big Bob and Alan Gurney were logging more than a few late, smoky nights at the bar in the Captain's Charthouse. They were a couple of jazzed-up R&D guys building a prototype.

"Alan was as much a rogue as my dad," says Fritz "Fritter" Johnson, Big Bob's younger son.

Carl Chapman (left) and Passage's *first captain, Peter Garbani (right) of Switzerland*

A fair hull required more than a fair amount of work. —image courtesy of Alistair "Tosh" McIntosh

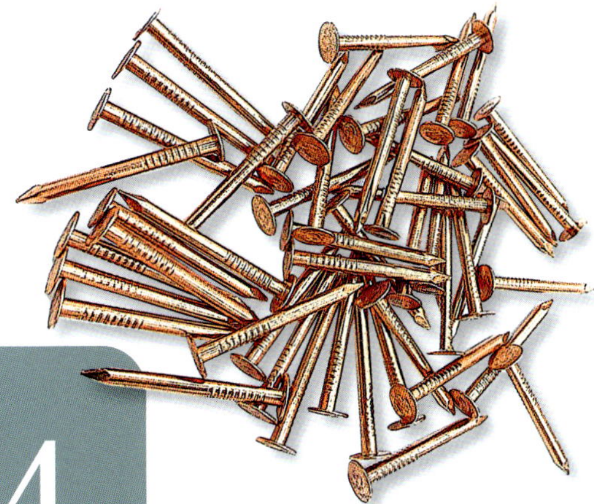

4

Island Girl

Life was not all a party for Big Bob's gang. They poured a concrete slab over the crushed coral next to Freeport Harbour as a lofting floor, and raised a tent over the top (until it blew away and they had to build a roof) to keep the sun and tropical showers off the project. Then the team set up their ring frames, primary bulkheads, and molds. Next, they began stirring up mixes of industrial epoxy and laminated the fir centerline timbers as well as stringers to run the length of the hull, which was being built upside-down.

The crew spaced the stringers about 3 feet apart and notched them into the ring frames and bulkheads. Then they began planking the hull with three layers of 7/16-inch spruce veneer set in epoxy and fastened with copper ring nails (bronze screws were added in later years during various restoration projects). Finally, they skinned the hull with Dynel saturated in epoxy to give extra strength and prevent moisture intrusion in case of hard knocks.

Initially built upside-down, the hull was then turned right-side up for decking and finishing. "Rolling-over day" was a big deal for everyone involved.—images courtesy of Fritz Johnson

In less than six months, Chappy and his minions had a completed hull. They rolled it right-side up with the help of a crane. While some of the gang laminated beams for the flush deck, others started laying down the decking. They installed two layers of ½-inch plywood, scarfed and bonded with epoxy and copper ring nails. Next, they "'glassed it over" with two layers of fiberglass cloth and epoxy, then added a stubby bowsprit. They dug a hole in the sand, made a mold, and poured a massive 33,800-pound, lead fin keel. Tosh remembers that it took "bloody weeks" to grind the keel fair.

Windward Passage*'s hull is triple-diagonal-planked aircraft-grade Sitka spruce with a Dynel sheath over the exterior. The keelson, floor timbers, stringers, and deckbeams are all spar-grade Douglas-fir.*

The planks are approximately 7/16 inch thick and glued together with epoxy. The hull planking, which is susceptible to rot, is in very good condition, largely due to the Dynel sheathing on the exterior. The inside was saturated with epoxy resin. Dynel, softer than fiberglass, has a much higher shatter resistance upon impact than fiberglass.

As for the interior, Chappy and Tosh used their shipwright's skills to install a double fore-and-aft bulkhead over the keel in the middle of the boat. They added two additional keelbolts down through the deck to the lead ballast to help carry the loads on the rig and keel. On opposite sides of this structure, they built a rudimentary galley and a dinette. There was a navigation station back aft with berths for the skipper and navigator. The rest of the boat was a shell with bins for sails up forward. Basic wooden bunks and aluminum pipe berths provided sites for sleeping for an ocean racing crew that generally numbered twelve.

For auxiliary power to get the yacht in and out of tight spaces, Chappy mounted a small, Westerbeke diesel (soon to be replaced with a heartier Volvo) in the middle of the boat. It had an offset hydraulic drive in a tube that could be retracted for racing.

In November 1968 Dotty Johnson tied a red scarf around her hair, climbed a make-do wooden scaffold while *Windward Passage* dangled from a crane, and christened the Big Dinghy with a bottle of champagne. When built at Grand Bahama, *Windward Passage* was called the second-largest spruce structure in the world, after Howard Hughes's six-engine *Spruce Goose* seaplane. In truth, *Passage* was the largest. Hughes's monster was mostly built of birch. The yacht's total cost to this point was less than $350,000.

After Peter Garbani, her first professional skipper, finished rigging the Proctor aluminum spars, the crew launched *Windward Passage* by crane into Freeport Harbour. They hanked on headsails repurposed from Big Ti and a new mainsail from Hood. Then they took off under sail to pay import duty on the new boat, to document her under a U.S. flag, and to complete her at the Spencer boatyard in West Palm Beach. During the start of the 80-mile reach across the Gulf Stream, *Passage* was pounding into the Gulf Stream seas. Gurney was along for the voyage, wearing his iconic "duck" hat.

Dotty Johnson christens Passage—*November 1968*

The canvas tent was a great idea—until it wasn't.
—image courtesy of Alistair "Tosh" McIntosh

"I can still picture him," remembers Peter Garbani. "He was back against the stern pulpit, chain smoking as usual. I could see in his eyes the gears turning in his head. Bob was at the helm."

Mark Johnson was aboard with Dotty and their two oldest sons, and Mark asked Gurney how he liked the boat.

"I don't know," said the designer between drags on his butt. "I've never sailed a 73-foot boat before."

After the foredeck crew hanked on a bigger jib, *Passage* heeled over and took off like a derby winner. Although the boat had no instruments, everybody aboard now knew that they had created something a whole lot sportier than *Ticonderoga*.

Big Bob's dream boat, his island girl, would become the prototype that inspired Alan Gurney's design for the 77-foot maxi *Great Britain II*, which Chay Blyth sailed to victory in the first Whitbread Round the World Race in 1973. But unlike Big Bob, Gurney lost his enthusiasm for the accolades of grand prix ocean racing. Despite his success as the architect of some of the mid-twentieth century's most celebrated racing yachts, Gurney left the world of yacht design shortly after drawing "GB2." He dedicated the rest of his professional life to the study of polar exploration and authored several books on the topic. He died of esophageal cancer in 2012 at his home on the island of Islay, Scotland.

But on that night in November1968 as *Passage* blasted toward Florida, Alan Gurney and Bob Johnson must have felt far from death. Gurney was thirty-two years old. Big Bob was fifty-six. They were both mavericks in the eye of some of the old guard who dominated yacht racing at the time. But they had just designed and built a vessel Olin Stephens would call a "masterpiece" when he saw it later in Jamaica.

▲ *Finishing the new keel*

◀ *After a storm destroyed the canvas roof over the hull, a new sturdy roof was constructed.*
—images on pp 38–39 courtesy of Alistair "Tosh" McIntosh

▼ *With the new roof in place over the cold-molded hull, "Tosh" McIntosh hoists a piece of spruce veneer while Bob Johnson and Alan Gurney inspect the work to this point.*

▼ *Getting closer with the keel now ready to be attached*

WINDWARD PASSAGE
LAHAINA

5

DEBUT

Even before Bob Johnson had *Passage* ready to race, the yachting press was afire with scuttlebutt concerning the "Bahamas beach boat." Newspapers as well as the yachting publications of the time turned a spotlight on the glamour and adventure of ocean racing. Helmsmen like Bill Ficker, Buddy Melges, Dennis Conner, and the brash, young Ted Turner became celebrities. Then there was the surfer/sailor Hobie Alter who gave birth to huge fleets of small catamarans and legendary post-regatta beach parties. Sailmakers like Ted Hood, Lowell North, Robbie Doyle, and Kenny Watts gained near-rockstar status in the nautical world.

In 1969 the magazine *One Design & Offshore Yachtsman* weighed in on *Windward Passage*:

> As a rule we don't get very excited editorially over a boat design until it has been turned into a successful, well-campaigned boat . . . . So here, contrary to this policy, we present plans for a boat that has barely gotten her bottom wet. A quick glance at the plans for Windward Passage will assure you she is no ordinary sailboat, to be bound by ordinary rules. Also rumors, questions, and speculation about her have been so persistent that to deny her would be to add to her mystery beyond all reasonable proportion . . . .

As this story on *Windward Passage* was going to press, Big Bob entered her in the 1969 SORC series, the premier grand prix ocean racing event of the time. In her first outing *Passage* won line honors and first place in the short St. Petersburg–Venice Race. She followed this victory with line honors and a record time in the 1969 St. Petersburg–Fort Lauderdale Race. She also won line honors in the Lipton Cup and the Fort Lauderdale–Palm Beach Race.

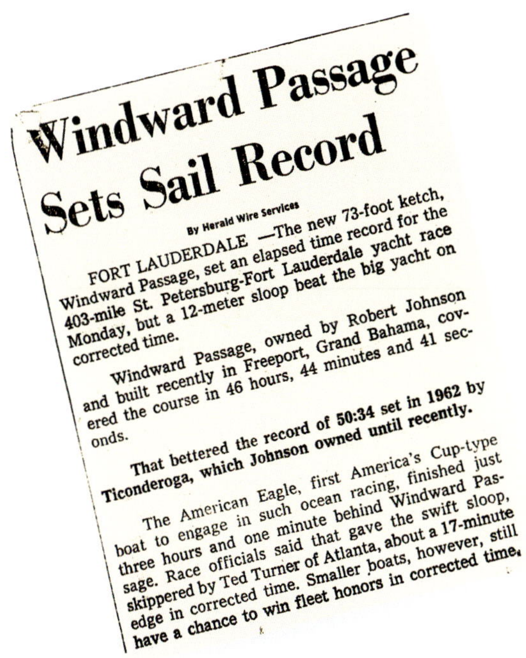

Windward Passage Sets Sail Record

By Herald Wire Services

FORT LAUDERDALE —The new 73-foot ketch, Windward Passage, set an elapsed time record for the 403-mile St. Petersburg-Fort Lauderdale yacht race Monday, but a 12-meter sloop beat the big yacht on corrected time.

Windward Passage, owned by Robert Johnson and built recently in Freeport, Grand Bahama, covered the course in 46 hours, 44 minutes and 41 seconds.

That bettered the record of 50:34 set in 1962 by Ticonderoga, which Johnson owned until recently.

The American Eagle, first America's Cup-type boat to engage in such ocean racing, finished just three hours and one minute behind Windward Passage. Race officials said that gave the swift sloop, skippered by Ted Turner of Atlanta, about a 17-minute edge in corrected time. Smaller boats, however, still have a chance to win fleet honors in corrected time.

Early times with no whale! In 1968 Passage *was new and ready to be tested.*

Clearly, there was an aura of glamour gathering around this 73-foot, cold-molded ketch. The Big Dinghy gained additional colorful nicknames like "Passing Wind" and "The Effing Whale" from envious competitors such as the hard-charging "Jungle Jim" Kilroy in his multiple maxis named *Kialoa*, "Huey" Long in his yachts called *Ondine*, and Ken DeMeuse in *Blackfin*. But to her loyal crews and admirers, she has always been simply "WP" or *Passage*.

The New York Times

Windward Passage Takes Lead in Miami-Nassau Sailing Race in Heavy Seas; FLEET IS BUFFETED BY RAIN, WAVES American Eagle, Ahead in Series, Closest Pursuer of Johnson's Yacht

The next race was the crown jewel of the SORC series, the Miami–Nassau charge. A March 4, 1969, headline in *The New York Times* says it all.

> ***Windward Passage*** Takes Lead in Miami–Nassau Sailing Race in Heavy Seas; Fleet Is Buffeted By Rain, Waves

Over a hundred yachts, the largest fleet to ever join an SORC event, took off from Governor's Cut across the Gulf Stream. Their first turning point on the 184-mile race course would be Great Isaac Light in the Bahamas, then on to Great Stirrup Cay before the final sprint to Nassau on New Providence Island. On the bulletin board in *Passage*, Big Bob had written, "If we can't win, we shouldn't sail."

Thirty-one-year-old Mark Johnson was aboard for the race with his dad. He remembers conditions at the start of the race were squally with building southeasterlies ahead of an advancing cold front. According to the *Atlanta Journal*, *Passage* crossed the starting line with "cool John Rumsey at the helm." He scooted ahead of Ted Turner, sailing his 12-Meter yacht *American Eagle*. An hour later *Passage* caught and passed the entire Class B fleet, which had started a half hour before her. By nightfall the cold front had stormed over the yachts. Winds were now gusting to at least 40 knots, but *Passage* kept driving forward through the dark at 11 knots.

Meanwhile a U.S. Coast Guard cutter was dispatched to the area around Great Isaac Light in the northwestern Bahamas to assist a number of racers with their rigs and sails torn up by the wind and seas. A Nassau newspaper called it a "night of terror." Aboard *Passage*, Big Bob perched in the companionway and stared into the black night with his eyes flashing and teeth set as if to say, "Bring it on."

Sailor and author Robert Rubadeau was on watch that evening aboard another racer surging through the dark toward Great Stirrup Cay.

"This great, white phantom blew by me like an express train, just a few yards to leeward," says Rubadeau. "It was *Passage.* She was there and gone before I even had time to be scared she might hit us."

Journalist Furman Bisher who was aboard *Passage* that night wrote that "nautical chaos" occurred at about 4:00 A.M. When the moon broke through the clouds on the back side of the cold front, Big Bob decided it was time to set the "balloon," the boat's biggest kite, "as big as a circus tent."

> A sheet broke loose, leaving the spinnaker flopping out over the bow and the pole banging against a [shroud] supporting the mainmast. Suddenly, *Windward Passage* veered sharply to port. Half the deck was awash. Peter Garbani, working desperately at a winch, was up to his waist in water. Mark Johnson, Bob's son, and another crewman working furiously on their knees on the stern, were soaked to their hips. Chip Cleary was fighting the rudder like a boxer trying to stay alive in the 15th round. The wind was howling. The sea was everywhere. The mast looked like the Tower of Pisa had finally decided to come down.

Eventually, the crew tamed the beast, and *Passage* took off at 18 knots on the home stretch to Nassau. The next morning she crossed the finish line off Paradise Island ahead of the rest of the fleet. The Big Dinghy finished in

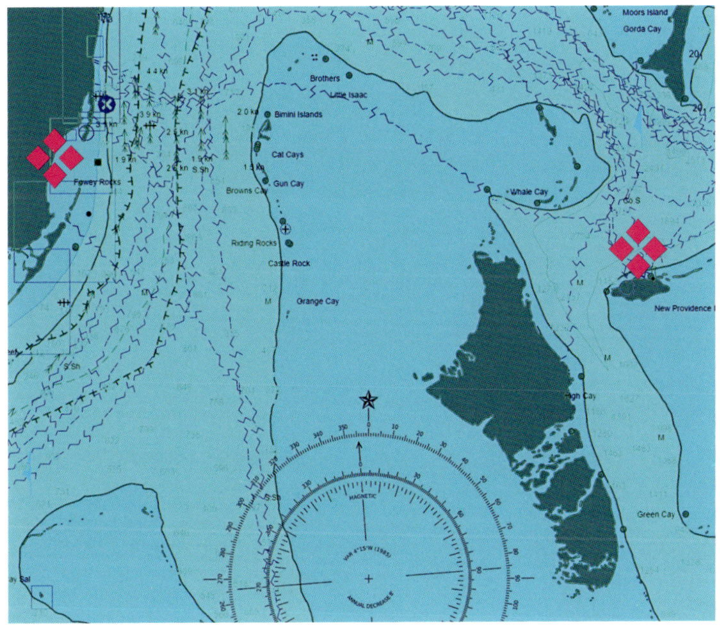

Miami–Nassau Race

Jim Kilroy, Big Bob Johnson, and a very young Ted Turner discussing tactics in detail

a record time of 15 hours, 54 minutes, 17 seconds, lopping off nearly three hours from the previous record for the race. She also finished a half hour ahead of *Kialoa II*, setting up a rivalry with the owner of "K2," Jim Kilroy, a Los Angeles real-estate developer, that would last for the next eighteen years and compel Kilroy to builder ever-bigger and more expensive *Kialoa*s to try to beat "The Effing Whale." Ted Turner's *American Eagle* lost her mast and did not finish at all.

A couple of days later *Passage* was first to finish, first in class, and first overall in the Governor's Cup sailed off New Providence Island. Following these triumphs, she sailed back to Miami and took off in the 800-mile Miami–Montego Bay Race. This was her first long ocean race, and once again she finished first.

So it was that *Windward Passage* began her career as a superstar. She had been either the winner or first to finish in her first eight ocean races, demolishing the previous record times in two of her outings. And these competitions and the glory were just rehearsals for the race she had been built to dominate. After the Montego Bay Race, *Passage* boarded her delivery crew and headed through the Panama Canal for Southern California to make the July start of the 1969 Transpac.

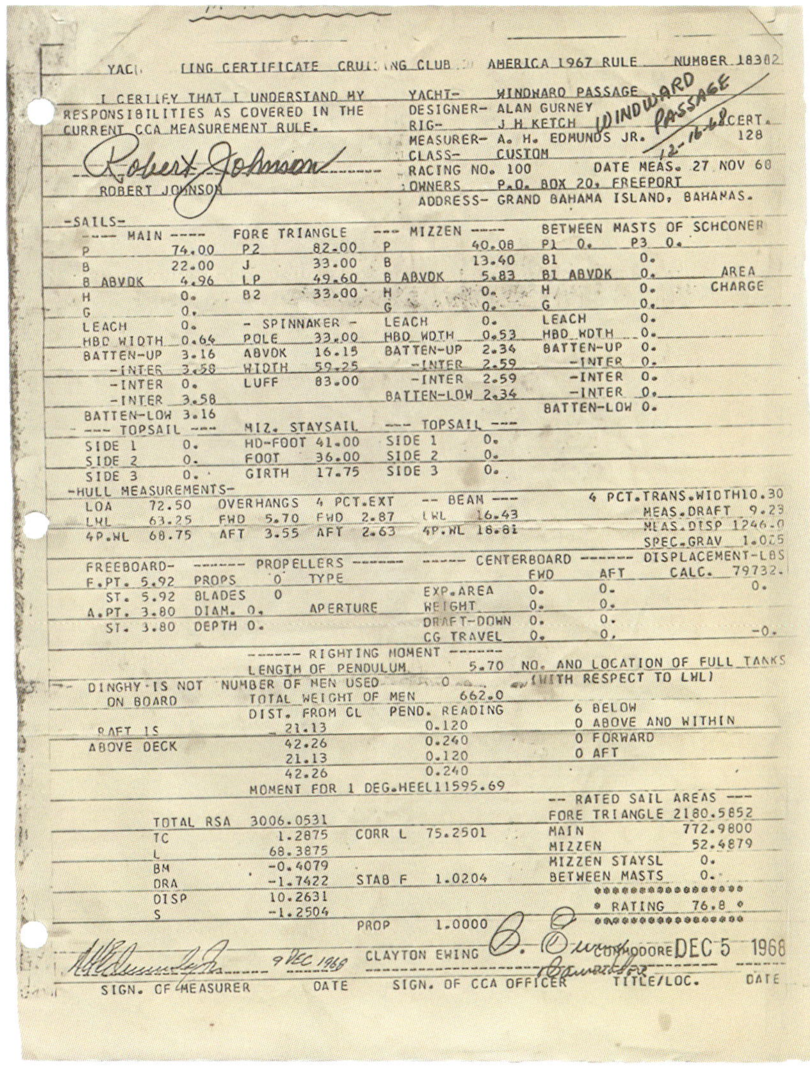
YAC[illegible] [illegible]LING CERTIFICATE CRUI[illegible]NG CLUB [illegible] AMERICA 1967 RULE NUMBER 18382

I CERTIFY THAT I UNDERSTAND MY RESPONSIBILITIES AS COVERED IN THE CURRENT CCA MEASUREMENT RULE.

Robert Johnson
ROBERT JOHNSON

YACHT- WINDWARD PASSAGE
DESIGNER- ALAN GURNEY
RIG- J H KETCH
MEASURER- A. H. EDMUNDS JR.
CLASS- CUSTOM
RACING NO. 100 DATE MEAS. 27 NOV 68
OWNERS P.O. BOX 20, FREEPORT
ADDRESS- GRAND BAHAMA ISLAND, BAHAMAS.

WINDWARD PASSAGE 12-16-68 CERT. 128

-SAILS-

---- MAIN ----		FORE TRIANGLE		--- MIZZEN ----		BETWEEN MASTS OF SCHOONER	
P	74.00	P2	82.00	P	40.08	P1 0.	P3 0.
B	22.00	J	33.00	B	13.40	B1	0.
B ABVDK	4.96	LP	49.60	B ABVDK	5.83	B1 ABVDK	0. AREA
H	0.	B2	33.00	H	0.	H	0. CHARGE
G	0.			G	0.	G	0.
LEACH	0.	- SPINNAKER -		LEACH	0.	LEACH	0.
HBD WIDTH	0.64	POLE	33.00	HBD WDTH	0.53	HBD WDTH	0.
BATTEN-UP	3.16	ABVDK	16.15	BATTEN-UP	2.34	BATTEN-UP	0.
-INTER	3.58	WIDTH	59.25	-INTER	2.59	-INTER	0.
-INTER	0.	LUFF	83.00	-INTER	2.59	-INTER	0.
-INTER	3.58			BATTEN-LOW	2.34	-INTER	0.
BATTEN-LOW	3.16					BATTEN-LOW	0.
--- TOPSAIL ---		MIZ. STAYSAIL		--- TOPSAIL ---			
SIDE 1	0.	HD-FOOT	41.00	SIDE 1	0.		
SIDE 2	0.	FOOT	36.00	SIDE 2	0.		
SIDE 3	0.	GIRTH	17.75	SIDE 3	0.		

-HULL MEASUREMENTS-
LOA 72.50 OVERHANGS 4 PCT.EXT -- BEAM --- 4 PCT.TRANS.WIDTH10.30
LWL 63.25 FWD 5.70 FWD 2.87 LWL 16.43 MEAS.DRAFT 9.23
4P.WL 68.75 AFT 3.55 AFT 2.63 4P.WL 18.81 MEAS.DISP 1246.0
SPEC.GRAV 1.025

FREEBOARD- ------ PROPELLERS ------ ----- CENTERBOARD ------ DISPLACEMENT-LBS
F.PT. 5.92 PROPS 0 TYPE FWD AFT CALC. 79732.
ST. 5.92 BLADES 0 EXP.AREA 0. 0. 0.
A.PT. 3.80 DIAM. 0. APERTURE WEIGHT 0. 0.
ST. 3.80 DEPTH 0. DRAFT-DOWN 0. 0.
CG TRAVEL 0. 0. -0.

------ RIGHTING MOMENT ------
LENGTH OF PENDULUM 5.70 NO. AND LOCATION OF FULL TANKS (WITH RESPECT TO LWL)
DINGHY IS NOT ON BOARD NUMBER OF MEN USED 0
TOTAL WEIGHT OF MEN 662.0
DIST. FROM CL PEND. READING 6 BELOW
RAFT IS ABOVE DECK 21.13 0.120 0 ABOVE AND WITHIN
42.26 0.240 0 FORWARD
21.13 0.120 0 AFT
42.26 0.240
MOMENT FOR 1 DEG.HEEL11595.69

-- RATED SAIL AREAS ---
FORE TRIANGLE 2180.5852
MAIN 772.9800
MIZZEN 52.4879
MIZZEN STAYSL 0.
BETWEEN MASTS 0.

TOTAL RSA 3006.0531
TC 1.2875 CORR L 75.2501
L 68.3875
BM -0.4079
DRA -1.7422 STAB F 1.0204
DISP 10.2631
S -1.2504
PROP 1.0000
* RATING 76.8 *

9 DEC 1968 CLAYTON EWING COMMODORE DEC 5 1968
SIGN. OF MEASURER DATE SIGN. OF CCA OFFICER TITLE/LOC. DATE

WINDWARD PASSAGE

Fast Ketch Headed Here

By HARRY MONAHAN

Bob Johnson's new 73-foot, lightweight speed demon, **Windward** Passage, is now in the Pacific cruising northward for a **possible** appearance in the Newport Beach-Ensenada stampede **May 1, and** she will not head back to the Atlantic until she **competes in** the San Diego-to-Acapulco race in February, 1970.

The new ketch was at Balboa, the Pacific terminus of the Panama Canal, on Monday. She must check in here on reentering U. S. waters and it is possible she may spend time at a local shipyard having some housekeeping chores done after the trip from the Atlantic.

Monahan

Windward Passage's Pacific date book includes a California Cup duel with Ken DeMeuse's Blackfin off Marina Del Rey June 20-22, another joust with Blackfin in the Transpacific Race in July, and the big boat scramble for the St. Francis Challenge Cup at San Francisco in the fall.

In her brief racing career (she was launched in November), Windward Passage has already wiped out elapsed time records in three races. Given good winds she could add two or three Pacific marks to her log. Johnson will be particularly anxious to post a new Transpac record because his former racer, Ticonderoga, owns the present standard of nine days, 13 hours, 51 minutes, two seconds.

* * *

Johnson's announced intention to enter her in the San Diego-Acapulco race injects some early challenge and excitement into that biennial event. The San Diego Union Perpetual Trophy, emblematic of the Acapulco elapsed time record, hasn't had a new name engraved on it since 1964 when the late Howard Ahmanson's swift greyhound, Sirius II, covered the 1,430 miles in 8:09:15:54.

The Transpac and the California Cup apparently have lost Sumner Long's aluminum swiftie, Ondine, sister ship to Blackfin. Long reportedly has decided to go in the Transatlantic Race, beginning June 22, instead.

6

Ready to Rock

In 1969 adventuring under sail—whether ocean racing or cruising—was capturing the interest of the general public in America. These were the Glory Days before grand prix yacht racing became dominated by billionaires, corporations, and all-professional crews. Sailors were largely unpaid for racing. They earned money by delivering yachts from race to race. A genre of pop music, later to be known as "Yacht Rock," emerged from the wave of nautical escapism that was surging over the United States and around the world during the Vietnam War era.

Music critics see the origins of Yacht Rock in the harmonies of The Beach Boys' "Good Vibrations" and "Sloop *John B.*" Christopher Cross's "Ride Like the Wind" and "Sailing" are two prime examples of the laid-back vibe about to emerge in California pop music of the era. Steely Dan, The Doobie Brothers, and Toto would be memorably innovators. Songs like "Brandy" by Looking Glass and Player's "Baby Come Back" would become essential elements of the Yacht Rock canon as would Robbie Dupree's "Steal Away," Bertie Higgins's "Key Largo," "Cool Change" by The Little River Band, the Commodores' "Easy (as a Sunday Morning)," and anything by Hall & Oates. David Crosby, Neil Young, Jimmy Buffett, and others sang about their nautical adventures in songs like "Southern Cross."

Even before *Passage* reached Southern California, the press was tuning in on the sailing vibes and proclaiming "Fast Ketch Headed Here" and "*Windward Passage* Sited Off Baja Tip." The *Los Angeles Times* hyped the coming race as a duel between "three new yachts designed primarily for speed in long-distance racing and causing considerable eyebrow raising among officials of the Transpacific Yacht Club," sponsors of the Transpac. Those yachts were *Passage*, Huey Long's *Ondine II,* and Ken DeMeuse's *Blackfin.*

On July 4, 1969, *The Register* proclaimed:

> Today is the day so many have been waiting for—the start of the biennial Trans-Pacific race to Honolulu.
>
> A record seventy-two boats will start today off Point Fermin outside Los Angeles Harbor to begin what at 2,225 miles is one the world's longest sustained athletic endeavors.
>
> Never before has such an incredible array of the finest long-distance, ocean racing boats and equipment money can buy ever assembled at the same time and same place. Since the last race over $85 million has been spent by the skippers of this armada . . . .
>
> Two men, Bob Johnson and Ken DeMeuse, have spent over $1 million between them. But only one of these boats—*Windward Passage* or *Blackfin*—will cross the line first, in a possible record time.

C6 The REGISTER Friday (m) July 4, 1969

Trans-Pacific Yacht Race To Honolulu Begins Today

By FRED MILLER
Register Boating Editor

Today's the day so many have been waiting for—the start of the biennial Trans-Pacific race to Honolulu.

A record 72 boats will start at noon today off Point Fermin outside Los Angeles harbor to begin what, at 2225 miles, is one of the world's longest sustained athletic endeavors.

Never before has such an incredible array of the finest long-distance ocean racing boats and equipment that money can buy ever assembled at one time and place.

Since the last race, well over $5 million has been spent by the skippers of this armada, whether on new boats built specifically for it, on modifications of existing craft or in sails, hardware or supplies.

Two men, Bob Johnson and Ken DeMeuse, have spent over $1 million between them. But, only one of the boats—Windward Passage or Blackfin—will cross the line first, in a possible new record time.

"There are SO many new boats in this race," said Tom Corkett of Newport Beach, skipper of Tahiti race winner Salacia and overall winner of the Trans-Pac with Islander in 1963, "you can honestly say that 60 out of the 72 have a chance of winning it."

For the kind of race it is, this is probably true. All the past racing records of any boat or skipper go out the window. Only two Whitney Series champions—Peter Grant's Nalu II and Chuck Ullman's Legend—have ever won the Trans-Pac in its long history.

Besides being a sailing race, Trans-Pac is a guessing game called "dodging the eye of the Pacific high." The high is a huge, invisible column sitting right in the middle of the race course in the eastern Pacific. Inside this column there is no wind at all, while around it the strong trade winds blow forever.

The real problem with it is that it moves around all the time, changing shape constantly, elongating and contracting and sometimes splitting in two. Because it is so big (hundreds of miles across in the absolutely windless "eye" of it), its slightest movements cover huge distances over a 24-hour period.

The shortest distance to Honolulu, because the earth is round, would not be a straight line but a northerly curve known to the airlines and motor vessels as the Great Circle Route.

Only in 1936, when the Pacific high was unusually far north did a Trans-Pac racer ever get away with sailing this shortest possible course.

This year all the weather experts say it is going to be a light-wind, slow race. I say they are in a worse position than the usual Trans-Pac racer's navigator, who knows full well that when he plots the isobars from the day's weather report, it matters not where the high is today, but where it is going to be tomorrow? The next day, and the day after that?

The answer is that it should be almost an exact relay of the 1955 race. It was very light the first part of the race, but the wind blew harder than ever before for all the rest of it.

The particular weather we are talking about happens to run in 7-year cycles. It has been 14 years since 1955, thus Ticonderoga's elapsed time record should fall.

But, which boat would be the one to break the record?

There are equally-divided camps (both very knowledgeable, too) on whether it will be Blackfin or Windward Passage to surf across the finish line off Diamond Head.

This issue is somewhat cut-and-dried. Obviously, Blackfin can beat the pants off WP on any point of sail if the wind's under 12 knots. Even if the wind got up to 15, once Blackfin was through with the only windward work of the race and had rounded the west end of Catalina, she could hold off WP the rest of the way. But, what if the wind stars to howl? WP on all ballots.

The irony of it all is that, no matter how hard the wind blows, Blackfin COULD beat WP but, she won't. Why? Two of her best helmsmen "jumped ship" because of her tender qualities. They didn't relish the thought of living in "a world turned on its side" for however many days it would take to get to the point out in the trade winds that Blackfin would be direcly before the wind and sailing upright again.

In any kind of wind Blackfin (moving very fast nonetheless) sails on her side. With all her free-board, her rail is under the water. Her portholes are so far under the water she becomes a true "glass-bottomed boat."

Until talking to "Super Henry" Sprague, the Congressional Cup winner, is some detail about Blackfin, I didn't know that HE had been sailing the boat all three times she broke race records.

"The boat IS as tender as everyone says," he said, "but off the wind she is NOT an unmanageable as many think. That retractible rudder aft isn't the main rudder at all. The thing on the keel isn't a trim-tab either; it's the main rudder. When it blows hard, they put the after rudder down and the boat tracks like a big missile."

"I've never gone so fast under sail in my life as on Blackfin. But, you have to have nothing but the very best helmsman in the world on the wheel at all times in that kind of going. The boat has a huge tendency to broach on waves.

"But, to me it's just like sailing Finn dinghies downwind off the San Francisco city front; if you are very good, you don't capsize, even though the rest of the fleet does. Finns have a tendency to capsize to windward, Blackfin has a tendency to broach. But, sailed properly, both are very fast. They asked me to go on Blackfin to Honolulu, but I told them I'd rather sail my Finn dinghy."

The only tendency Windward Passage has in heavy wind and sea conditions is to go faster than ever before. All it needs is wind: it's a "heavy-weather stomper," in Finn class phraseology.

When *Passage* sailed out of the Angel's Gate at the mouth of Los Angeles Harbor to line up for the start of the race, she carried the image of a red whale on her transom. It was known as the "Lahaina whale" because it was a symbol on the burgee of the Lahaina Yacht Club on Maui where Bob Johnson was a long-standing member. In the years and decades to come the whale would become the yacht's iconic identifier. Even though the hail port on her transom would change from Lahaina to Miami to Portland to Atlanta to Sydney to Newport Harbor over the next six decades, the image of a whale would remain.

Beside the whale, Johnson's yacht sported a lot of new sails. Her primary sails had been cut by the North loft in San Diego, and she carried a North representative in the person of John Rumsey with a sewing machine for on-the-spot modifications and repairs. Some of the heavy-air sails came from Ted Hood with his special weave of low-stretch fibers. Almost all the spinnakers came from Kenny Watts. The crew had eleven of them. When running before the wind with spinnaker, blooper, mainsail, mizzen spinnaker, mizzen staysail, and mizzen set, *Passage*'s crew could fly an astonishing 13,000 square feet of sail.

What they didn't have were enough toilets (two) and anything like the modern navigation equipment and radios that would soon become standard fare for ocean racing.

"We had Dad and his sextant," says Mark Johnson, "a rather basic radio direction finder, an old-fashioned Walker log to measure speed, a VHF radio for line-of-sight communications, and a single-sideband for long-distance radio messages. Pretty basic stuff for a 2,000-mile race across the biggest ocean on the planet." If the crew on *Passage* couldn't see their opponents or the sky was too overcast to get a noon sight of a star shot, they were dueling blind.

7

Beating the Odds

From the very start of the twenty-fifth Transpac in 1969, *Windward Passage* seemed to struggle against dark fates. Following the race, Big Bob penned a letter to designer Alan Gurney. It was published in the 1969 Lahaina Yacht Club yearbook and deftly articulates Big Bob's pride in his boat and his crew. It also unfolds the challenges they faced.

"I believe we have the greatest ocean racing crew to be assembled anywhere . . . *Windward Passage*'s crew is *Ticonderoga*'s crew," he writes near the top of his letter. "We all felt that if *Ticonderoga*'s record [in the Transpac] was to be broken, we wanted *Windward Passage* to be the boat to beat it . . . . We built *Windward Passage* with the '69 race in mind." Big Bob wanted to see if he could "get there fastest with the leastest instead of trying to win by spending the most money . . . ." He added, "*Windward Passage* cost only a fraction of some of the other 73-footers or large boats in the race. She's built of wood and plywood, and we built her ourselves. She's 'backyard,' but the work is not of 'backyard character.' We had excellent boat builders on the job, and some of them were in our crew. So they can say 'we built her and we sailed her and she won.' So I have always saluted them for it . . . . As for what *Windward Passage* actually cost, suffice to say we spent less building her than we spent remodeling and repairing *Ticonderoga* for racing after buying her in 1963. We are all proud of that fact, and as you designed her, you are no doubt proud of this fact, too."

Johnson's letter spends several paragraphs describing the start of the race—with all seventy-two boats starting together at a short starting line that was atypically *not* perpendicular to the rhumb line. He called it "the most ill-conceived one I have ever seen in all my ocean racing years."

Big Bob Johnson—based on an image in the Lahaina Yacht Club's 1969 Transpac program

Poster appearing on the cover of the 1969 Transpac program

Then Big Bob gets to the race.

> Coming up to the line *Windward Passage* dodged a Cal-40 coming the other way. The committee's photos show that. And if that doesn't indicate confusion, what does?
>
> We crossed the starting line late but clear of everyone, with a small boat ahead and slightly to leeward. To our astonishment he started coming up right in front of us yelling "on the wind." We put the helm hard over to avoid hitting him, came up in the wind and called to him that we were "hard over" and could not respond any quicker.
>
> After coming up into the wind, the small boat (later identified as *Esprit* of San Francisco) then fell off and resumed course. He had two fiberglass man overboard poles sticking out at least 8 feet over his stern. As he swung back on course and our bowsprit swung past his stern as we tacked in response to his luff, our man on the pulpit pushed one of those poles out of the way.
>
> As he touched it, someone on *Esprit* yelled, "That man touched our boat. Get his name and his picture . . . ." Then, "We'll get you . . . hotshots!" *Esprit* got on the radio to advise the committee they had been fouled and were filing a protest against *Windward Passage*.
>
> At the start and afterwards the wind was light. We chose to go up the coast before we tacked. We made a bad choice. At the west end of Catalina we were at least five miles behind *Blackfin*. She had tacked earlier and caught the wind first and disappeared over the horizon.
>
> We weren't very happy about that fact. As the wind increased, we reefed the main and went to smaller headsails. In a couple of hours we passed *Pursuit* and *Baruna* and had only *Blackfin* ahead of us. She's a fast, fast boat, and we wondered if we could catch her.

ORANGE COUNTY, CALIFORNIA WEDNESDAY, JULY 9, 1969

Terror on Passage After Spinnaker Breaks

By ALMON LOCKABEY
DAILY PILOT Boating Editor

ABOARD THE WINDWARD PASSAGE — After a night of terror Tuesday night Windward Passage is still in the race for first to finish in the Transpacific Yacht Race.

Shortly after midnight the spinnaker started splitting and before the watch on deck could cut it down, it crashed down on the deck. Also the spinnaker pole footing crashed down on the deck.

The watch below turned-to to help clear the net but to no avail.

In the following two hours two men were aloft with the boat wallowing in heavy seas trying to cut the huge spinnaker free.

Peter Garbani was lashed to the masthead and then lowered down to the snarled sail where he worked nearly one hour.

John Rumsey went aloft twice to clear and retrieve halyards. Both men perform extraordinary feats of seamanship under extremely dangerous conditions.

Just before the hassle Blackfin was less than one mile ahead of Windward Passage.

There was gloom aboard the Windward Passage as all hands figured Blackfin had pulled far ahead.

But the gloom vanished this morning when Blackfin was spotted six miles to the south. So the big match race is still on.

Both yachts are ahead of Ticonderoga's time in the record 1965 year. Also both boats have now passed the halfway mark in the Honolulu race.

The battle was joined early Saturday morning when Windward Passage overtook Blackfin for the first time since the start of the race. Windward Passage slowly passed Blackfin and left her nearly one mile astern and at nightfall Blackfin was heading up toward the north.

On Sunday the boat was not in sight but Blackfin reported position three miles astern and two miles behind Windward Passage and 30 miles to the north.

Monday morning the watch on deck reported her off the starboard bow and saw Blackfin all day long as the boats sailed neck and neck with Blackfin in the lead.

On Monday night Blackfin was still barely ahead, but Windward Passage was moving up fast. About 10 p.m. Monday night Blackfin lost a spinnaker during a squall. The crew took care of the mishap and had a new one flying within 15 minutes.

TRANSPAC REPORT

Blackfin was again about two miles ahead of Windward Passage's port beam by daylight.

The two boats have been running bow and bow with Windward Passage moving up during the squalls when the wind is better and Blackfin edging away in the night time.

To most observers, the Windward Passage crew pulled a unique feat of seamanship when they sewed up a foot of a spinnaker while it was still flying in a rain squall.

Our answer came at sun-up. There she was about three miles to leeward and slightly ahead. As the day wore on, we overhauled her and pulled directly ahead of her. By sundown we had her almost down over the horizon astern. We were happier.

At noon we figured we had made 212 miles from the start. This would be our shortest day's run during the race . . . . We were on track with where "Big Ti" had been four years before.

Next day we didn't see *Blackfin*. We continued our course with a reacher and shook out the reef in the main . . . . On the morning of the fourth day, *Blackfin* reached down across our bow carrying a spinnaker . . . . We went to a spinnaker and followed her.

It was to be a frustrating three-day chase. We were always behind. Each day we gained on her during the day, up to within a mile or so. Then each night something would happen. Twice the fitting on the spinnaker pole opened and the pole crashed down on deck and in the water.

The third night we wrapped the spinnaker and lost a couple hours jibing back and forth to get it down. John Rumsey and Pete Garbani spent a couple of real dangerous hours aloft in big rolling seas at night.

Pete finally cut the spinnaker into shreds, got it down, and we were underway again. [Some fifty years later Garbani would say it was "the worst night I ever spent at sea."]

In the morning *Blackfin* was a dot on the horizon far to leeward. Soon she jibed and vanished on a port tack going south. We hung on to our starboard tack.

I know a lot of very good sailors believe you should "cover" your competition if you are ahead and "stay with him" if you are behind. That's okay around the buoys, but in an ocean race I believe you sail your own race and that's what we decided to do . . . .

> So we gambled, perhaps, by sailing to our lay line . . . . As we went, the wind increased and we had 12-knot hours on our old-fashioned Walker log. Coming down toward Molokai we listened to *Blackfin*'s estimated morning position and they were pretty discouraging . . . even though from 500 miles out we had only our best four helmsmen steering the boat . . . .
>
> We got a radio report that said *Blackfin* would finish at 5:02 for a new record. It looked like 7:00 P.M. for us . . . . But everyone said let's quit listening to these estimates and sail the boat . . . .
>
> As we came down on Ilio Point, we called Honolulu and asked what time *Blackfin* had finished. Bill King answered and said there was no *Blackfin* in sight from Diamond Head. So we put a man up in the rigging and spotted *Blackfin* coming down along Molokai about 6 miles away *behind* us . . . . We'd cut her off at the pass . . . .
>
> A 95-foot Coast Guard cutter came out and raced along with us . . . . "We can do 22 knots with the big surfing seas, and that's what you were doing," [they said]. Not bad for just a wood sailboat, Alan!

Over 3,000 citizens came down to Diamond Head to watch *Passage* cross the finish line at 6:44 P.M. She was down to her last usable spinnaker, a 1964 relic from *Ticonderoga*. *Blackfin* made it at about 8 P.M. Big Bob's wooden whale's elapsed time was 9 days, 9 hours, 24 minutes, 59 seconds. This was more than three hours faster than Johnson's line-honors victory with Big Ti in 1965.

But there was a problem. Two yachts were filing protests against *Windward Passage*.

The "Hot Shots" Crew

Robert F. Johnson—*skipper*
Sandy McKenzie—*cook*
Chip Cleary
John Rumsey
Mark Johnson
Albert Gooch
Irmin Stawicki
Ron Young
Robert Hoehn
Peter Garbani
Joseph Cronin
Robert Hanretty
Denny Dennison
Don Vaughan
Al Lockaby

Pan Am Clipper Cup, 1982
—©Phil Uhl

8910
8910

8

Robbed of Glory

After she finished, *Blackfin* claimed *Passage* had given false position reports, leading the crew of *Blackfin* to believe they were far behind. Because of this misconception, Ken DeMeuse said he had slowed his boat down and sailed cautiously in the stiff breeze typical of the home stretch to the finish line of the Transpac.

The race committee heard the protest and examined the position reports of *Passage* and *Blackfin* for the final three days of the race. A Coast Guard plane had overflown the racers during those days and found *Passage*, along with *Mir, Queen Mab*, and *Pursuit.* substantially where they said they were. But the Coast Guard could not find *Blackfin*.

"Ken didn't know where he was," says Mark Johnson.

"End of protest," Big Bob wrote to Gurney.

Meanwhile, *Passage* filed a protest against the race committee for what Johnson considered an unsafe and irregular starting line. In hindsight this protest seemed to not have been the best idea, because it put the committee on the defensive. They rallied, according to Big Bob, proclaiming "they had done everything about the start just right." Next, the race committee heard *Esprit*'s protest about the *Passage* sailor touching her man-overboard pole at the start, despite her having nothing to gain since she had won Class D. Meanwhile, the newspapers were spilling lots of ink over the "controversy." Finally, in a split decision, the race committee decided to penalize *Passage* two hours on her elapsed time. It was just enough of a penalty to rob the Big Dinghy of her record time and line honors.

Big Bob Johnson did not take the news well. He wrote Gurney, "I was called a liar by *Blackfin*'s protest. A Mainland newspaper came out with '*Windward Passage* first to Honolulu, but Johnson accused of cheating' . . . .

◀ Blackfin *sailing off the coast of Honolulu—©Phil Uhl*

D2 The REGISTER Friday (m) July 18, 1969

Blackfin's Protest Not Valid Against Windward Passage

HONOLULU (UPI)—The 39-ftoot sloop Argonaut was declared the overall winner of the 25th Biennial Transpacific Yacht Race Thursday as class "C" boats walked away with all the hnoors in the 1,225 mile race from Los Angeles to Hawaii.

The protest committee for the race also met Thursday and ruled there was no evidence to show that any position was intentionally given in error by Windward Passage, the first yacht to cross the Diamond Head finish line.

Skipper Kenneth DeMeuse of the Blackfin, which sailed out of the St. Francis Yacht Club of San Francisco, had filed a protest against Windward Passage skipper Bob Johnson claiming Windward Passage filed "erroneous" position reports. DeMeuse urged the protest committee to disqualify Windward Passage, which sailed under the colors of the Lahaina Yacht Club of Maui.

The five-member committee met for more than two hours Thursday and, in absolving Windward Passage, also stressed the importance of position reports because of the safety factor.

However, The Esprit, class D winner of the Aeolian Yacht Club and skippered by George W. Phillips, also has made a charge against Windward Passage for making contact at the beginning of the race. The protest committee was to m[illegible] again today to consider latest charge.

The contact protest was signed by Tom Wailey, a navigator aboard The Esprit.

While a handful of boats were yet to finish, race officials named The Argonaut, skippered by owner Jon Androm of the Santa Barbara Yacht Club, winner of the fleet standings according to handicap.

The Argonaut, which crossed the finish line early Wednesday, was given the corrected time of six days, 20 hours, 54 minutes and seven seconds. It had an elapsed time of 11 days, 16 hous, 35 minutes and 23 seconds.

A race spokesman said the boats still on the waters didn't have a chance of displacing the first three places of the overall divisions.

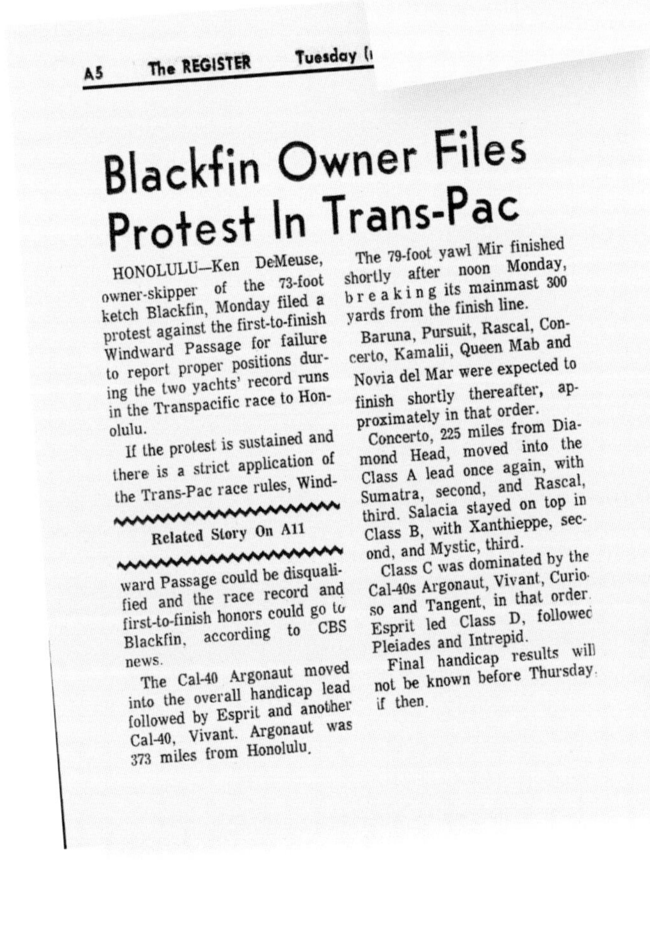

A5 The REGISTER Tuesday (

Blackfin Owner Files Protest In Trans-Pac

HONOLULU—Ken DeMeuse, owner-skipper of the 73-foot ketch Blackfin, Monday filed a protest against the first-to-finish Windward Passage for failure to report proper positions during the two yachts' record runs in the Transpacific race to Honolulu.

If the protest is sustained and there is a strict application of the Trans-Pac race rules, Wind-

Related Story On A11

ward Passage could be disqualified and the race record and first-to-finish honors could go to Blackfin, according to CBS news.

The Cal-40 Argonaut moved into the overall handicap lead followed by Esprit and another Cal-40, Vivant. Argonaut was 373 miles from Honolulu.

The 79-foot yawl Mir finished shortly after noon Monday, breaking its mainmast 300 yards from the finish line.

Baruna, Pursuit, Rascal, Concerto, Kamalii, Queen Mab and Novia del Mar were expected to finish shortly thereafter, approximately in that order.

Concerto, 225 miles from Diamond Head, moved into the Class A lead once again, with Sumatra, second, and Rascal, third. Salacia stayed on top in Class B, with Xanthieppe, second, and Mystic, third.

Class C was dominated by the Cal-40s Argonaut, Vivant, Curioso and Tangent, in that order. Esprit led Class D, followed Pleiades and Intrepid.

Final handicap results will not be known before Thursday, if then.

SANTA ANA REGISTER · JULY 19, 1969

Blackfin Named First-To-Finish In Trans-Pac

HONOLULU (AP) — The yacht Windward Passage Friday was denied first-to-finish honors in the 25th Transpacific Yacht Race.

The Transpac Protest Committee upheld a complaint filed against the 73-foot ketch by the yacht Esprit and a two-hour penalty was lodged against Windward Passage, owned and skippered by Robert Johnson, a retired Oregon lumberman.

As a result, the first-to-finish honor went to the yacht Blackfin which waged a close race with Windward Passage at the windup of the 2,225-mile race from Los Angeles.

Blackfin crossed the Diamond Head finish line Sunday evening nearly an hour behind Windward Passage, the first yacht across.

But the two-hour penalty applied against Windward Passage's elapsed time made Blackfin the official first finisher and holder of the new record.

Blackfin's new elapsed time was announced as 9 days, 10 hours and 21 minutes flat, beating the previous record set by the Ticonderoga in 1965 by about 5½ hours.

Earlier, the Transpac Protest Committee had disallowed a protest filed against Windward Passage by Ken Demeuse, owner and skipper of the Blackfin. Demeuse claimed owner Johnson of Windward Passage falsified his position reports.

Skipper-owner George Phillips Jr., of the yacht Esprit accused Windward Passage of violations that occurred shortly after the start of the Jul[y] 4 race at San Pedro, Calif. That protest was upheld.

Then we were read out of the race and the new record by a protest we believe would be called 'frivolous' anywhere else in yacht racing. So I doubt I would ask a crew to again sail 7,000 miles to run the chance of being disqualified another time on this sort of stuff. I don't need any more of it . . . so that's enough. For me it's Transpac, *Aloha, Mahalo,* and Goodbye. "

But then Johnson seemed to get control of his tantrum and wrote, "Alan, you should know from all of us that your boat's just great . . . . You can still take pride . . . . We demonstrated we could get here first in record time with a great boat that, while immensely strong, light, and fast, cost only a fraction of some of its principal competitors. The crew did it, and you did it."

"After the protest committee ruled against *Passage*," remembers Mark Johnson, "Ken DeMeuse, *Blackfin*'s owner, came to my dad and said he told the committee he didn't want the trophy or the record. It belonged to *Windward Passage*. The committee told DeMeuse if he didn't take the trophy he would never be allowed to compete in another Transpac."

Big Bob had always known that some of the old guard in the yachting community considered him a backwoods lumberjack from "East Ducksquat," Oregon. They saw him as an interloper—like the young Atlanta media mogul Ted Turner—into their august fraternity, and thought of his boat as a wooden aberration.

Transpac '69

(Yachts listed in order of arrival)

Yacht	Elapsed time D	H	M	S	Corrected time D	H	M	S	Class Stand.
*Windward Passage	9	9	24	59	7	18	33	33	A-8
Blackfin	9	10	21	0	7	13	11	42	A-4
Mir	10	3	47	35	7	16	39	5	A-7
Pursuit	10	8	31	2	8	4	39	44	A-10
Baruna	10	10	49	22	7	13	51	6	A-5
Rascal	10	12	30	18	7	2	59	21	A-2
Concerto	10	14	10	22	7	0	48	47	A-1
Kamalii	10	21	12	29	8	5	19	33	A-11
Queen Mab	10	21	31	2	8	13	21	39	A-12
Novia Del Mar	10	22	41	23	8	19	44	59	A-13
Sumatra	11	0	40	7	7	4	16	32	A-3
Whirlwind II	11	4	48	47	7	22	24	1	A-9
Salacia	11	5	24	44	7	3	15	9	B-1
Mystic	11	7	34	26	7	7	56	10	B-2
Dare	11	9	18	59	7	15	27	49	A-6
Jubilation	11	12	0	38	7	12	39	47	B-6
Nimble	11	15	34	14	7	7	59	38	B-3
Argonaut	11	16	35	23	6	20	44	7	C-1
Quasar	11	17	53	24	6	21	16	9	C-2
Vivant	11	18	4	55	6	23	35	14	C-3
Moccasin	11	18	43	45	7	9	44	24	B-4
Curioso	11	21	17	59	7	1	58	59	C-4
Simoon	11	21	43	19	7	11	40	56	B-5
Marionette	12	0	34	16	7	17	39	5	B-9
Amorita	12	1	22	25	7	17	5	43	B-8
Tilt o' Kilt	12	1	47	44	7	8	21	28	C-6
Intrepid I	12	1	56	47	7	2	31	55	D-1
Chita III	12	2	11	21	7	21	41	58	B-14
Cygnus	12	2	11	44	7	16	22	42	B-7
Ya Turko	12	2	15	25	7	18	0	12	B-10
Numsee II	12	2	29	9	7	6	36	2	C-5
Tangent	12	2	43	38	7	10	25	13	C-9
Intermezzo	12	2	54	55	7	18	59	21	B-13
Montgomery Street	12	3	2	11	7	8	49	11	C-7
Esperance	12	3	22	47	7	9	4	13	C-8
Westerley	12	4	28	34	7	18	17	36	B-11
Xanthippe	12	4	39	15	7	18	35	0	B-12
Ashante	12	5	3	33	7	10	39	25	C-10
Chiriqui	12	5	21	28	8	17	50	46	A-14
Hawaiiana	12	6	57	34	7	13	44	16	C-12
Starling III	12	7	0	6	7	23	12	42	B-16
Typee	12	7	12	8	7	13	21	45	C-11
Ranger	12	8	36	11	7	22	31	56	B-15
Americana	12	8	50	11	7	20	7	13	C-16
Loco Viente	12	10	55	53	8	2	27	41	B-17
Val o Van	12	11	0	39	7	16	4	38	C-14
Rowena	12	12	48	6	8	4	55	26	B-18
Dakar	12	11	53	52	7	16	57	51	C-15
Esprit	12	11	36	4	7	2	43	58	D-2
Intrepid I	12	1	56	47	7	4	15	0	D-2
Hawaiiana	12	6	57	34	7	13	44	16	C-13
Typee	12	7	12	8	7	13	21	45	C-12
Americana	12	8	50	11	7	20	7	13	C-17
Esprit	12	11	36	4	7	2	41	58	D-1
Pleiades	12	14	40	42	7	7	25	15	D-3
Blanquita	12	20	0	39	8	9	53	4	B-19
Mamie	12	18	48	52	7	12	26	26	D-4
Ano Nuevo	12	21	43	13	7	12	46	53	C-12
Destiny II	12	21	51	51	7	23	1	6	C-16

*Set record for first to finish.

You win one and you win one more . . . and then you lose "the biggie."

Mark Johnson

9

Taking Control

A few months after his disappointment in Hawaii, Big Bob Johnson died on September 19, 1969 (age fifty-seven) while toasting the new arrival of a godchild in San Francisco. Johnson had been battling heart disease for several years, but the death of the jovial maverick still came as a shock to the sailing world as well as his family. His wife Ramona died shortly thereafter in 1970, leaving Mark, Dotty, and Fritz Johnson to carry on. *Passage* now belonged to them, and Big Bob had left provisions in his will to fund campaigning the boat, at least for a while.

Grieving but undaunted, the Johnson brothers teamed up to complete the multi-year racing campaign Mark and his father had set up for the boat. Mark was thirty-two. Fritz ("Fritter") was just twenty-two.

In November, with Mark Johnson in command, they went nose-to-nose with rival *Blackfin* in the Long Beach to La Paz, Mexico, race. *Passage* and *Blackfin* traded the lead over the 900-mile course, but in the final stretch from Cabo San Lucas north to La Paz, Ken DeMeuse took *Blackfin* close inshore, expecting better thermal breezes.

"I decided not to follow him and sailed the rhumb line for La Paz," says Mark. "It paid off. We got a strong norther and *Blackfin* was becalmed." Mark Johnson had won his first race, and once again the Big Dinghy proved she could rock. There was one hell of a fiesta ashore.

From Mexico, a delivery crew sailed *Passage* back east through the Panama Canal for another SORC series plus local races in Florida and the Bahamas. Before the start of the Miami to Palm Beach race, Chip Cleary, the senior member of the crew and the crew manager, took Mark aside and said, "Take the helm at the start this time, otherwise the crew won't see you as the captain."

THE NEW YORK TIMES, SUNDAY, NOVEMBER 2, 196

Will to Win Spurs Windward Passage

Late Skipper Put Ketch in 960-Mile Race Saturday

If Windward Passage [illegible] [illegible]day's [illegible] race from Long Beach, Calif., to La Paz, Mexico, there will only be one way to describe it: she had the will to win.

For when her late skipper, Robert F. Johnson, died last Sept. 19 of a heart attack at his Portland, Ore., home, he left a will providing that his 72-foot superswift ketch be sailed in at least 10 major blue-water races following his death.

Mark Johnson, his 31-year-old son, will be at the helm of Windward Passage when she renews her fued with the equally rapid Blackfin—and 31 other yachts—in the third biennial race. The younger Johnson served as crewman on the boat's successes in the Southern Ocean Racing Circuit and the Trans-Pacific race. He will fly the burgee of the Lahaina Yacht Club of Hawaii.

Rascal in Class A

Blackfin, a 73-foot flush-deck ketch, will be skippered by Kenneth DeMeuse of San Francisco's St. Francis Yacht Club. The boat was awarded first-to-finish honors in last summer's Transpac after Windward Passage had been penalized two hours for a foul that occurred at the starting line, costing her the elapsed-time record for which she was designed.

Although class designations are still pending, race officials indicated that Class A entries, in addition to Blackfin and Windward Passage, would include Bill Wilson's Rascal, a 59-footaluminum yawl; George Sturgis's Columbia 57 sloop Dorothy O; John Hall's Concerto, also a Columbia 57, and Jack K. Hamilton's Jacarol II, a Cal 48 sloop.

Although Argonaut, the Transpac corrected-time winner, isn't entered, the swift and sure Cal 40 class, which did so well in the midsummer event, will be represented by three sloop-rigged entries and by a fourth one rigged as a yawl.

The race, which originated in 1963, is an unusual challenge to seamen in that the first 770 miles from Long Beach Harbor to Cabo San Lucas is usually a fast run with strong, steady winds.

However, after rounding the cape at the tip of Baja California, sailors are confronted by powerful, swirling currents and rapidly changing wind conditions, making the final 190 miles one of sailing's greatest challenges.

Windward Passage is entered in next Saturday's race from Long Beach, Calif., to La Paz

Pictorial Parade

Article from the New York Times, *November 2, 1969*
Image courtesy of Tad Belknap

Mark had usually been a sail trimmer in previous races. Although he had been messing around in sailboats since age eight on Lake Oswego in Oregon, and he had plenty of blue-water racing experience in his father's yachts, particularly Big Ti and *Passage*, Mark had never been through the relentless racing drills common to yacht club junior sailing programs or gotten involved with dinghy racing. The starts of sailboat races made him anxious. He wondered why he couldn't let John Rumsey take the helm to start the race as his father had always done.

Cleary said, "You're not your father. You have to find a way to gain the crew's respect. This is it."

Mark Johnson took a deep breath, then walked to the helm. He told Rumsey he might need a little help.

"He said it might be easier, if he just handled the start," says Mark. "I told him thanks, but we were going to do this my way."

Mark had a team to build. And after the next series of first-place finishes, none of the crew would be jumping ship. There was a season of serious racing ahead with the new skipper. Once again the Big Dinghy dominated the SORC fleet when it came to winning line honors. After a winter of tropical victories, *Passage* sailed north to Newport, Rhode Island, in June 1970 and was first to finish in the Cruising Club of America's classic Newport Bermuda Race.

"Gurney was aboard in his duck hat, smoking away as usual," says Mark Johnson. "The boat started to heel over more than 20 degrees. 'I believe if you put a smaller jib on her, she might go a bit better,' said Gurney. We switched out the jib. She came up a bit flatter in the water and took off." That's the night Mark Johnson learned *Passage* had a sweet spot for speed going to weather right at 20 degrees of heel.

During the winter of 1970–71, *Windward Passage* was once again in the vanguard of SORC fleet, but then she broke her mainmast in a race from Florida to Lucaya in the Bahamas. Meanwhile, the new Sparkman & Stephen's–designed 60-foot, aluminum sloop *Running Tide* grabbed top honors in the SORC.

With his boat in pieces, Mark Johnson tried to focus on a new challenge, the 800-mile Miami–Montego Bay Pineapple Cup race. It has run every other year since 1961 and is one of the oldest races on the grand prix ocean-racing circuit. After the start, racers cross the Gulf Stream for the Northwest Providence Channel. The middle of the race features a fetch down the eastern side of the Bahama Islands chain toward the tip of Cuba. The final stretch is a 240-mile downwind slide from Cuba's eastern tip to the finish at Montego Bay on the west coast of Jamaica.

"We had to hurry up and sleeve our broken mast in the Bahamas and get back to Miami for the start," remembers Mark Johnson. "The whole race we worried we would break the thing. It was blowing like hell, and I wasn't going to slow down. The first part of the race was a close reach, but the wind kept veering around behind us as we turned to the south. It was crazy."

The crew set what they called the "storm spinnaker," a kite with no shoulders, as they rounded the Bahamas and dashed for the east end of Cuba.

With the arrow on the Walker log pegged at 20 knots for most of the race, they left other maxis like *Ondine* to fade away over the horizon astern. At one point, according to Fritz Johnson, they outran a Cuban gunboat that was chasing them through—where else?—the Windward Passage.

During the last 240 miles of the race, the crew hoisted a large kite and surfed all the way to Montego Bay. The result was a course record: 3 days, 3 hours, 40 minutes, 7 seconds. *Passage* had beaten her '69 record-setting run by an astonishing 31 hours. It was a record that would stand for thirty-two years, through assaults by later generations of maxis until *Zephyrus V* beat *Passage*'s record run in 2003.

After Robert McNeil, the owner of *Zephyrus V*, broke the record, Mark Johnson called him to congratulate him.

"He told me he felt there should be separate trophies because his boat was so different from *Passage,*" says Mark. "It was longer, weighed half as much, and had a water-ballasted, retractable keel. There is no comparison."

10

Winning It All

By the summer of '71 the Johnson brothers had *Passage* lined up near Point Fermin off Los Angeles Harbor for the race Big Bob had said he would never again sail, the Transpac. The world's six fastest 73-footers had come together for this race: *Windward Passage, Blackfin, Kialoa II, Ondine, Graybeard*, and *Buccaneer.*

"Everything we had learned about the boat in dozens of races over the last two years, told us she could win this thing," says Mark Johnson, "and we wanted to do this for Dad."

More than a score of first-to-finish performances in major ocean races over the last year of competition had given Mark growing confidence in not just *Windward Passage* but in himself. And the boat's expanding reputation as a sorceress under sail attracted a crew of some of the best racing sailors alive.

Chip Cleary was the "Old Man" on the boat and one of the watch captains. At the request of his shipmates, he kept a running log of the race that captures the drama with matchless immediacy. Eventually, it appeared in the Lahaina Yacht Club's 1971 magazine.

> SUNDAY, JULY 4. Mark gets off to a very good start on starboard tack along the middle of the line, which had been set approximately right-angles to the course to Honolulu. Wind is SSW at about 5 to 6 knots. We have taken an extra foot in rating—71.6 IOR—in order to carry a 170-percent jib. On corrected time this will cost us more than two hours. But we believe the Honolulu race is won or lost in the first 26 miles, getting to, and around, the west end of Catalina. We do not intend, as we had to do in '69 with less powerful sails, to play "catch-up" after Catalina . . .
>
> By 2000 [ship's time] we are sailing in light and fluky winds, with *Graybeard* and *Blackfin* holding up high of us. But we

begin to foot faster as the winds freshens. We sail through *Graybeard*'s lee, with *Blackfin* on her weather quarter. And that's going to be our goodbye to our temporary "friends . . . ."

MONDAY, JULY 5. Before the race we spent about three months studying and keeping track of the Pacific weather and the prognostications of the Pacific High. The weather history cranked into our pre-race strategy discussions . . . . Mark decides we'll sail the rhumb line, the shortest, most direct course to the Diamond Head finish . . . . It is against the grain of customary tactics. Our trick will be to sail the boat to maximum speeds possible in the winds that come to us.

TUESDAY, JULY 6. At 0900 we do what we have been anxious to do for hours. Up goes the 2.2 [ounce] reaching spinnaker and our speed climbs back up to 11 and 10 plus on a heading of 235 degrees. One hour later we change to the bigger-shouldered regular 2.2 Hood and sail a course between 230 to 240 degrees. The course to Honolulu is 242 degrees . . . . Our speed holds at a steady 10 plus.

WEDNESDAY, JUL 7. It is squally during the night watches. Rain begins to drag down on the spinnaker, so at 0500 we drop the 2.2 and fly the dry 1.5 to keep the boat speed to 10 knots or better . . . . Slow going creeps over into our afternoon watch . . . . As everybody knows, this is no way to win a race. Depression begins to fog in the crew, and we concentrate on sailing WP like a dinghy with shifting ballast . . . . We do manage to get another 250-mile run for the 24-hour period . . . . By noon we figure to be about 1500 from Honolulu.

THURSDAY, JULY 8. This is a bad day at Black Rock for sure. The going is slow. And more slow . . . . The Hawaiian wind god, Kahuna, really should be embarrassed by his poor showing—not to mention the heretical remarks about him freely offered by all hands. In retaliation the rascal let the winds slump to 10 knots in the afternoon. There is only one way to fight back. The ¾-ounce spinnaker comes out for its workout . . . .

Approaching the Transpac finish line at Diamond Head, 1977 —©Phil Uhl

7099
7099

Despite our depression about the reduction in the day's run and all of our gloom about the failure of Kahuna to come up with some really good wind goddammit, everyone on board is quite jubilant about what has happened in our race with the other 73-footers up to this point . . . . We are 32 miles ahead of *Blackfin*. *Graybeard* is 50 miles south of us. *Kialoa II* is seventy-six miles astern. *Ondine* is 90 miles below us and 100 miles astern. If this weren't such a dry ship, we would break out a triple tot of rum for all hands. Since we are denied the rum, we get back to bitching about the winds . . . .

FRIDAY, JULY 9. It's heavily overcast during the night and early morning hours. The wind hovering around 10 knots. Despite this, both watches manage to keep the boat speed up between 8.5 and 9 knots. At 0900 things begin to look up—there are patches of clearing blue skies ahead . . . . and the boat speed begins to edge up . . . . By mid-afternoon we are out from under the overcast skies and the wind begins to fill in and carry some heft to it . . . . We change from the 1.5 to the 2.2 chute . . . . We get a modicum of surfing at 13 knots . . . . Our fleet position according to the UCLA computer is 1st in Class A and 4th in fleet.

SATURDAY, JULY 10. We're keeping our boat speed up to an average of 10 knots or better for each watch. But it's not easy as the wind sags off in strength, comes back in and then goes off again. And again. right after roll call . . . . *Blackfin* says [she is] about 40 miles behind us. Our day's run is 235 miles . . . . The UCLA computer gives us first in Class A and 2nd in fleet. . . . Things are looking up . . . . In the process of a two-pole jibe, we try to do it too fast and snag the clew of the chute and rip the luff. Down comes the 2.2 and up goes the new maximum-sized 2.5, which Mark has bought with the idea of carrying it in winds up to 35 knots . . . . During all this our only loss in boat speed is about ½ knot.

SUNDAY, JULY 11. A ketch on the far horizon is sighted in midmorning. And for a crew so psyched up since the start off

Sandy McKenzie was a large and beloved part of many of Passage*'s successes.*

Keeping on, keeping on. Transpac 1977 —©Phil Uhl

Fermin last Sunday that they can hardly stay put for a second, it's inevitable that one of them will claim it is *Blackfin* . . . . The rumor runs riot. Then a closer look is taken. It's a wandering cruising ketch not *Blackfin* . . . . Things quiet down and it's back to racing WP . . . We are 600 miles from the finish . . . . We have *Blackfin* by 60 miles. . . . We have *Buccaneer* by 130 miles . . . . We have *Graybeard* by 62 miles . . . . We have *Kialoa II* by 163 miles . . . . We have been keeping up our boat speed despite the fact the maximum wind has been 15 knots . . . . By 1900 we have about 500 miles more to go and 50 hours to do it if we are to set a new record.

MONDAY, JULY 12. It's slow going again—comparatively—for our two early morning watches . . . . We put up the 2.2 to see how well the portable sewing machine crew has done. Their repair job looks very good . . . . Our days run is 251 miles . . . . *Blackfin* doesn't answer her call the first time around, but later reports . . . 70 miles behind us. *Buccaneer* says on a relay from *Graybeard* [she is] 170 miles behind us . . . . With that report out of the way, she coolly says she's lost her rudder and is proceeding under jury rig at 6 knots. By 1245 *Graybeard* says she is taking on water very fast, faster than her own pumps can handle it, and she needs help urgently. *Pakeha* heads toward her and maydays the Coast Guard, which reacts promptly with an airdrop of pumps, etc. *Graybeard*, as it develops, lost her skeg soon after the rudder stock sheared off, and she's got a hole the size of a football in her . . . . We have a maximum of 250 miles to go and a maximum of 24 hours to beat *Blackfin*'s "record."

TUESDAY, JULY 13. We have first to finish tucked away, unless a catastrophe occurs . . . . We are facing the same old light to medium and back to light winds. But we assure ourselves there's always the run down the Molokai Channel to give us that extra surge and a chance to surf and pick up hours of bonus time on our competition . . . . By 1610 we're abeam the Molokai Light at Kalui Point . . . . We decide to douse the 2.5 and set the 2.2 reaching chute . . . . We hope for heavier winds and better surfing seas, and for a short time

Don Vaughn Perpetual Memorial Trophy—given to the most outstanding crewmember each year. John "Gargle" McClure was the recipient in 1985.—©Phil Uhl

Don Vaughn, Sailing Master, who ran the crew for many years

DAYS
NEW COURSE RECORD
HOURS
MINUTES
SECONDS
Transpacific
Yacht Race

> the wind does get up to 22 knots . . . . The best we are able to do is an occasional 13 to 14 knot slider . . . . It ain't the hard-driving, wind-banging finish we wanted desperately. Then we are in the middle of beach cats, the powerboats, the Hobie cats and EVERYBODY afloat. It seems to us everyone escorting us to the finish is able to run as fast as *Windward Passage*. It would be humiliating if we didn't know we were going to beat *Blackfin*'s official "record," and even shave a few minutes off our own '69 first-to-finish time! We cross the finish line with the largest collection of escort boats ever seen for a Honolulu Race finish—at least 150 of them . . . .

So it was that Mark and Fritz Johnson, along with an amazing crew, fulfilled what Chip Cleary called "the impossible dream" that started with Big Bob, Alan Gurney, their cocktail napkins, and their pens one night at the New York Yacht Club. *Windward Passage* set a new Transpac record time of 9 days, 9 hours, 6 minutes, 48 seconds.

As *Passage* docked Mark Johnson was at the bow pulpit. Dotty was dockside with an orchid wreath in her hair. She was waving a bottle of J&B scotch to her man. *Windward Passage* had arrived in Honolulu first to finish, first in Class A, and first on corrected time. She had won the triple crown. At the award ceremony she claimed the six most-prized trophies.

When asked by a reporter what he would change if he could sail this Transpac over again, Mark Johnson said, "I wouldn't want to try it over again and improve on it because it would be pretty hard to do." He added, "Our crew was as efficient as any I have ever seen. I think it is one of the finest racing crews ever assembled."

Donated by Roy E. Disney and created by Andrea Favilli, the clock in the Transpac trophy is always set to the best record time. The hands are digitally modified to reflect Passage's *1971 record.*
—image ©Phil Uhl

The Champion Crew

Mark Johnson–*skipper*
Sandy McKenzie–*cook*
Skip Allen
Rex Banks
Tom Blackaller
Charles Blair
John Boulton
Chip Cleary
Paul Cook
Peter Garbani
Albert Gooch
Richard Haskell
Chandler Hovey
Curtis Jackson
Fritz Johnson
Irmin Stawicki
Don Vaughn

11

A 6,000-MILE DUEL

TO SOME OBSERVERS THE TRANSPAC record and victory seemed hard to top, but when *Windward Passage* met *Blackfin* in September, 1971, for the St. Francis Yacht Club's Perpetual Trophy, generally called "The San Francisco Big Boat Series," California newspapers as well as the yachting press gave the duel vast coverage. This was not an ocean race. It was a series of buoy races, and some of Mark Johnson's first. But he out-maneuvered *Blackfin* at the start of the first of three races around San Francisco Bay. At one point, the Big Dinghy was so far ahead that winch-grinder Don Vaughn lowered John Rumsey over the side to water-ski behind *Passage* along the city waterfront just to add an exclamation point to the boat's speed.

Some onlookers saw the drubbing as *Passage*'s way of asserting her winning ways in the buoy racing game (as well as in blue-water competition) after she had lost to "Blackie" in a light-air match race for the Cal Cup off Marina del Rey in 1969. The press was not kind to *Blackfin*, which hailed from the St. Francis Yacht Club and was a local favorite. They wrote about "*Blackfin's* Bleak Day," saying "*Passage* Whips *Blackfin* Handily." One writer gushed, "*Windward Passage* added to her expanding reputation as the world's fastest ocean racing yacht . . . ."

The so-called "friendly feud" between *Passage* and *Blackfin* mushroomed into a running battle when Blackie's owner, Ken DeMeuse, signaled to the press that he was planning a four-race duel with *Passage* as the maxis looked toward to their 1972 racing schedules. The competition would start with a match race off Long Beach, followed by the San Diego to Acapulco race, the Newport, Rhode Island, to Bermuda race, and a transatlantic marathon from Bermuda to Spain. Those events added up to 6,000 miles of racing and a 25,000-mile voyage for the yachts to make the round trip back to California.

Windward Passage *was always in the mix in the San Francisco Big Boat Series, 1980.—©Phil Uhl*

John Rumsey water-skiing behind Passage *just to prove a point.*

To try to seize the advantage, Ken DeMeuse sent *Blackfin* to the Stephens Brothers yard in Stockton, California, for a new bow that added 34 inches to the foredeck and 18 inches to the waterline. Meanwhile, Mark Johnson was taking life one race at a time. He ordered some new sails and entered his ketch in the Cal-Coastal Race from San Francisco to Los Angeles.

Windward Passage took off in the coastal race, chasing the smaller yacht *Warrior* (also cold-molded of wood) down the California coast, but when the wind piped up, Mark Johnson and his crew rallied to claim line honors off Los Angeles. Then *Blackfin* showed up with her new bow, but she could not best *Passage* in the three match races sponsored by the Long Beach Yacht Club.

After the dashes around the buoys, the yachts sailed to San Diego for the start of the 1,430-mile race to Acapulco, Mexico. Once again, *Windward Passage* took the lead from the start, but *Blackfin* was close on her heels. Halfway through the race, off Cabo San Lucas, *Passage* and Blackie were side-by-side.

"We were so close, we could hear the gears on their winches clicking during the night," remembers Mark Johnson.

Blackfin pulled into the lead as the wind went light. But when the breeze freshened to 8–14 knots, *Passage* charged ahead and stayed there. Due to light winds in the middle of the race, this was no record run, but *Passage* had added yet another first-to-finish to her résumé.

The 6,000-mile duel was not all glory and limelight for *Passage* and her crew . . . but what adventures they shared. After a memorable fiesta ashore in Acapulco, the two big ketches took off for the long delivery trip through the Panama Canal, then north to Newport, Rhode Island.

ST. FRANCIS YACHT CLUB
ON THE MARINA — SAN FRANCISCO 94123
931-2700

COMMODORE, ALBERT T. SIMPSON
VICE COMMODORE, ROBERT D. FORD
REAR COMMODORE, HAYS A. MCLELLAN

BOARD OF DIRECTORS
ROBERT D. FORD, CHAIRMAN
FRANCIS A. SOOY, M.D., SECRETARY

Tuesday, September 21, 1971

To : Commodore Alber t T. Simpson
Fr o m : R. C. Keefe, Regatta Chairman
Sugject: Results, Second Race St. Francis Perpetual Series

Th· Yachts sailed Course "D" (24.I Miles)

·dw ard Passage........Elapsed Time 2-37-05

Black fin...............Elappsed Time 2-41-09

Windward Passage won todays race and consequently the match for the St. Francis Perpet.:ual Trophy.

The final result

As *Passage* prepared for the so-called "Thrash to the Onion Patch," the 1972 Newport Bermuda Race, she had her "A-listers" of the era aboard, including Mark (skipper), Fritz Johnson, Peter Bowker, Don Vaughn, Rex Banks, John Rumsey, Kirk Elliott, and Dick Haskell among others. Sandy McKenzie and Dotty Johnson were the cooks.

Passage blew out two sails before the start in a northeast gale, but she led the fleet of 178 boats as they slogged across the Gulf Stream over 600 miles through storm-force winds in the tail end of Hurricane Agnes. Throughout the trip Dotty strapped into a galley harness for hours on end and whipped up her signature chili, Bolognese, and fried rice for the guys who weren't fighting seasickness while doing battle with the wind, rain, and high seas. A former competitive skier and the daughter of loggers from the mountains of Grande Ronde, Oregon, Dotty was no stranger to hard living. But after days with the boat rocking and rolling, and the combers rumbling over the deck, she began questioning the cost of extreme adventures like ocean racing.

"I wondered if my children [she and Mark had four by now] would ever see me again," she remembers. She knew this was her last ocean race. She needed to put being a mother to her own children above her natural tendency to nurture the *Passage* crew. But it was sad, she says. "I felt like we had built that boat."

"At one point, we were going 10 knots with just a jib staysail up," says Mark Johnson. "There were 110-knot gusts. You had to wear a diving mask to see where you were going."

By the time *Passage* was 35 miles out from Bermuda, the weather had shredded the last of her racing sails. The crew had been driving her hard through brutal 14 foot seas and hurricane-force winds. Now they had to

◀ Passage *burying the rail*
—©Phil Uhl

deploy the only sail they had left, the storm trysail, to make headway while her competitors clawed by to deny her victory. *Blackfin* did not finish in the money either, but she came in ahead of *Passage*. The 61-foot sloop *Robon* was first to finish and first in Class A. Eleven competitors were dismasted or disabled. It was at a moment like this that Mark Johnson remembers navigator Peter Bowker reciting a traditional bit of English doggerel, "All around is desolation, and life is like an open tomb . . . ."

After the race Ted Turner took Mark and Dotty to dinner. When the subject of an impending protest hearing from *Running Tide* against *Windward Passage* came up, Turner told Mark he should "go in there with a tommy gun hidden in a violin case and shoot all the bastards." Johnson chose a calmer tack instead. The Big Dinghy was just getting started on her climb to stardom, and she had bigger challenges ahead.

Bill Bowers joined the crew in Bermuda following the "Thrash to the Onion Patch." As he tells it, Mark Johnson was bent on redemption when they crossed the starting line in *Passage* on the Regatta Del Descubrimiento Transatlantic Race from Bermuda to Bayona, Spain, retracing Columbus's second voyage home in the *Pinta* in 1493. The navigator thought the yacht's best course to victory was to sail the rhumb line straight to Spain. But it took them through an immense high-pressure dome in the central Atlantic that had filled in after the hurricane passed. Not even new, light-air sails and the yacht's sleek profile could carry her through the Sargasso Sea at times.

"Sometimes the seaweed seemed to be moving faster than we were," says Bowers. The highlights of the day came at the top of the forenoon watch when the boat's 'porn captain' posted a new risqué photo in the sail locker.

Each evening the crew gathered to listen to Peter Bowker read a chapter from *Stuart Little* in his rich English accent.

As *Passage* neared the Flores mark, gentle breezes began to fill the twin spinnakers off and on. On one occasion Rex Banks was standing on the foredeck when a squall popped open the collapsed main chute. His foot was in a bight of the sheet, and he was instantly flipped upside down by the ankle, smashing his cheek into a stanchion. The crew unloaded the clew with the lazy guy and lowered Rex down to the deck. Bowers, acting ship's surgeon, cleaned and sterilized the gash and closed it over the exposed cheekbone with butterfly bandages. Banks wore the scar of surviving his duel with the Atlantic high as a keepsake.

Windward Passage logged more than twenty-one days on that trip, besting Christopher Columbus's time on the passage by one day, and arrived a week behind yachts that had traveled north around the high.

Passage's crew had bet on sailing a rhumbline course, a strategy that had served them well in the Transpac and other victories, but in this race, the rhumb line proved a bad bet.

"We just went the wrong direction," admitted Mark Johnson. "It happens."

When the crew sailed the Big Dinghy to the dock under staysail and mizzen (the engine was out of commission), her provision lockers were empty except for a few cans of food and some bottles of Beck's beer. *Blackfin* and Ken DeMeuse had been there waiting for days.

"I danced with him at the awards party," remembers Dotty. "My husband was still somewhere over the horizon." Bowers's fiancée Linda recalls meeting Dotty and also three young ladies who were all there waiting to greet Don Vaughn.

WINDWARD PASSAGE
PORTLAND OREGON

After Mark and his bedraggled crew finally cleared customs and immigration, they found a *bodega,* poured cups of sangria, took heart, and toasted the boat. In a matter of weeks she had endured a hurricane and a deadly calm, as well as two spectacular and unexpected losses. *Windward Passage* was starting to claim a new role. She was not just a winner, she was a survivor.

During the 1976 Sydney Hobart Race, a bronze swivel attached to the headsail halyard on Passage *failed, causing the halyard to snap back against the mast and break the stainless steel snap-shackle as well. John Rumsey remembers, "As we raced forward to retrieve the sail before it went under the boat, these fittings landed near me on the deck. I now keep them around to remind me how lucky we are at times." —image courtesy of Patsy Bolling*

Image taken from a calendar—photographer unknown

Blackfin, Passage in 6000-Mile '72 Duel

By Jack Schmale
Boating Writer

NEWSY NEW YEAR: The friendly 1971 feud between famed 73-foot speed ketches Windward Passage and Blackfin, in which the former prevailed over 2225 miles of ocean and another 60 on San Francisco Bay, will be resumed with a shift into overdrive in 1972.

The renewal will find Ken deMeuse's aluminum Blackie from St. Francis Yacht Club opposing Mark Johnson's sleek wooden rival of Hawaii's Lahaina YC in a travelogue duel involving four boats and four countries, over 6000 nautical racing miles, and—at least for Blackfin—a 25,000-mile round trip consuming a minimum eight months.

The local queen will be rejuvenated by a new facelift, or nosebob. She's scheduled for relaunching almost any day now, following installation of a redesigned bow at Stephens Brothers yard in Stockton. The alteration, replacing the one-foot rounded vertical surface with a much sharper point of entr... to increase boat spe... adv...

THE OPERATION will also add 34 inches to Fin's foredeck and 18 to the waterline, permitting a larger spinnaker for her Jan. 28-30 closed course match series with passage off Long Beach. It will also qualify her just within the new International Offshore Rule's handicap rating of 70.

Passage, which currently rates approximately 73, will be unaffected in the 1430-mile San Diego-Acapulco biennial, in which the pair squares off February 6. Johnson will be obliged to sacrifice some of WP's potential power and whittle down to 70, however, for the Transatlantic 2500-mile marathon from Bermuda to Spain, in which the twain again shall meet in late June, also ... up, the New York-Ber... June 6.

★ ★

PORT 'N' STARB... news—with ... approval—for tenants ... house Cove annex of S... Marina. The Board of ... scheduled to vote nex...

reduce the surge problem drastically. The city would match Federal funding for the approximately $125,000 Army Engineers project, closing the western channel to Gashouse berthers, but allowing access to the largest west harbor.

One of the first showboats to tie up at the Cow Palace indoor marina for the huge S.F. Natonal Sports & Boat Show next week will be the exposition's swank flagship, the 57-foot Carri-Craft catamaran cruiser. In keeping with the tradition of squeezing the big babies through the doors first, the all-new super-houseboat will moor on Tuesday, three days before Friday's grand opening

Part III—Tues., Feb. 8, 1972 Los Angeles Times ★

WINDWARD PASSAGE HEADED FOR RECORD

Mark Johnson's record-smashing, 73-foot ketch, Windward Passage, of Lahaina, Maui, appeared on her way to a... elapsed time m... day as she took th... the 1,430-mile San... to-Acapulco race.

Windward Passag... the lead from Ke... Meuse's 76-foot ke... Blackfin, St. Fra... Yacht Club, before d... Sunday and at the Mond... roll call was five mil... ahead.

Both boats bettered the first-day run of the 83-foot cutter, Sirius II, in her record-setting 1964 race. The record is 8 days, 9 hours, 15 minutes 54 seconds.

In this race Sirius II, now owned and skippered by ... nch, Newport ... t Club, was

third in elapsed ti... miles behind ...

Los Angeles Times

14 Part III—Thurs., Feb. 10, 1972

WINDWARD PASSAGE KEEPS RECORD PACE

BY ALMON LOCKABEY

Light southwest winds along the Baja California coast slowed the Acapulco yacht race fleet to a virtual crawl Wednesday.

Still leading with 589 miles logged since the start off Point Loma Sunday was Mark Johnson's Windward Passage, but her progress had been slowed to a 135-mile day's run. She still is 97 miles ahead of the pace set by Sirius II when she established the race record in 1964.

...iling Windward Pas... ...miles was Ken ... from

ius II from Newport Harbor Yacht Club was 25 miles behind Blackfin.

The light airs allowed the smaller boats to move up on the leaders. Thalia IV, a Cal-43 sloop skippered by John Barbey of San Diego took the handicap lead with 531 miles logged since the start.

The leaders were about 100 miles from Cape San Lucas, halfway point in the 1,430-mile race. The bulk of the 26-boat fleet was bunched between Point Lazaro and Magdalena Bay.

Standings (overall handicap):

OVERALL—1. Thalia IV; 2. Sangrita ... Tzchak II; 4. Windstar; 5. Vixen. ... 1. Atorrante; 2. Vector II; ... Nalu IV; 5. Barca de ... Windstar;

Part III—Wed., Feb. 16, 1972 Los Angeles Times ★

Windward Passage First to Finish Acapulco Race

BY ALMON LOCKABEY

ACAPULCO — With three yachts safely in port, the long waiting game to determine the handicap winner in the 1,430-mile San Diego-to-Acapulco yacht race has begun.

Mark Johnson's 73-foot ketch Windward Passage was first to finish at 7:28 a.m. (PST) Tuesday. She was followed at 12:13 p.m. by Ken DeMeuse's 76-foot ketch Blackfin of San Francisco, and Bob Lynch's 83-foot cutter Sirius II, Newport Harbor Yacht Club, finished at 1:37 p.m.

Windward Passage missed the elapsed time record by 10½ hours. She saved her handicap time on both the other finishers but was still in jeopardy by some of the Class B and C yachts still at sea.

Bob Beauchamp's Columbia 57 Dorothy O was expected to finish by dawn today with no chance of saving her time over the three top finishers.

Johnson and DeMeuse told of a thrilling boat-for-boat battle between Windward Passage and Black-fin—with Sirius II in sight astern—most of the day Monday. It wasn't until nearly midnight that the wind freshened along the shore, allowing Windward Passage to pull steadily ahead and finish first.

Handicap standings:

OVERALL: 1. Nemesis; 2. Alegre; 3. Tzchak II; 4. Atorrante; 5. Vixen; 6. Dorothy O; 7. Malu IV; 8. Thalia IV; 9. Sigame; 10. Vector II.

CLASS A: 1. Atorrante; 2. Dorothy O; 3. Malu IV; 4. Vector II; 5. Windward Passage.

CLASS B: 1. Alegre; 2. Thalia IV; 3. Windstar; 4. Thera; 5. Rainy Day.

CLASS C: 1. Nemesis; 2. Ezchak II; 3. Vixen; 4. Sigame; 5. Tatei.

E6 The REGISTER Thursday (e) February 10, 1972

IN S.D.-ACAPULCO RACE

'Windward Passage' Holds Lead

SAN DIEGO—Windward Passage was still running well ahead of Sirius II's 1964 record pace in the Acapulco race Wednesday as winds resumed an 18-20 knot velocity.

However, the wind was out of the south-southwest, meaning the 27-boat fleet was reaching and sailing slightly into the wind instead of directly before it as it had the first three days out.

WP had logged 589 miles from San Diego as of Wednesday's ...oon radio roll call. Blackfin ...oved back into second spot, ...t trailed WP by some 24 ...les from 565 miles out from ... Diego. Sirius II moved back ... third position 15 mil... Blackfin. ...lia IV ...

running fourth in the fleet with 531 miles logged. Second on overall handicap was the class C leader, the Cal-30 Sangrita II which is the smallest boat in the race. Atorrante was the class A leader.

The highly touted Mexican entry, Tzchak II, which has Olympic champion and former Star class world champion Lowell North in her crew, was again third on overall handicap and could very well be winning since discrepancies in posi... reporting have been ... according to S... Club.

The REGISTER Tuesday (e) February 8, 1972

Windward Leading In Acapulco Race

By FRED MILLER
Register Boating Editor

SAN DIEGO — Mark Johnson's 73-foot ketch Windward Passage took over the lead of the XI San Diego-Acapulco race Monday, and held a six-mile lead over Ken DeMeuse's 76-foot ketch Blackfin at fleet roll call time.

The race record holder, Bob Lynch's 83-foot cutter Sirius II from Newport Beach, was unable to keep up with the other two when the point of sailing became dead downwind and slowly slipped astern.

WP has logged 229 miles from San Diego since Sunday's start.

Blackfin 223 and Sirius II 202.

Running fourth boat-for-boat is the Mexican entry Barca de Oro, a Cal-48 sloop owned and sailed by Enrique Braun, Acapulco. Barca de Oro had logged 193 miles while in fifth place was Herb Johnson's radical New Zealand sloop Vector II from San Diego, which had logged 189 miles.

Although it is really too soon to tell anything, the reported overall handicap leader was Bill Jonas' 37-foot custom sloop Meltemi from San Francisco.

Winds were 18 knots under an overcast sky Monday, with seas running six feet in height.

Two Straight

Passage Sweeps St. Francis Cup

By Jack Schmale
Boating Writer

Windward Passage added to her expanding reputation as the world's fastest ocean racing yacht yesterday when Hawaii's Mark Johnson masterfully wheeled the handsome 73-foot ketch to a second straight victory over rival Blackfin and wrapped up the St. Francis Perpetual Cup match series.

The triple crown winner and record-breaking champ of July's Transpacific race slipped through the starting line almost as if the gun were fired to salute the feat.

The precision starboard tack carried the white hulled beauty on a heeling bee-line sprint to the beach. And as if to entertain the thousnds of fans swarming host St. Francis Yacht Club, Johnson flipped her onto the port reach a thin 100 feet off-shore and boomed off for the Crissy weather mark.

Ken DeMeuse's local queen, of similar rig, length and color, valiantly pursued Passage into the freshening 15-knot breeze and looped the buoy 35 seconds in debt. If there was an imperfection in the winner's performance, it occurred at this point, when a stubborn spinnaker stop refused to free the big balllooner.

12

Challenged

As the winter of 1972–73 loomed, *Windward Passage* had been on the ocean-racing circuit for three years. She already had dozens of first-place finishes in grand prix events to her credit, and by most estimates, she was the fastest modern ocean-racing yacht the world had ever seen. She was also the most glamorous if you judged her by the volume of her press coverage or the number of spectators who showed up by boat to watch her compete or ogled her at the dock. Women gathered to welcome her all-male crew ashore. Despite her fluke losses in the Bermuda and the Transatlantic races, one had to wonder what *Windward Passage* could do for an encore.

After she once again bested the competition for line honors in the '73 SORC races, *Passage* seemed nearly invincible. But her rivals were hardly giving up. If anything, they were more energized than ever to knock her out of the spotlight by throwing money at the problem. Sick and tired of looking at "The Effing Whale" (on *Passage*'s transom), Jim Kilroy started building *Kialoa III*. She was a ketch designed by David Pedrick at Sparkman and Stephens. At a cursory glance "K3" looked to be similar to *Passage*. But under the new (1970) International Offshore Rule (IOR) governing ocean racing, maxis were no longer constrained by the former 73-foot limit. So K3 was being built 6 feet longer by Palmer Johnson in Wisconsin with a launch date of 1974. She was made of aluminum and cost well over twenty times what the Johnsons spent to build *Windward Passage*.

Likewise, Huey Long had been digging deep into his pockets. He had just built his fourth *Ondine*, a 79-foot, Britton Chance–designed yawl, with the hope of putting *Passage* in her place. There were also other competitors like *Running Tide*, sometimes skippered by Ted Turner, on the hunt. And then there was a dark horse that wasn't really a maxi at all . . . .

13751
13751
1375

Built as *Infidel* in 1963–65 to the design of New Zealander John Spencer, she was now called *Ragtime* and hailed from Southern California. But unlike *Passage*'s other challengers, she was neither state-of-the-art, expensive, larger, or designed with a racing rule in mind. Her brilliance was that her design mimicked old-school, simple, hard-chined, racing keelboats like the Star Class sloop. And like *Passage* she was made of wood (a double layer of ⅜-inch sheet plywood to be exact) in an era when racing yachts were built of anything but former trees.

People called her a "freak boat," just as they had dubbed *Windward Passage.* Her crews said she had a curious way of flexing as she moved through the water, but they also said that when running off the wind, she was fast as hell. *Ragtime* was a 62-foot sled, the forerunner of what would eventually be called ULDBs (ultralight-displacement boats). She had the potential to get up on a plane and surf the whole way to Honolulu if she didn't break apart. One other thing, she weighed less than half as much as *Passage* did.

Mark knew that this freak boat flying the burgee of the Long Beach Yacht Club was a threat. *Passage* had raced around the buoys a couple of times with "Rags," and sometimes the plywood wonder had won. For the '73 Transpac she was being sailed by a syndicate of six owner-skippers: Bill Dalessi, Barney Flam, Dr. Mort Haskell, Stan Miller, Chuck Kober, and Jack Queen. She also had Olympic medalist Dick Deaver sailing aboard.

"In those days," says Mark Johnson, "you just didn't get better than Deaver."

On July 4 *Windward Passage* got off to an excellent start for Honolulu amid sixty other yachts at Point Fermin. She led the race for nine days with *Blackfin* unable to catch up. It would be the last match between the two rivals. In January 1974 Ken DeMeuse and two of his children would die in a crash after the Beechcraft Duke DeMeuse was piloting

Arch-nemisis: Jim Kilroy's Kialoa III
—©Phil Uhl

RAGTiME
BEHR
RAGTiME
HONOLULU, HI.

crashed in Utah during a snowstorm on the family's return from a ski vacation in Colorado.

Unlike the 1971 Transpac, this year's race never subjected the fleet to sustained light air. As they charged for Honolulu, *Ragtime* began to show her ability to surf in the following seas. Instead of chasing *Passage* along the rhumbline course, "Rags" pointed a bit up to windward ever so slightly to get a better angle on the breeze and waves so she could pick up speed and surf. Her crew was downwind tacking her back and forth across the rhumb line like Deaver did when he was racing dinghies.

"On the last morning of the race," remembers Mark, "we heard *Ragtime* reporting in with her position. She said she had *Windward Passage* in sight. We could see her coming on. She went lower on the course from us, but when she jibed for the final run through the Molokai Channel for the Barn Door, she had a faster angle on the wind than we did. She was going quicker than we were. And she was surfing, really surfing. Every time she slid down the face of a big wave, she gained another 100 yards on us. Maybe I should have tried to cover her, but I don't know if I could have blocked her. This is what she was built for. So I went straight for the finish line and hoped for the best."

In the end *Ragtime* nosed out *Windward Passage* by 4 minutes, 31 seconds at the Diamond Head finish. This would be called "the most exciting elapsed-time finish since the races started in 1906" by the officials who came out to watch. But it was no record. *Ragtime*'s elapsed time was 10 days, 14 hours, 40 seconds. *Warrior*, Al Cassel's 50-foot, cold-molded cutter from Newport Beach, which had challenged *Passage* in the Cal-Coastal Race a year ago, came first in Class A on corrected time. Most of the big boats, including *Passage*, placed well down in the overall (corrected time) category.

Yet another head-to-head nemesis, Ragtime*: smaller, lighter, damn fast —©Phil Uhl*

ONDINE
NEW YORK
BLACKFIN
HONOLULU

13

Down Under

IT SORT OF HAPPENED WITH A CASUAL CONVERSATION in my brother's driveway," remembers Fritz "Fritter" Johnson. The year was 1974, and he was twenty-seven years old. "It wasn't like 'Here, younger brother. Now you take over the boat.' We just both saw that Mark had a wife and five young kids. Jetting off on airplanes for weeks at a time to race just didn't make good sense. It was time for me to shoulder some of the load with the boat."

As the brothers agreed, Fritz Johnson would take the helm of *Windward Passage* for a while. But first they had to make an immediate decision about the 1975 Transpac. Neither of the brothers was in an easy position in terms of their personal or professional lives to commit to the race. But there was another option. A filmmaker wanted to charter *Passage*, put his own crew of sailors and photographers aboard, and make a movie about racing to Honolulu.

"It seemed like a good idea at the time," recalls Mark. "But they didn't get it done as far as racing went."

By all accounts the 1975 Transpac was a slow and forgettable race. *Ragtime* won again. But she finished about 14 hours off *Windward Passage's* 1971 record run, *Ondine II* crossed the line 8 hours later, *Passage* showed up off Diamond Head 16 hours behind "Rags." Some ocean racing observers said that the Big Dinghy's ho-hum finish was evidence that she was becoming obsolete and tired (the normal course of events for ocean racing yachts after four or five years of competition), and it was time for her to move over for a new generation of maxis being designed specifically for the IOR. Jim Kilroy wasn't so sure. He knew *Passage* could be a fierce competitor. Her problems in the current Transpac might well have been because the Johnsons and their A-team were not aboard.

◄ *Yet more competition:* Ondine *and* Blackfin *at Ala Wai Yacht Harbor —©Phil Uhl*

▲ *Fritz Johnson*

▶ *Boxing Day 1977—Sydney Hobart Race —©Phil Uhl*

Scuttlebutt in the sailors' bars of Honolulu had begun circulating a story that some of *Passage*'s regular crew, like Rex Banks who came from Down Under, had lobbied the Johnsons to take the boat to Australia for the Sydney Hobart Race in December 1975.

"If you can get her there, we'll race her," they said.

This would be Fritter's debut, and he was ready.

Jim Kilroy saw this as his chance to start evening his score against "The Effing Whale," and he began prepping his new yacht, *Kialoa III*, for an epic battle. Before arriving Down Under, K3 had already won line honors in the English Channel race, the Miami–Montego Bay race, the Governor's Cup race, and the Transatlantic race. In fact, she had been first to finish in every race she had entered prior to arriving in Australia. Mark Johnson joked with his brother about "Jungle Jim and his new boat Rin Tin Tin," but the Johnsons knew K3 was going to force *Passage* to up her game.

A number of inshore, Southern Cross Cup Series races precede the Sydney Hobart Race, and *Passage* was in the thick of it. As the story goes, there was a night race in Sydney Harbour as *Passage* was dueling in the dark with another maxi. On the downwind leg, one of the boats had a projector and was playing a XXX porno film on the spinnaker to distract the opposition. No one aboard *Passage* ever owned up to the mischief, but *Passage* was there off Bondi Beach . . . while the love scenes sizzled.

The Sydney Hobart Race, like the Transpac, is one of the crown jewels of ocean racing. It is only 628 miles long, but after running down the east coast of Australia, it crosses the Bass Strait, notorious for some of the most challenging weather and sea conditions in the world, before finishing in the harbor at Hobart on the island of Tasmania. Virtually every running of the race sees yachts disabled and withdrawing from competition.

Coming on Boxing Day, December 26, amid the summer Christmas holiday season in Australia, the annual "Sydney Hobart" is a major spectacle in Australia. Along with 102 racing yachts jockeying for position before the start in Sydney Harbour in 1975, there were hundreds of spectator boats bobbing about for the racers to dodge.

"My god, it was distracting," remembers Fritz Johnson. "All I remember is bosoms everywhere." It seems there's a tradition of women in the spectator fleet flashing their breasts at the sailorboys who are about to do battle with each other, the Bass Strait, and fierce winds called "Southerly Busters." But despite the immense spectator fleet and the mermaids, Fritz got his boat off to a clean start in light easterly winds. She beat K3 across the starting line and ran down the leader *Ballyhoo*. With the wind veering northeast behind the yachts, *Passage* set three kites pulling from her main and mizzen masts. She held off K3 for two full days and was leading as she ran before the wind toward Hobart.

But then, according to *The New Times*, "*Windward Passage*, making more than 15 knots, was hit by a squall as she rounded Tasman Island and was 'laid on her beam end.'"

Kilroy and K3 pulled ahead in what Australian TV was reporting as "the clash of the giants" to the millions of racing fans ashore tuning in on the telly to see aerial footage of both yachts surfing toward a new record at over 20 knots.

Covering the finish, *The New York Times* wrote, "The two American yachts, each more than 70 feet in length, staged an exciting duel as they neared the finish, blowing out spinnakers in the fresh northeasterly winds."

US
7099
7099

During the final hours, K3 held off "a desperate challenge from *Windward Passage*" and finished at 2:36 am, beating the record by almost 11 hours. Fritz Johnson and his crew crossed the finish line 23 minutes later. No boat would beat these record runs by K3 and *Passage* for the next twenty-one years.

With barely enough time to decompress, the giants took off for New Zealand in the 1,500-mile Tasman Sea Race from Hobart to Auckland across the Southern Ocean. The race no longer exists.

"For good reason," says Fritz Johnson. "You get crosscurrents against each other and the wind out there. Seas shaped like houses. We got the hell beat out of us. The boat got the hell kicked out of her. I don't know what happened to *Kialoa*. I never saw her. That's an adventure I could have skipped."

"I think we actually won that one," remembers John Rumsey who was a watch captain. "The guys sure were pretty excited when we got to Auckland."

It was during this race that Fritter gained a new nickname from his crew. They started calling him the "Prince of Darkness" because he only seemed to rally from his berth during the night. But if he was feeling a touch of *mal de mer*, he wasn't alone, according to Gargle McClure who was aboard for the start of his eleven-year hitch on the boat he calls "the old girl."

"I've never sailed in anything as bad as that weather," says Fritz. "The ocean looked like a washing machine. Then we had this old New Zealand fisherman aboard that told us we needed to post an iceberg watch. An iceberg watch? It was complete madness. I got a lesson down there."

It seemed *Passage* had reached her limit, and so had her crew. They couldn't go on like this. But they would not give "Jungle Jim and his boat Rin Tin Tin" bragging rights forever.

◀ *Southern Cross Race, 1977—off North Head*
—©Phil Uhl

▼ Passage *off Sydney in 1977*
—©Phil Uhl

WINDWARD

WINDWARD PASSAGE

After the Tasman Sea Race, a delivery crew (including Rex Banks, Peter Bowker, Gargle McClure, Ridley Buttrose, Paul Buttrose, and others) sailed *Passage* 7,000 miles home to the U.S. via Tahiti and Hawaii to Newport Beach, California, where she had Sparcraft add taller main and mizzen masts and fit a triatic strut to the backstay to keep the mizzen from sagging off to leeward when going to weather. Paul Buttrose took over as her professional skipper and sailed her up to San Francisco for the St. Francis Yacht Club Big Boat Series. She got beaten by *Ballyhoo* and K3.

"Following the Big Boat Series, *Passage* was tied up at St. Francis Yacht Club for the winter," remembers Buttrose. "My lengthy work list included replacing the original, unfriendly, cranky, and battle-scarred Volvo with a Perkins. Seizing the opportunity, I decided to paint the entire bilge (Bilgekote gray), which included removing all the water tanks singlehandedly, a sizable chore. Once completed and prior to replacing the main water tank, I painted, 'Welcome. Congratulations on getting here. Either the boat is sinking or you are extremely conscientious. Either way, good luck mate.'"

The message has cheered crew, shipwrights, and mechanics who have found themselves deep in the bowels of *Windward Passage* over the years.

Charterers from Newport Beach, California, raced *Passage* in the 1977 Transpac. She beat her 1971 record, but there were three other boats ahead of her, including arch-rival Jim Kilroy's *Kialoa III* and Bill Lee's new breakthrough boat, the ULDB *Merlin*. It was only 5 feet shorter, but it weighed a third of what *Passage* weighed. It surfed most of the way to Honolulu and crushed the competition and the old record by 22 hours.

14

Crash & Bash

▲ *Cheer up! Paul Buttrose was here before you.*

◀ Passage *just after finishing the 1977 Transpac —©Phil Uhl*

From Hawaii *Passage* sailed for Australia again. In Sydney the competition started with Fritter back aboard for the Southern Cross Cup. The crews of K3 and *Passage* were eager to do battle again after a tight race in the Transpac. The wind was cranking 18–20 knots and building during the first race. It was a four-leg, triangular course starting and finishing to windward. *Kialoa III* led *Passage* during the first leg to the weather mark. Fritter and his crew made up ground during the first of the reaching legs, but K3 rounded the second mark still ahead. The next leg was a broad reach and both maxis set large kites and full mizzens. Seasoned Australian sailor Rob Vaughan, who had come aboard back in Hawaii as the professional captain, was at the helm.

At the leeward mark as the foredeck crews prepared to set jibs and douse the chutes for the final upwind leg, the boats were nearly neck-and-neck with *Passage* starting to overtake *Kialoa III*. Approaching the mark, Fritz thought he could get an "inside overlap," force K3 to give *Passage* "buoy room," and thereby take the lead.

The crew on K3 did not believe *Passage* had an overlap as they closed to within two boat-lengths of the buoy (the distance at which an overlap must be established), so the tactician on *Kialoa III* told Jim Kilroy, who was at the helm, to start his turn around the mark but not get too close "so that when the bow reached the mark, the boat already [would] be established on its 'close hauled' course going upwind."

"Basically, they tacked right in front of us," says Rob Vaughan.

"We hit them at the steering station," remembers Fritz. "It was a grave misfortune."

Passage's bowsprit and bobstay tore right through the aluminum skin on *Kialoa III*'s port rail. Two of her men, including John Kilroy (the owner's son), went overboard. At the helm Jim Kilroy dove for the cockpit sole

Southern Cross Series, Kialoa III *and* Windward Passage, *Sydney Harbour—©Phil Uhl*

US
7099
US

and barely missed being impaled as *Passage*'s bowsprit crunched the wheel on K3 and tore the mizzen. After *Passage* fell away from the collision, leaving a ragged, 3-foot hole in *Kialoa III*'s rail, she picked up one of the two men in the water. Then Fritz and his men began to quickly get sails off their yacht. With the bobstay broken and the bowsprit bent, the headstay was at risk of failing and letting the whole rig come down.

So ended the Southern Cross Cup inshore series for the two American maxi rivals. So began the protests with Jim Kilroy blaming *Windward Passage*, and claiming the accident was, according to Fritz Johnson and Rob Vaughan, "a blow to the dignity of yachting."

"I couldn't go up against that kind of talk at a protest hearing," remembers Fritter, by way of saying that Kilroy was an iconic, fifty-five-year-old yacht-racing veteran and a persuasive speaker. Fritz was a thirty-year-old still trying to find his way in the world.

The protest committee decided in favor of K3.

"But as it turned out later, Sandy McKenzie had a picture that showed the truth," says Vaughan.

McKenzie, the cook on *Passage*, had popped up out of a hatch with his camera just before the crash and snapped a picture. When it was developed weeks later, it seemed to show that the sails on K3 were not full.

"She was still in her tack," says Vaughan.

The boat was not established on her new course at the time of the crash. If such were the case, then K3 was culpable. No matter. The two maxis made their repairs, licked their wounds, and prepared to line up for the race to Hobart.

Passage *noses out "K3" off Sydney Harbour, 1977.*
—©Phil Uhl

As more than 130 yachts jostled for position for the start of the 1977 Sydney Hobart, there was an even more mammoth spectator fleet than usual. International ocean racing was squarely in the media spotlight these days, following the hard-fought races in September for the *America*'s Cup with Ted Turner skippering *Courageous* to four close wins over Alan Bond's *Australia*. At nearly the same time, the press was following Chay Blyth's *Great Britain II* (another Gurney design, of course), saying she was destined to be the elapsed-time winner for the second running of the Whitbread Round the World Race.

Amid the public fervor over big-boat racing and a lot of blarney about K3 being the boat to beat, *Passage* rose to the challenge. Fritz Johnson took the lead almost from the start in light easterly breezes, and, after clearing Sydney Heads, *Windward Passage* started to stretch her legs. *Kialoa III* was flying a mizzen staysail and full mizzen while *Passage* had no mizzen staysail and a reefed mizzen, but in the freshening breeze she continued to hold more than a quarter-mile lead over K3.

By the second morning *Kialoa III* had overtaken *Passage*. Both boats were sailing in sight of each other as they approached the Bass Strait. They were tight-reaching under spinnakers with *Passage* abeam of K3 and to weather, close inshore. The seas were calm and both yachts were clipping along at almost 11 knots, but the crews had their eyes on the sky for any clouds heralding the sudden onset of a forecast southwest gale in the vicinity of the Bass Strait.

"I saw *Kialoa* get hit with a clear-air blast just as she was getting down her kite," says Fritz.

Bruce Kendall repairing damage to K3
—©Phil Uhl

"You could see it coming toward us," remembers Rob Vaughan. "I told the guys to bring up the number three or number four jib. We need to douse the chute. But the guys back aft weren't ready. Until you've been hit by one of these Southerly Busters, you have no idea."

Before the cockpit crew in *Passage* truly sensed the danger, the buster roared down off the cliffs and blew the big red-and-white kite backwards over the rig. Out of control, and with the mainsail boom dragging in the water, *Passage* slewed around to the north to put the wind behind her while the crew tried to duck and tame whipping sheets that could kill a man.

"People were shook up," says Fritz. "It took us a while to get back on course."

By the time *Passage* was under control with a tangle of four sails and a spinnaker pole cleared away, K3 had put several miles on her as a gale settled over the Bass Strait and the seas built. Both boats beat toward Hobart under storm jibs and double-reefed mains. For the next 30 hours the mission was to keep moving forward without breaking anything or killing someone in winds gusting over 60 knots. Astern the rest of the fleet was being ravaged. Dozens of boats dropped out.

Later the winds eased and the sun came out as Fritz Johnson chased Kilroy across Storm Bay and into the River Derwent. By nightfall the maxis had a drift to the finish line. K3 took line honors. It was not a record run. Kilroy smiled and shrugged off the bash like the veteran he was.

"Well, it was a pretty bumpy road coming down," he said. "But it was simply a case of going to work and sailing the boat well . . . . No nasty moments. A few interesting waves . . . . We've been in all kinds of conditions all over the world. Not unusual."

In the bars of Hobart, people were calling Kilroy a "smug Yank."

◀ Passage'*s crew weighting down the bow to help tighten the bobstay turnbuckle —©Phil Uhl*

"He ran a well-trained, professional operation," says Vaughan who had raced with Kilroy on K3 in the 1975 Sydney Hobart against *Windward Passage*, "but he was not very charitable, especially when it came to *Passage*."

Two hours and 25 minutes later *Passage* finished. Speaking to the cameras about his second-place finish, Fritz tried to be a bit more humble than his rival. He called Kilroy a "great competitor," with a "great piece of hardware," and a "really good crew." Then he reminded himself that although he had not beaten K3, he had come in at the extreme vanguard of a fleet of 150 racing yachts, including a number of other maxis. His boat was a veteran of nine hard years of constant ocean racing, but she could still run with the swift.

So it was during the second Austral summer *Passage* spent Down Under with Fritz Johnson. She was about to say goodbye to the Southern Ocean for a while. But not before she headed north for the start of the Hong Kong to Manila race . . . with more drama on the way.

◀ *Pan Am Clipper Cup, 1982,* Passage *off Koko Head, O'ahu*
—©Phil Uhl

US
7099
7099
WINDWARD PASSAGE
PORTLAND OREGON

15

Delivery from Hell

I left *Bravura* after the 1977 Sydney Hobart Race," remembers Bill "Noodle" Leary, "and joined the crew of the 73-foot ketch *Windward Passage*, which had also competed in the Hobart race, to help deliver the boat north to Hong Kong."

His story continues as he describes what was often the life at sea of delivery crews in maxis of that era the world over:

> Rob Vaughan . . . had moved on to skipper *Windward Passage*, and he invited me along for the delivery. It was a great opportunity to sail on the iconic vessel, visit a part of the world I hadn't seen, and voyage again with my friend and mentor.
>
> *Windward Passage*'s crew for the delivery north was a mix of experienced ocean sailors and some rookies. There were four of us with offshore experience: Rob and his girlfriend Debbie, both of whom I had sailed with previously on *Bravura*, Mogan, a Californian who had been a part of the crew since the boat left the U.S., and myself. Les, an elderly friend of Rob's father, and Peter and John, two Tasmanians my age, were all aboard for their first offshore adventure.
>
> We had a leisurely and uneventful cruise up Tasmania's eastern coast, across the Bass Strait, and up the east coast of Australia stopping in Sydney and Mooloolaba, just north of Brisbane.
>
> It was overcast when we departed Mooloolaba, but otherwise the weather seemed fair as *Windward Passage* headed north outside of Fraser Island and into the Coral Sea towards New Guinea. Shortly thereafter though, Rob heard a warning on the shortwave radio that a deep low-pressure area was brewing in the waters northwest of our position. The wind and seas were starting to build with the influence of the weather system, but the breeze was from the south and pushed us in the direction we were headed anyway. Unfortunately, we were already well offshore and there was nowhere to hide from the storm. To our west lay the jagged and dangerous Great Barrier Reef.

◀ *Southern Cross Series, just before the Sydney Hobart Race, 1977 —©Phil Uhl*

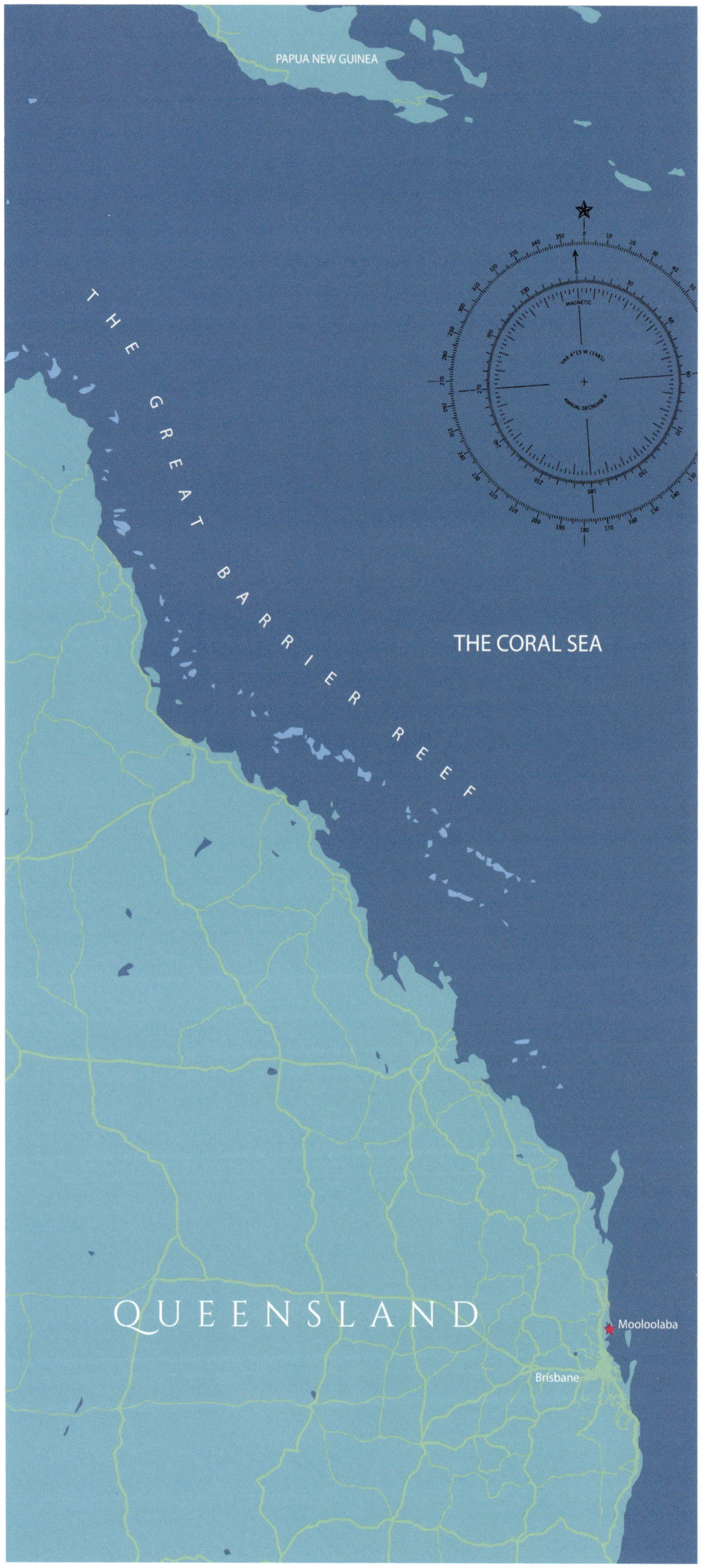

We didn't want to turn around and head back south into the wind and sea, and there was no shelter to the north or east. We kept going.

The crew had settled into three, two-person watches. Rob was standing watch with Les, Mogan with John, and I was with Peter. That put one experienced guy with a rookie on each watch. Debbie was doing most of the cooking so she didn't stand a watch.

The wind and seas continued to build, fortunately still from behind us, and we shortened sail as conditions worsened. First one reef in the mainsail, then two. We shifted through smaller and smaller jibs until we removed them entirely and then dropped the mainsail so we were running under bare poles. This progression through the sail inventory took just over a day. We continued to track the reported location of the storm as it moved slowly to the east ahead of us and we approached it from the south. Fortunately, in the southern hemisphere the wind in these lows has a clockwise rotation, and this kept the breeze behind us as we danced with the devil.

The wind continued to increase and the size of the seas increased with it. *Windward Passage's* anemometer had broken during the Sydney Hobart Race so we had no idea how windy it was, but standing on deck without holding onto something wasn't possible with so much wind pressure. The sound of the wind in the rigging increased from a howl to an incessant scream.

Navigation was a problem too. Rob hadn't been able to take a sextant sight due to the complete overcast since our departure from Mooloolaba days earlier, and we were determining our position by dead reckoning, not reassuring in an area littered with hazards. At one point we had to zigzag to the west through a 50-mile-wide channel between two coral reefs. Both shoals had lighthouses on them, and we didn't see either one, so our navigation was apparently good enough. Right in the middle of the channel Rob sighted a freighter heading in the other direction idling along slowly, barely maintaining steerage way and taking the huge seas head on. Rob called them on the VHF radio and spoke to the captain who confirmed that our DR position was accurate and lamented that these were the worst conditions he had experienced in more than forty years at sea.

Conditions continued to deteriorate as we closed to within a hundred miles of the low's reported position, our closest point of approach. The system was now directly north of us and moving in an easterly direction. The storm's huge waves were breaking and threatening to broach the boat. Running under bare poles, *Windward Passage* would hit 10 knots as she surfed on the face of each passing wave and then slow down to four knots as she slid down their backs. The boat was moving fast enough with just wind pressure on the bare spars to steer easily though, and as long as the helmsman took the breaking seas directly on the transom, she was handling the conditions just fine.

Windward Passage's 10-foot-wide crew cabin, separated from the saloon by a centerline bulkhead, had four berths against the starboard hull, two sets of upper and lower bunks. Four of us occupied these outer berths. The centerline bulkhead had another upper/lower bunk set in front of a large built-in chest of drawers, but these berths were empty. Our accommodations were cozy, but sleeping in those conditions was next to impossible. The screaming wind was terrifying enough, but laying in my aft lower bunk against the skin of the hull, I could hear the breakers as they approached and I'd tense up as they engulfed the boat and she squirted out from under each one.

In the middle of the night, I heard a particularly large breaking wave approaching, and I instinctively held on to the bunk frame as it hit us. The helmsman did not get the boat headed directly downwind before the wave hit, and the breaker picked *Windward Passage* up and threw her down on her side, mast in the water. I managed to stay in my bunk until the boat righted itself, but the rest of the cabin's occupants were not as fortunate. Peter, above me in the after upper berth, flew across the cabin and landed on top of the dresser chest. Mogan, in the forward lower, landed in the lower centerline bunk with John

above him in the upper centerline bunk. All were uninjured except John, who couldn't move and we feared he may have broken his neck upon landing.

The boat righted itself after a few seconds, and as soon as she came up, I rushed into the aft cabin to find Rob, who was on watch with Les, standing at the foot of the aft companionway. Les was driving and Rob had been below entering the log when the broach occurred. Rob and I rushed up the ladder to find Les tangled in the mizzen rigging on the port side of the boat.

Les had been thrown out to the end of his 10-foot safety harness tether during the knockdown, but since *Windward Passage* was so beamy and he was clipped into a centerline pad eye, he ended up on deck when the boat righted itself. He appeared to be uninjured but was in shock so we carried him below and put him in his bunk.

We had lashed the doused (but still hanked on) storm jib to the perforated aluminum toerail on the port side of the foredeck, but the force of the broach had broken the jib's lashings, torn the two forward most lifeline stanchions on the port side right out of the deck, and bent the bow pulpit. The folding seats in *Windward Passage*'s small crew cockpit just aft of the mast were also ripped from their hinges by the force of the broach. That was amazing considering the sides of the cockpit were more than six feet inboard of the deck's outer edge. All of this damage was superficial, though, and once we got the jib re-secured and broken stanchions under control *Windward Passage* was back underway heading north.

The storm started abating shortly thereafter, and within a few hours it had moved off to the east. A day later, it was flat calm and we were powering. John's neck wasn't badly injured after all, and after a few days of bed rest, he was out of his bunk and standing watch again.

Just another day in Paradise.

16

STAYING ALIVE

By the time *Passage* arrived back in Seattle in 1978 (after placing second again behind *Kialoa III* for line honors in the race to Manila), she was tired. In the previous ten years she had raced over 50,000 miles at a grand prix level and traveled more than five times that distance on deliveries around the globe.

"We couldn't believe she was still holding together," says Gargle McClure.

Windward Passage arrived at Seattle's Vic Franck's Boat Company for more than R&R. Before biotech and software companies dotted the shores of Lake Union, Vic Franck built and repaired boats here. The yard began in 1927 with Franck's father and was the oldest boatbuilding company in Seattle. It had over 250 vessels to its credit, from fishing trawlers to megayachts. Franck was known as a master of wooden boat construction and repair.

"It was the kind of place you could feel at home," says Fritz Johnson, possibly referencing his own roots in neighboring Oregon, "and it *was* home. I lived out of the back of my car there for months while we were trying to set the boat right."

There was a long punch list of repairs for the yard to make on *Passage*, but the Johnsons wanted more than repairs to their battle-weary veteran. They wanted to make state-of-the-art changes to her so she could show Kilroy, Long, and a collection of newly minted maxi owners a thing or two. They wanted to prove *Windward Passage* could still "float like a butterfly and sting like a bee," just as boxer Mohammed Ali was shouting as he promoted his 1976 bout with Leon Spinks.

"The first thing we did," says Fritz Johnson, "we got Doug Peterson [a star among the competitive sailboat designers at the time] to come up. We wanted to do something with the keel to make her point higher."

The Vic Franck Shipyard in Seattle, 1970s

Main construction shed, image courtesy of John Caldbick

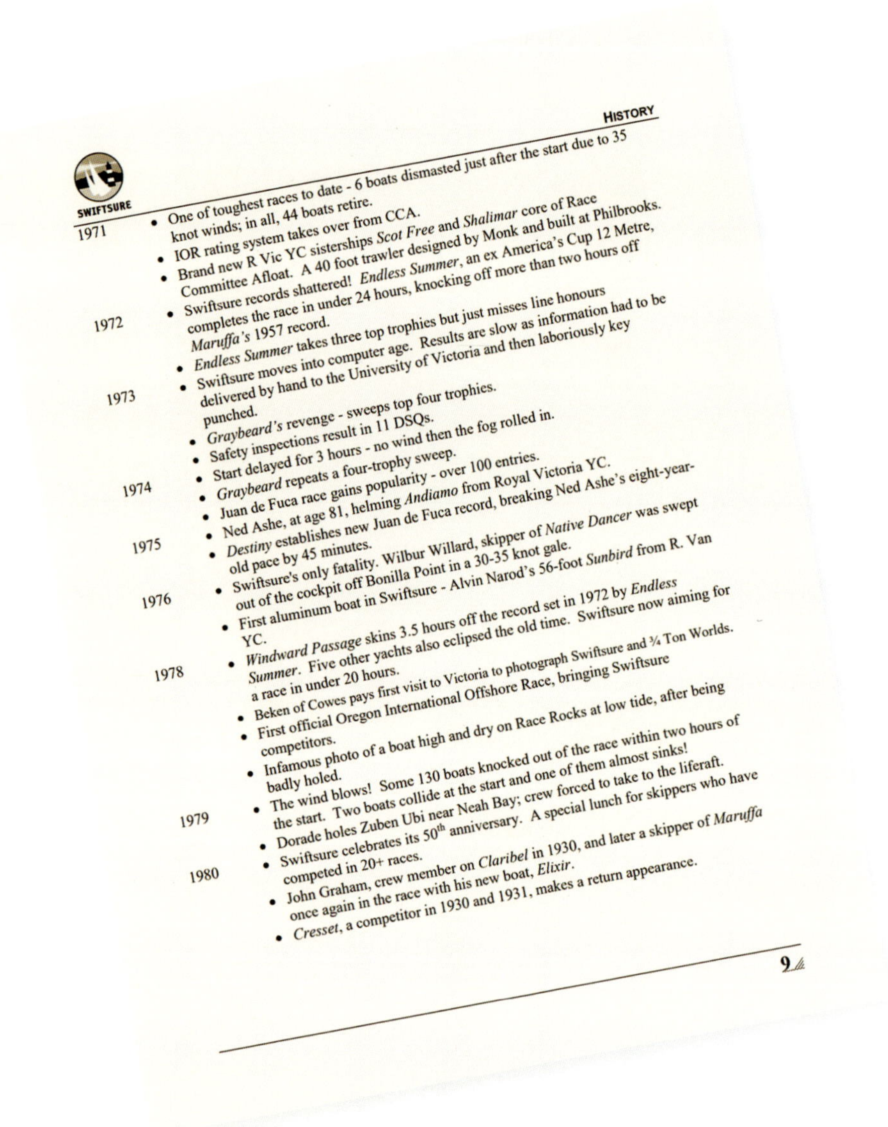

SWIFTSURE

HISTORY

1971
- One of toughest races to date - 6 boats dismasted just after the start due to 35 knot winds; in all, 44 boats retire.
- IOR rating system takes over from CCA.
- Brand new R Vic YC sisterships *Scot Free* and *Shalimar* core of Race Committee Afloat. A 40 foot trawler designed by Monk and built at Philbrooks.
- Swiftsure records shattered! *Endless Summer*, an ex America's Cup 12 Metre, completes the race in under 24 hours, knocking off more than two hours off *Maruffa's* 1957 record.

1972
- *Endless Summer* takes three top trophies but just misses line honours
- Swiftsure moves into computer age. Results are slow as information had to be delivered by hand to the University of Victoria and then laboriously key punched.

1973
- *Graybeard's* revenge - sweeps top four trophies.
- Safety inspections result in 11 DSQs.
- Start delayed for 3 hours - no wind then the fog rolled in.

1974
- *Graybeard* repeats a four-trophy sweep.
- Juan de Fuca race gains popularity - over 100 entries.
- Ned Ashe, at age 81, helming *Andiamo* from Royal Victoria YC.

1975
- *Destiny* establishes new Juan de Fuca record, breaking Ned Ashe's eight-year-old pace by 45 minutes.
- Swiftsure's only fatality. Wilbur Willard, skipper of *Native Dancer* was swept out of the cockpit off Bonilla Point in a 30-35 knot gale.

1976
- First aluminum boat in Swiftsure - Alvin Narod's 56-foot *Sunbird* from R. Van YC.

1978
- *Windward Passage* skins 3.5 hours off the record set in 1972 by *Endless Summer*. Five other yachts also eclipsed the old time. Swiftsure now aiming for a race in under 20 hours.
- Beken of Cowes pays first visit to Victoria to photograph Swiftsure and ¾ Ton Worlds.
- First official Oregon International Offshore Race, bringing Swiftsure competitors.
- Infamous photo of a boat high and dry on Race Rocks at low tide, after being badly holed.

1979
- The wind blows! Some 130 boats knocked out of the race within two hours of the start. Two boats collide at the start and one of them almost sinks!
- Dorade holes Zuben Ubi near Neah Bay; crew forced to take to the liferaft.

1980
- Swiftsure celebrates its 50th anniversary. A special lunch for skippers who have competed in 20+ races.
- John Graham, crew member on *Claribel* in 1930, and later a skipper of *Maruffa* once again in the race with his new boat, *Elixir*.
- *Cresset*, a competitor in 1930 and 1931, makes a return appearance.

9

Peterson didn't have any drawings, so when the Johnsons asked him what he had in mind, he started making sketches on the back of a green door in the office. The result was a Peterson-designed shoe for the old keel to add righting moment and better performance going to weather.

While *Windward Passage* lay in Seattle for repairs and modifications at Franck's and at the Cadranell Yacht Landing, Mark and Fritz Johnson were taking note of changes in the ever-growing global maxi fleet. Jim Kilroy was already building *Kialoa IV.* He and other maxi owners were talking about forming an association to organize, promote, and govern their racing. The Aga Khan invited the Johnsons, Jim Kilroy, Huey Long, and other prominent maxi owners to Sardinia to discuss making the island a locus for maxi racing and the seat of a governing organization. Among the owners there were discussions and debates about corporate sponsorship, "show-up" money, purses for winners, and syndicate ownership of the yachts.

The new boats were bigger than *Passage*. They now averaging 80 feet in length, but they seemed fragile and ephemeral to the Johnsons. Wealthy owners were beginning to put their yachts in cradles to send them on freighters as deck cargo to each new racing destination instead of risking their considerable investments during long-distance deliveries like Bill Leary's brutal trip to Hong Kong. Instead of paying delivery crews, owners were beginning to hire professional racing sailors for regattas. The days of sailors like *Passage*'s Chip Cleary, who paid his own way to race aboard a maxi, were coming to an end.

"You could see a change away from Corinthian maxi racing coming," says Mark Johnson. "They wanted to pay me to bring *Windward Passage* to the Mediterranean. I thought about it for a while. Then I turned down the invitation. I wasn't interested."

But the Johnson brothers were not willing to give up on their ten-year-old warhorse or the sport of maxi racing just yet. They gave *Passage* a complete going-over in Seattle. They pulled off all the deck hardware and made repairs to the boat's Dynel skin. They asked Maine boatbuilder Paul Luke to engineer and build new jibsheet cars to run sheets inside the shrouds to help the boat point closer to the wind. Then they removed the mizzen.

"Doug Peterson told me having that mizzen up there was like having a Volkswagen Beetle hanging 10 feet up in the rigging," says Fritz Johnson. "We got it down. Then we gave the boat a new Imron paint job."

In typical Johnson "can-do" fashion, Fritz found a bodybuilder at a local gym to do the painting, not a professional boatyard paint whisperer.

"You have to keep the flow going with Imron, so we needed someone who could balance on a raft next to the boat and hold a spray gun for hours at a time," recalls Fritz. The bodybuilder was "the ticket." *Passage* looked great.

Against this background the Johnsons entered *Passage*, now as a sloop, in the 1978 Swiftsure Race.

"A friend, Tiger Warren, told me it was a matter of honor that we enter, so we went," remembers Fritz. "We didn't even have all the hardware back on the boat. Some of it was still in plastic milk crates when we headed out for the starting line."

Since the1930s, sailboats have been racing from Cadboro Bay, British Columbia, around the lightship on Swiftsure Bank, at the entrance to the Strait of Juan de Fuca and return. By the 1960s, at least four dozen yachts were lining up for the 256-mile Lightship Classic in late May. It's a race that is rife with fog, capricious winds, and strong tidal currents. Following the U.S. removal of the lightship in 1961, a Royal Canadian

Swiftsure Race, 1978—the end result

7099
US

Navy or Coast Guard ship has been temporarily moored at the lightship station for the race.

Mark Johnson took the helm of *Passage* for the start of the race, and he was hopeful that all her repairs, along with her new sloop rig, would make her competitive against a fleet of newer yachts. The Big Dinghy did not disappoint. In the end *Passage* sets a new race record by 3.5 hours. It would stand for the next seventeen years.

"That current out there was really something," remembers Mark. "It will sweep you sideways. I had to go 300 yards beyond the lightship [Canadian Coast Guard cutter] to get around her. We had a flood tide, and it was the middle of the night."

"We beat *Merlin* in," says Rob Vaughan. "*Windward Passage* was the best boat I ever sailed on. She was pretty basic. Not a Rolls Royce, but definitely an Aston Martin."

Feeling really good about their boat, the Johnsons entered her in the September 1978 San Francisco Big Boat Series. Widely regarded as the West Coast's premier regatta, the Big Boat Series attracted world-caliber competitors for four days of buoy racing on San Francisco Bay. This is the St. Francis Yacht Club's signature event, and *Passage* dominated the maxi class with Mark at the helm. *Sail* magazine writer Jay Boze summed up the spectacle in the title to his humorous piece, "The Year *Passage* Took *Kialoa* to the Men's Room."

The Johnsons chartered *Passage* for the 1979 Transpac, and the boat made a dismal showing in an extremely light-air race, coming in 18th in Class A. Longtime crewmember Dave Palmer remembers the race as "light, light air." He says that when *Passage* arrived in Honolulu "the only water left on the boat was in the teakettle."

Look, Ma—no mizzen! Just one of her many new rigs—©Phil Uhl

But the Johnson brothers were undaunted. They knew *Passage* was capable of much more, so they pulled together an A-list crew. Then Fritz took her to Hawaii to race in the 1980 Pan Am Clipper Cup series. Fritter and the crew got off to a great start in the series, taking line honors in two of the first three races and first place in all three races on corrected time. After the third victory, Fritz, a lot of his crew, and their girlfriends went out to celebrate at a restaurant Fritz remembered fondly as his father's favorite Honolulu eatery. The place was called Wo Fat Chop Suey Restaurant. It was on Hotel Street in Chinatown, an area with a longstanding reputation for crime at night.

After dinner the *Passage* gang went bar-hopping. Eventually, they ended up at The Swing Club, a dance hall, pool palace, and former WWII sailors' bar. Fritz was an ace billiards player, and seeing the pool tables, he just had to have a game or two.

"People say I was playing for money, and I was trying to hustle this local guy. But that isn't what happened," he says. "It was a casual game of eight-ball. My wife-to-be and I were playing this fellow and his girlfriend."

Passage had just won her third race in the Pan Am series. The boat's name and Fritz's picture were all over the front pages of newspapers that were lying on the bar.

"I think the guy saw those newspapers, recognized me, and decided he'd take me down off my high horse. When I pocketed the eight-ball, he didn't like it. He went outside and came back in with a .38 Saturday Night Special. Then he shot me at point-blank range an inch above my navel and ran out the door. It was five minutes before midnight."

Mike Farley was part of the crew with Fritz that night.

Before playing some pool
—©Phil Uhl

"A funny thing happened that evening, yet I don't really talk about it much," he says. "When I ran after [the shooter] down the street yelling for the cops, at one point he turned back at me with the gun still in his hand, and I ducked back into a doorway out of sight. But I soon came to the conclusion that if he continued back at me, I would have nowhere to go and would have been an easy target myself . . . . Fortunately, he didn't and when a cop finally did show up, I was saved. Have you ever heard the phrase 'It scared the shit out of me' . . . ? It was quite noticeable, the brown stains on my pants!"

Meanwhile, in the bar people were trying to get Fritz to lie down so they could put direct pressure on his wound while they waited for an ambulance.

"I was having none of that. I was in shock, and I didn't want to die on a barroom floor in front of my crew and the woman who I was going to marry."

By the time he got to the hospital, he was on the verge of bleeding out when a trauma surgeon who had treated a lot of gunshot wounds in Vietnam got to Fritz.

"I think his name was Dr. Francis Odda, and he saved my life, no question," says Fritz.

"The next morning we all went to the hospital and gave blood," says Dave Birchenough who was the professional captain on the boat at the time. "But you have to wonder if any of the blood was usable, given the partying the night before."

The same morning both Mike Farley and his future wife Suka picked the shooter out of a police lineup.

Farley remembers, "A few months later, the State of Hawaii flew both Suka and me out to Hawaii all the way from Holland, where we were getting

Mike Farley had T-shirts made with an image of Yosemite Sam with guns a-blazing on the front. On the back of the shirt Farley had printed, "When sailing, we're hot. In pool, we're shot." Shown with Mike's wife, Suka, and Gordo Johnson.—©Phil Uhl

Mark Johnson welcoming back Fritz Johnson as he returns from the hospital still wearing his patient wristband—©Phil Uhl

PASSAGE

Alaska Eagle ready for the upcoming Whitbread Race, to give testimony in the trial. He paid for his actions."

In the days following the shooting, Mark Johnson flew to Honolulu to skipper *Passage* for the Around the State Race. When it was clear that the police had the shooter, Fritz would recover, and *Passage* had secured yet another bundle of trophies, Mike Farley had T-shirts made at the International Market Place at Waikiki with an image of Yosemite Sam with guns a-blazing on the front. On the back of the shirt Farley had printed, "When sailing, we're hot. In pool, we're shot."

These were far from the only gag T-shirts *Passage* crews wore. According to Birchenough, Fritz once supplied the crew with *Windward Passage* bowling shirts. Then there were the shirts reading, "Wayward Sausage; Your Air-Conditioning Specialists." At one point each of the crew had matching tank tops. On the back was the image of the Lahaina whale that was on the transom of the boat and the words "*Windward Passage.*" On the front it said "Captain."

"The plan was to wear the tank top while cruising the barrooms for women," says "Halfdeck" Johnson. "The only problem was the crew had to split up and go to different bars."

After the Clipper Cup *Windward Passage* returned to San Francisco for the Big Boat Series in 1980 to win line honors in the maxi division, nipping *Merlin* (now sailing in the new ULDB class) for line honors yet again. "Fritz was the skipper," says Birchenough, "with his colostomy bag."

But while *Passage* was barnstorming in San Francisco during September 1980, a fleet of six new maxis, led by the Australian *Bumblebee,* were meeting off Sardinia's Costa Smeralda for the first ICAYA (International Class A Yachting Association) World Championship. This was a maxi organization founded by John Kilroy, Baron Edmond de Rothschild, and others. It was the group Mark Johnson had decided not to join.

After just five years Jim Kilroy had put K3 out to pasture and launched his new Ron Holland–designed *Kialoa IV.* She missed the ICAYA World Championship in 1980, but she cleaned up in the line-honors category at the SORC in 1981. She would go on to win the maxi World Cup three times in a row.

The Johnson brothers knew that as long as *Passage* continued to win races, "Jungle Jim" would come gunning for her with ever-newer and more expensive racing yachts. Their hearts were no longer up for the challenge. Going forward maxi racing seemed like a "money game" dominated by wealth, corporations, and professional sailors. This new world order wasn't the Johnsons' idea of fun. They were done with maxi racing. But, of course, "the old girl" was not.

◀ *Big Boat Series, San Francisco, 1980, Mark Johnson at the helm with Fritz doing sibling supervision—©Phil Uhl*

OLD BAHAMA CHANNEL
BAHIA DE BUENA VISTA
GULF STREAM CURRENTS
CAUTION
NOTE X
GOLFO DE GUACANAYABO
MANZANILLO
HAMILTON
QUARTZ

17

MAKEOVER

SOON AFTER THEIR DECISION to give up racing (following *Passage*'s fourth-place finish in the 1981 SORC maxi division), the Johnson brothers sold *Windward Passage* to Bill Johnson (no relation). But there were lingering regrets.

"Not a year goes by that that my brother and I don't ask ourselves why we ever sold her," says Fritz Johnson. There was so much of their dad in her and so many good times. To this day Mark and Dotty's joint email address includes the numbers "7099." It's *Windward* Passage's official number, the one emblazoned on her sails.

"This was no straightforward yacht sale," remembers sailor, shipwright, and boat broker Courtney Ross of Clearwater, Florida.

He was in the mix. For some years he had maintained cruising boats at his Clearwater boatyard for Bill Johnson. Johnson was an Atlanta-based restaurateur, hotelier, entrepreneur, and real estate developer. He was frequently in Florida tending to business projects and visiting his vacation homes in Clearwater and Naples. Like a lot of people at the time with waterfront access, Johnson and his wife Sandra caught the sailing bug.

"The Johnsons never cruised," says Courtney Ross, "but they very much enjoyed daysailing and the pleasure of having a perfect boat at whatever was their getaway property of the moment—Hilton Head, Clearwater, Man-O-War Cay in the Bahamas, or Naples, Florida."

Their first boat was an Endeavor 37. They quickly moved up to a fully tricked-out Hinckley Bermuda 40, which they sailed in Florida and the Bahamas. They kept the boat most of the year near their home in Hilton Head, South Carolina, but moved the Hinckley to Clearwater and Naples, Florida, for the winter months. Whenever their boats needed servicing, the boats went to Courtney Ross in Clearwater.

Passage*'s ship's chronometer*
—image courtesy of John Rumsey

According to Ross, "Bill was a gentle giant" (6 foot 4) with a quiet nature, and a "down-home" Georgian drawl. He was also a "perfectionist among perfectionists who wanted the best of everything. That's how he was with his hotels like the Ritz Carlton in Boston, and that's how he was with his boats."

"My husband was truly a self-made man," says Sandra Johnson, his wife of more than fifty years. "He got up every morning at five o'clock, ran 8 miles, skipped breakfast, and got going with his businesses. He started with owning one Waffle House; by the time he was done, he owned 165. Then he got into hotels. I never knew what he was going to do next. But Bill could look at something like a mountain, a tired old hotel, or a used boat, and he could imagine what it might be. He really liked to take old things and make them shine again."

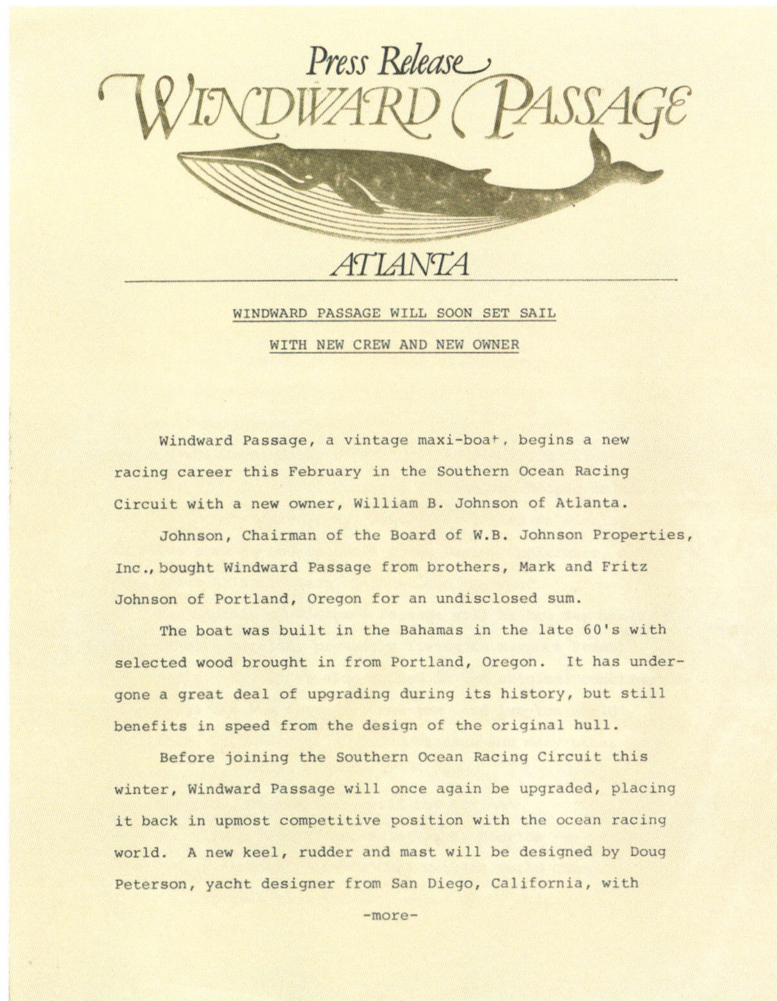

Press Release

WINDWARD PASSAGE

ATLANTA

WINDWARD PASSAGE WILL SOON SET SAIL

WITH NEW CREW AND NEW OWNER

Windward Passage, a vintage maxi-boat, begins a new racing career this February in the Southern Ocean Racing Circuit with a new owner, William B. Johnson of Atlanta.

Johnson, Chairman of the Board of W.B. Johnson Properties, Inc., bought Windward Passage from brothers, Mark and Fritz Johnson of Portland, Oregon for an undisclosed sum.

The boat was built in the Bahamas in the late 60's with selected wood brought in from Portland, Oregon. It has undergone a great deal of upgrading during its history, but still benefits in speed from the design of the original hull.

Before joining the Southern Ocean Racing Circuit this winter, Windward Passage will once again be upgraded, placing it back in upmost competitive position with the ocean racing world. A new keel, rudder and mast will be designed by Doug Peterson, yacht designer from San Diego, California, with

-more-

In the early 1980s cultural changes were afoot. The wistful and mellow days of yacht rock had been replaced by the pumping beat of disco. Rick James's "Super Freak" was an immensely popular song. Pack-man and MTV were vying for attention. Ronald Reagan was President of the United States. Madonna was about to give voice in "Material Girl" to a shameless fascination with social status and fashion in "a material world." More and more people were enjoying the luxury of carefree, discretionary spending.

Amid these trends business was booming for Bill Johnson's restaurant, hotel, and real estate ventures. He already owned Waffle Houses and Holiday Inns. But now he was taking over the entire Ritz Carlton chain, which he would eventually merge with Marriott's hotels. He was an impulsive man, and after six years of low-key yachting, he now felt the urge, and had the expanding financial horsepower, to change up his sailing game. During the 1980 *America*'s Cup, he chartered the Hinckley 64 *Skeets* to take friends and investors out to watch the cup races.

Bill Johnson

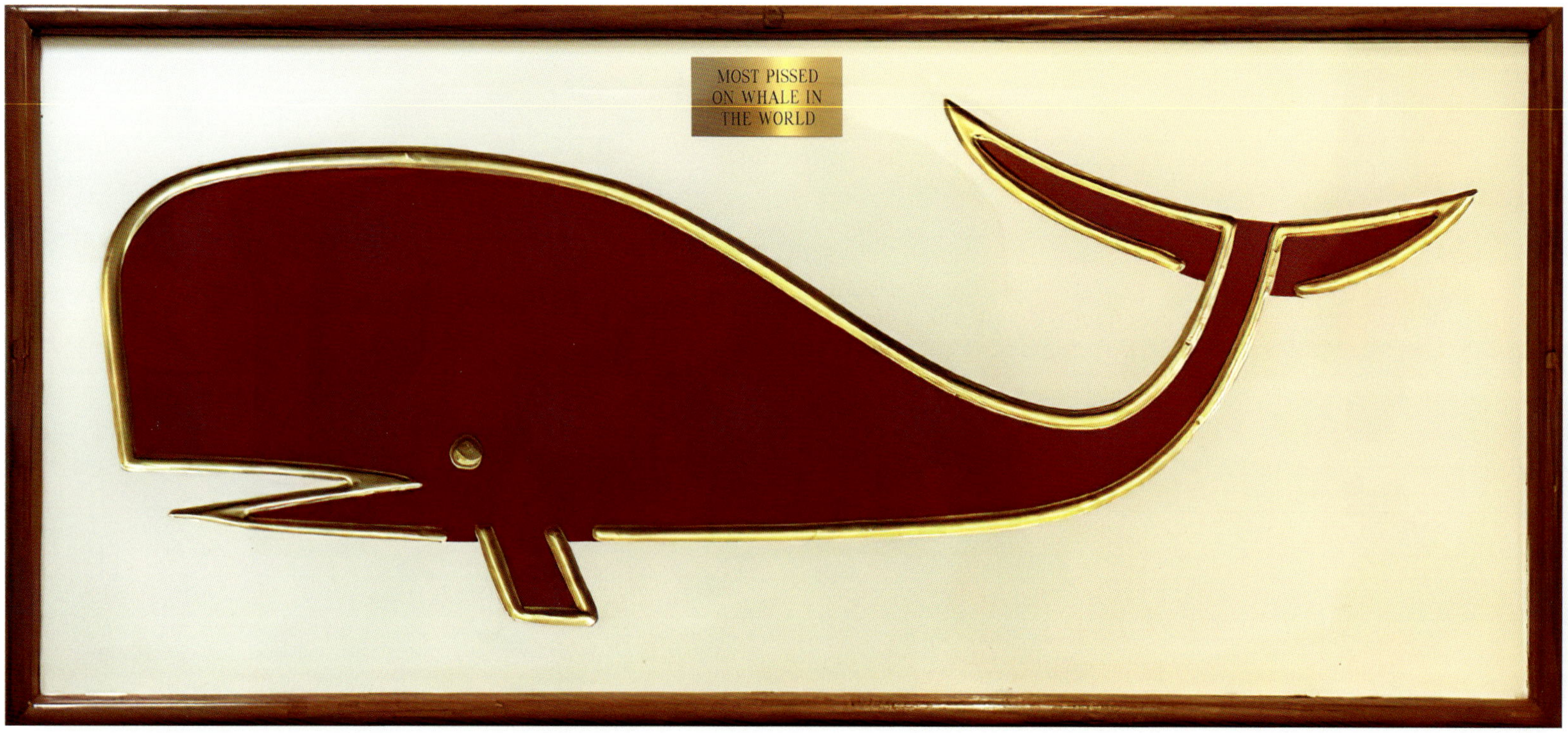

The old whale with its pieces glued back together upon removal —image courtesy of Courtney Ross

"Each day on the way out to watch the *America*'s Cup, we would pass several of the maxis moored nearby and Bill would come up to me," remembers Courtney Ross. "He would put his hand on my shoulder and say something like 'Buddy, we got to get one of them big boats.'"

After the event, Ross did not give much thought to Johnson's fascination with large racing yachts until he got an evening call from Johnson wanting to know if Ross had any leads on a maxi for sale. It seemed buying a maxi was something Johnson seriously wanted to pursue.

After checking out the potential market, Ross "came up with the thought that maybe *Windward Passage* would be right up his alley," if it could be bought and upgraded to make maximum usage of the old-age allowance. Johnson liked the idea, so Courtney Ross called John Rumsey to get his thoughts on whether the boat could be purchased. The plan would be a "no money spared" upgrade in order to take advantage of the old-age allowance. Johnson also wanted to pull together people who had crewed on her before, in order to create "a first-rate program to win."

"That's how what I call the 'Great Bandage [as in Johnson & Johnson] Deal' began," says Ross.

"He turned everything he did into a business," says Bill Johnson's wife. "That's what happened with *Windward Passage*."

At the time John Rumsey, along with Gargle McClure, were among the professionals overseeing *Passage* when the Johnson brothers weren't around. Once Courtney Ross was sure Bill Johnson was serious about buying a maxi, he asked Rumsey if he thought "the Johnson boys" would sell *Passage* and if the boat at her age could still be competitive "because Mister Bill likes to win."

▲ *Bill Johnson, ever the perfectionist, designed his own house flag —image courtesy of Courtney Ross*

▼ *1983 SORC off Miami—©Phil Uhl*

WINDWARD PASSAGE
ATLANTA

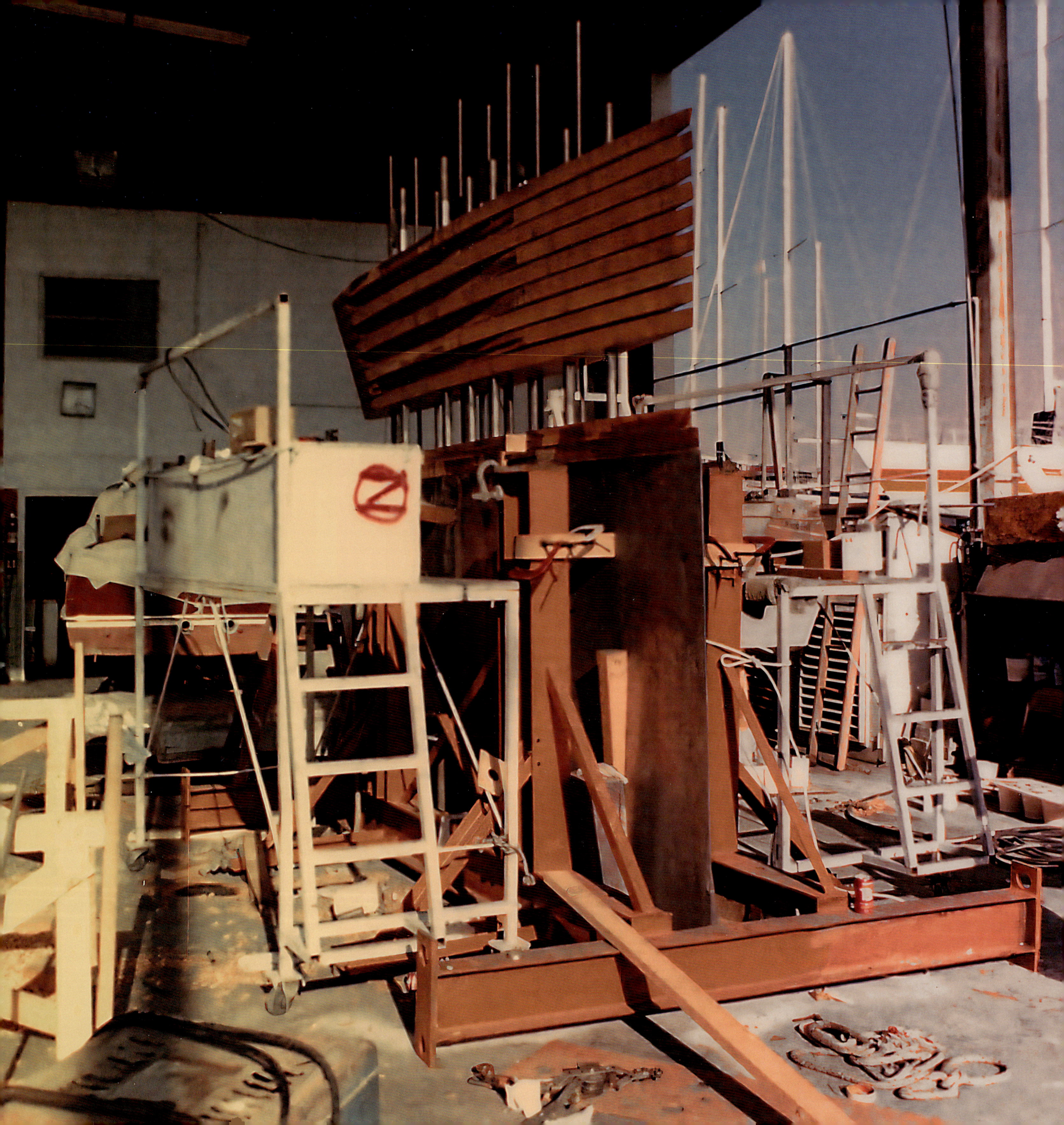

Discussions ensued that included yacht designer Doug Peterson.

"Dougy's mouth watered with the possibilities," remembers Ross. With upgrades to the keel, rudder, and rig, as well as the "age allowance" the boat would now get under IOR rules, Peterson thought *Windward Passage* "could kick some butt."

Johnson got pumped up. He thought he could make *Passage*'s star blaze brighter than ever, and he pitched an offer to the Johnson brothers to buy *Passage*. Money was no object. "This is a once-in-a-lifetime boat," Johnson told *Yachting* magazine.

"He had the interest and the capital to care for her. Caring for the boat was important to us. And he wanted to keep campaigning her," remembers Mark Johnson. "It seemed like a good fit, so Fritz and I sold him the boat."

As soon as the Johnson brothers said "yes" to the sale, Bill Johnson asked Rumsey, McClure, and others in the regular crew to stay on and "make her perfect . . . and fast as all get-out." He wanted to win the next SORC.

"After a search of yards that would have a schedule to get the boat modified and ready for the 1982 SORC, and getting no commitments better than 'maybe,'" says Ross, "my alligator mouth and tadpole ass came up with the idea that we could do the project at Ross Yacht."

In those days Ross Yacht Services would have forty or more racing yachts at the yard and nearby marinas during the late fall, all preparing for the start of the winter SORC. The yard, at that time of year, would be overflowing with race boats, both new or in the process of being updated. But it was a small yard with not enough water depth to handle a maxi. So to make the program work, Ross came up with a plan to haul *Passage* in Tampa, take the keel off, and bring the hull around to his yard in Clearwater to do the major part of the work.

Doug Peterson—image courtesy of Phil Uhl

The new Doug Peterson–designed keel being fabricated —image courtesy of Courtney Ross

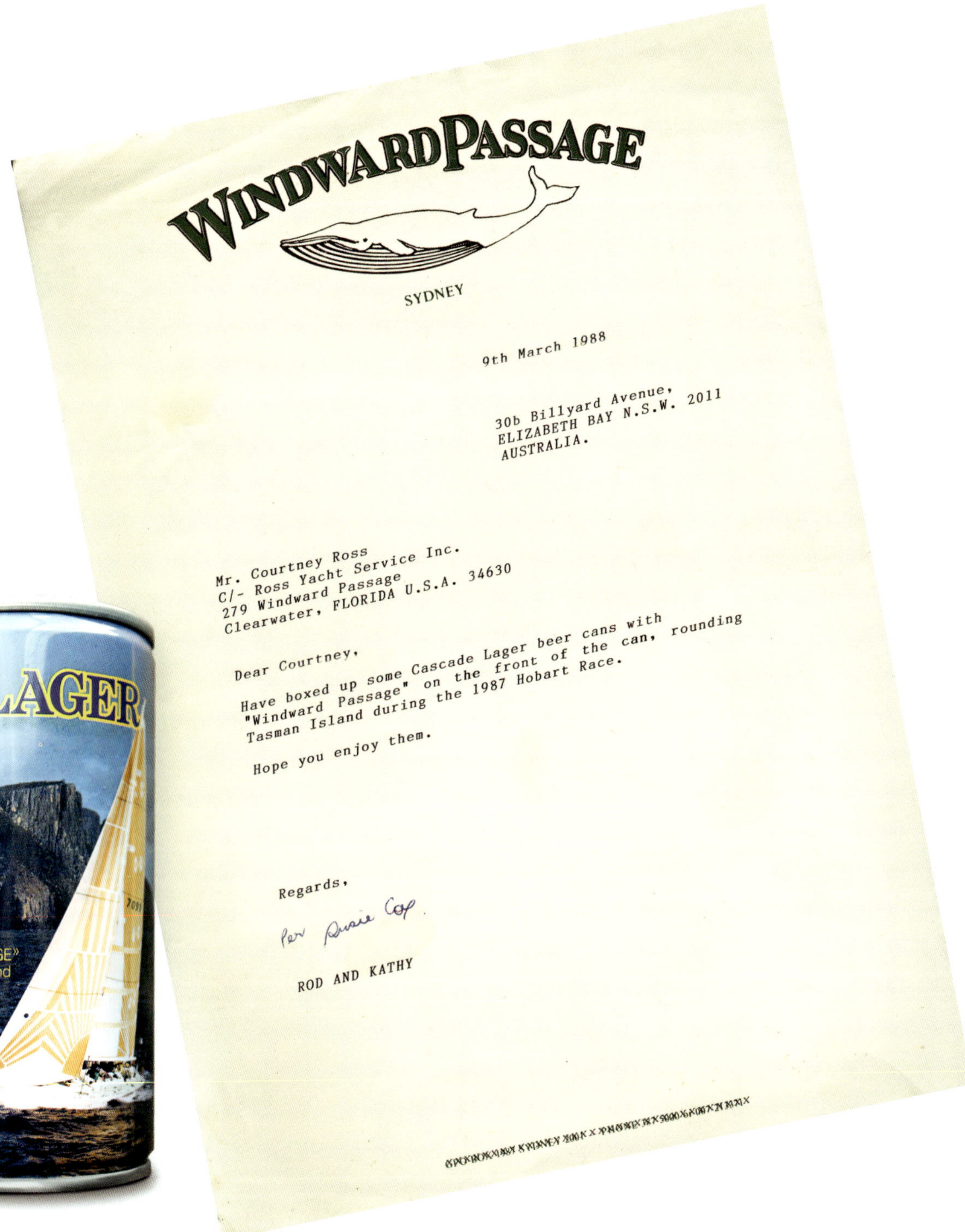

WINDWARD PASSAGE

SYDNEY

9th March 1988

30b Billyard Avenue,
ELIZABETH BAY N.S.W. 2011
AUSTRALIA.

Mr. Courtney Ross
C/- Ross Yacht Service Inc.
279 Windward Passage
Clearwater, FLORIDA U.S.A. 34630

Dear Courtney,

Have boxed up some Cascade Lager beer cans with "Windward Passage" on the front of the can, rounding Tasman Island during the 1987 Hobart Race.

Hope you enjoy them.

Regards,

ROD AND KATHY

Then Ross Yacht Services, Rumsey, McClure, and company went into high gear. They got Doug Peterson (with the help of Alan Gurney) to "redesign the underbody." Peterson came up with a sleeker, deeper (13-foot) keel that had to be fabricated and shipped from California. He drew a new rudder (with a new bearing system) to be fabricated in Switzerland and ordered a taller mainmast from Stearns.

Meanwhile, Ross, his craftsmen, and the *Passage* crew worked together to laminate a new keelson of Douglas-fir, reinforce the maststep, remove the old engine, and close up the "trap door" for the old hydraulic drive. Then they prepared the engine bed/shaftlog/strut/etc. for a conventional installation of a new Perkins 195-horsepower engine with a V-drive.

"Doug Peterson and Courtney Ross made her competitive for another decade," says Ron Holland.

Bill Johnson spared no expense. He gave his boat all new sails from North and Doyle, Barient winches (longtime crewmember Don Vaughn was a Barient dealer), Stearns and Navtec hydraulics, a Yacht Specialties wheel, Ritchie compasses, Brookes & Gatehouse instruments, Northstar and Trimble lorans, Magnavox SatNav, Alden weatherfax, and an Intech SSB radio.

One other thing. Bill Johnson wanted to put his stamp on the boat. He had a knack for branding things. He liked the whale on the transom, but the Lahaina whale had been Big Bob's signature, so Bill Johnson had Ross remove it and a new image of a whale created. It's the same whale today . . . and its iconic likeness has migrated to the sails, the hardware, and the decor on *Windward Passage*. It is even on jewelry Bill Johnson and other owners have given as memorabilia.

"It was a crazy amount of work," says Ross, "but somehow we got it done. With the hard work of a great group of people in every aspect of the

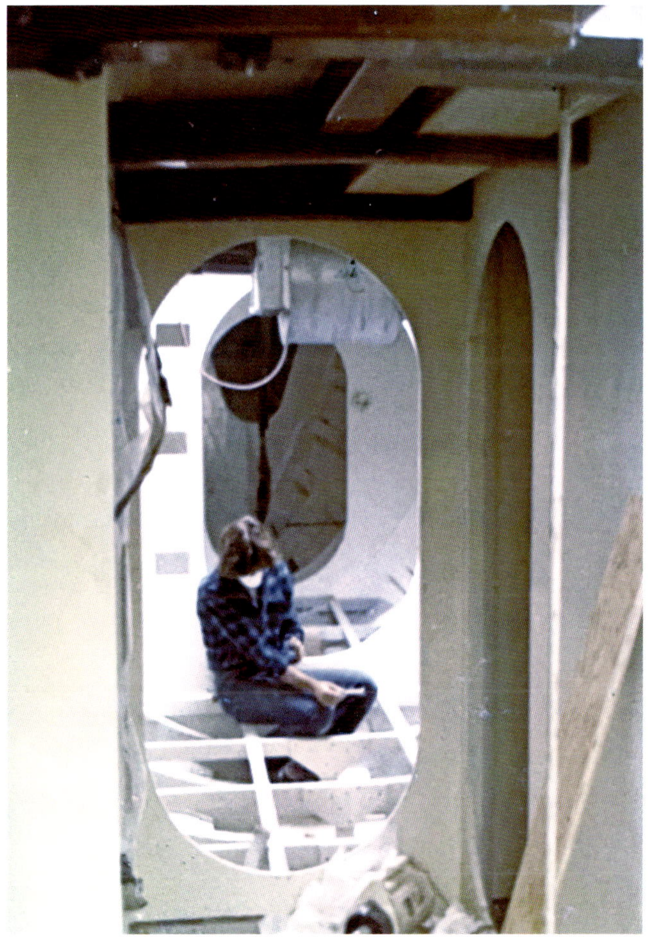

The refurbishment at Ross Yacht Services was extensive and meticulous.—images courtesy of Courtney Ross

Passage*'s transition from Australia back to the States included some* Windward Passage *beer, sent to Courtney Ross by Rod and Kathy Muir.*

project working together, the boat went back to Tampa to put the new keel on and assemble all the pieces in time to be ready to race." Jim Kilroy and *Kialoa IV* were waiting.

The "new" whale on the transom

Project manager Whit Batchelor looks on as Passage *gets her new 1980s keel.—image courtesy of Courtney Ross*

18

The Good Fight

Bill was hands off," says Courtney Ross. "He trusted us, expected the crew to keep his boat perfect, and get it done on the race course. At this point we were like family, but losing was not an option, especially against Jim Kilroy."

In 1982 *Windward Passage* headed for the starting line at St. Petersburg to face off with "Jungle Jim" and his latest "piece of hardware" yet again. For his first race Bill Johnson's had Rumsey, McClure, Ross, and the A-team crew (including Mark Johnson) aboard and ready to work their magic.

In anticipation of the race, the yachting press had been touting *Kialoa IV* and her near-sister *Condor* as "break-through boats." *Kialoa IV* had been tuned to a fine racing pitch after extensive matched competition against her predecessor K3 and battle-hardened after a year of impressive victories. Kilroy's new boat and *Condor* were in the vanguard of significant changes to maxis. Designed by Ron Holland, "K4" measured just over 80 feet in length. Kiwi Yachts in Florida built her with a composite sandwich-laminated hull and deck with aluminum reinforcing. Kilroy bragged that his new boat had lighter ends and deck, which made her superior to K3 in moderate air. But Bill Johnson's crew noted that at 84,000 pounds displacement, she was heavier than *Windward Passage* (about 79,500 pounds at the time).

To almost everyone's surprise except Doug Peterson and Bill Johnson's crew, *Passage* delivered the win Bill Johnson yearned for. When the series ended, "The Effing Whale" had won the maxi class, defeating *Kialoa IV*, *Bumblebee, Condor,* and *Ondine IV.* To the dismay of her longtime rivals like Jim Kilroy, *Passage* was proving that while victory for her was no longer as predictable as it had been back in the days of bell-bottoms, the Vietnam War, and a Richard Nixon presidency, she had the heart and soul of a champion. Bill Johnson and his crew were "all fired up."

◀ Passage *and* Kialoa III *crossing under St. Petersburg's Sunshine Skyway Bridge, SORC 1983—©Phil Uhl*

Following *Passage*'s class victory in the 1982 SORC, Johnson sent his boat to Honolulu to compete in the five races of the 1982 Clipper Cup Series held in August.

While her rivals cursed and muttered, she screamed in the first two buoy-racing events against the new and bigger racing machines like *Condor* and *Kialoa IV*.

Passage trounced the fleet in the second race with a record time in gale-force winds that damaged many boats and forced them to withdraw. Looking back on the race, *Condor*'s skipper Dick Deaver shook his head and mused, "*Passage* sailed a very, very good race, almost a flawless race. They had one problem at the first turning mark. They broke a spinnaker pole. To sail without a spinnaker pole in those conditions says a lot for their helmsman. They are very good seamen."

"It's amazing," says Bobby Steel, a professional sailor who logged a lot of miles in Jim Kilroy's *Kialoa*s as well as aboard *Passage*, "she took all the punishment the racing and the weather could throw at her. Just about the only problem that cold-molded hull has had in fifty-five years is the ding a boat-load of nuns put in her when they accidentally rammed her in their motorboat."

"When you think about it, *Passage*'s performance in the '82 Clipper Cup series was pretty incredible," says Gary Weisman. The former president of North Sails, he was a sailmaker and racing guru for North at the time, and he sailed aboard *Passage* often in the early 1980s. "She had been racing and winning at the highest level for fourteen years." Jim Kilroy was on his fourth *Kialoa*, Huey Long on his fourth *Ondine*. And they were still trying to beat the same old boat.

◀ *A rather busy time at the Pan Am Clipper Cup —Sharon Green/Ultimate Sailing*

▼ *The motley crew seen here in Honolulu sailed in the 1982 Pan Am Clipper Cup:*

1 Donny Anderson
2 Rex Banks
3 Mick Beaty
4 John Boulton
5 Peter Bowker
6 Richie Boyd
7 Bruce Cochran
8 Alan Crawford
9 Con Findlay
10 Nick Frazee
11 Doc Greenaway
12 Bill Johnson
13 Rob Maw
14 John (Gargle) McClure
15 Gary Milrimore
16 John Peschelt
17 Courtney Ross
18 John Rumsey
19 Arnie Schmelling
20 Tom Stewart
21 Gary Weisman

8
11
17
19
10
4
7
3
14
15
5

16
9
13
20
2
6
1
12
18

Weisman was aboard *Passage* for race three, the Molokai Race. This event was an ocean race of nearly 150 miles from Oahu to the eastern end of Molokai and back. The race started at midday with a long fetch to the east with K4 and *Condor* pulling ahead of *Windward Passage*. The wind was gusting over 35 knots in the Molokai Channel.

"That year we had strong trade winds," recalls Weisman, who was thirty-one at the time. "We were 10 hours going 75 miles upwind to the turning mark. By the time we got there it was nearly dark, and we were about 10 or 12 minutes behind."

After rounding the mark, clearing Molokai, and turning downwind, the *Passage* crew pulled out all the stops.

According to Gargle McClure, "Rumsey said, 'Hold onto your tits, boys. We're going in.'"

"We hoisted the 2.2-ounce kite," says Weisman. "That thing was nearly bulletproof. Probably something else would break before it let go."

With the 2.2 doing its thing, *Passage* took off and surfed past *Condor*. *Kialoa IV* fell behind with a blown-out spinnaker and a broken boom.

Weisman continues, "Only Rumsey and I drove that night. We were about 45 minutes on, 45 minutes off. This wasn't like driving *Merlin* [the record-setting ULDB] that went straight in these conditions. You were on the fine edge. If the boat got just slightly left or right [of the course], she would broach. Then you were going to do a whole lot of damage. It was kind of hairball, what we were doing, but Rumsey was amazing. He was the coolest. Nothing fazed him."

Keeping *Passage* running squarely behind her chute in building seas was not the helmsmen's only challenge. It was the middle of the night.

John Rumsey's business card can still be found pasted on the front cover of one of Courtney Ross's scrapbooks.

Pan Am Clipper Cup, 1982; left to right: Doug Peterson, Gary Weisman, Skip Allen, Bill Johnson, John McClure, Rob Maw (behind McClure), Alan Crawford (bending over), Doc Greenaway, Courtney Ross (looking through Alan Crawford's bend). Not pictured but very much there: Donny Anderson, Rex Banks (with back to us), Peter Bowker (behind Johnson's knee)—©Phil Uhl

They were charging downhill before the wind with almost no way to maneuver. Meanwhile, the fleet of slower boats in the race were still beating upwind across her course to the mark.

"We could see their lights and hoped we wouldn't hit them," says Weisman, "because we really couldn't change course."

It wasn't long before *Passage* seized the lead.

"We did the last 75 miles in about 5 hours," remembers Weisman, "and beat *Kialoa* and *Condor*. Both of them broke a bunch of stuff."

At this point it looked like *Windward Passage* could win the maxi class in the Clipper Cup for the second time in a row. But K4 bounced back to win the fourth race, another sprint around the buoys. Still, *Passage* remained ahead on accumulated points. The final standings came down to the maxis' performances in the last race of the series . . . the Around the State Race.

Following the start, Bill Johnson's boat engaged *Condor* in a tacking duel. K4 fell behind when a crewman lost the tip of his finger and Kilroy slowed for a rescue boat to come alongside. As the second night loomed, *Passage* held onto the lead, followed closely by *Condor* and K4, as the wind and sea conditions began to build.

"I was the bowman," remembers Gargle McClure. "We were right off Molokai, starting to crack off with a number three jib and one reef in the main. A sea came over the boat and swept me all the way down the deck. It was like I was swimming, but I wasn't swimming."

He ended up near the stern hanging over the side from the upper lifeline, shouting, "Get me the hell back on board." Afterward, the watch sent him below for 15 minutes to recover.

Pan Am Clipper Cup, 1982, Passage *off Koko Head, Oahu*
—©Phil Uhl

1982 Pan Am Clipper Cup, Molokai Race
—©Phil Uhl

WINDWARD PASSAGE
ATLANTA

"That was the beginning of a bad night," McClure says. "We could see *Kialoa* behind us. We were on port tack when, oh my word . . . the port lower spreader failed."

"The whole rig came down," says Weisman.

The mast snapped in two just below the lower spreaders. There were sails draped all over the side of the boat. Rumsey, ever the cool-headed leader, called a quick meeting to come up with a plan to disconnect and cut away the rig before the top of the broken mast punched a hole in *Passage*.

"It seemed like forever, but it probably only took us 15 minutes," says Gargle. "We all cheered after we cut away the last halyard and the whole mess sunk. *Kialoa* saw what happened. They offered to stop and help. We told them we had things under control, go finish the race."

As it turned out, K4 posted a record time. That record could have been The Effing Whale's if only . . . Weisman, who has raced and won hundreds of regattas all over the world in almost every superstar grand prix yacht on the planet, has one word to sum up the '82 Clipper Cup odyssey aboard *Windward Passage*:

"Unforgettable."

Ala Wei Harbor with the broken mast cobbled together —©Phil Uhl

S-32323
S-32323

19

On the Red Carpet

Following the '82 Clipper Cup, Bill Johnson had planned to send *Windward Passage* to San Francisco for the Big Boat Series," remembers Gargle McClure. "But we had to go back to Florida [for repairs] through the Canal."

He laughs at the memory. "Rumsey found a broken mast ashore from a boat called *Paragon*. We cleaned up the ragged edges and dropped *Paragon*'s mast inside what was left of ours and bolted the two together. Then off we went for California with that jury rig and ten barrels of diesel strapped aboard." After a stop for water, fuel, and provisions in San Diego, the crew took off for the Panama Canal with one stop in Mexico along the way.

They got beat up a bit in the Gulf of Tehuantepec, but going through the Panama Canal was "one big party," according to McClure.

The crew on *Passage* knew some of the American Canal pilots who lived in Panama. Their families lived with them in the Zone but had never been through "The Ditch."

"So we invited them along for the ride," remembers McClure. There was catered food and beverages of every description for the transit. The whole event felt like a Fourth of July boat picnic.

Once *Passage* completed her voyage back to Ross Yacht Services in Florida, she got a new Hood mast and entered the 1983 SORC. She had some flashes of brilliance, but K4 won Class A for the series. Still, winning isn't everything when it comes to the Big Dinghy. The November 1983 issue of *Yachting* magazine had an article by Ted Jones, celebrating *Windward Passage* in her fifteenth year. He called her "Everybody's Sweetheart."

Even Jim Kilroy might have agreed . . . but he was trying to focus on the future, not the past. That (1983) was the year he imagined a maxi world championship series, starting with the SORC, then moving on to Europe.

◀ Passage *passing* Nirvana *in the background, 1983 SORC —©Phil Uhl*

32323
S-13131
US-7099

At the same time, Kilroy and his maxi-boat cronies were evolving yet another organization to oversee their sport, the International Maxi Association (IMA). It started as "a small gathering of maxi yacht owners wishing to bring more co-ordination to their sailing." Over four decades, it has grown to manage maxi racing globally. Its honorary members include the King of Spain, the Aga Khan, and American industrialist Bill Koch. The inimitable Peter Bowker, *Passage*'s longtime navigator, also made the cut.

Maybe the Johnson brothers found such organizations superfluous, but *Windward Passage*'s current owner wanted in, all in. Bill Johnson yearned to run with the big ponies wherever they gathered, and he told his crew, "Saddle up, buddies. We're going to Europe."

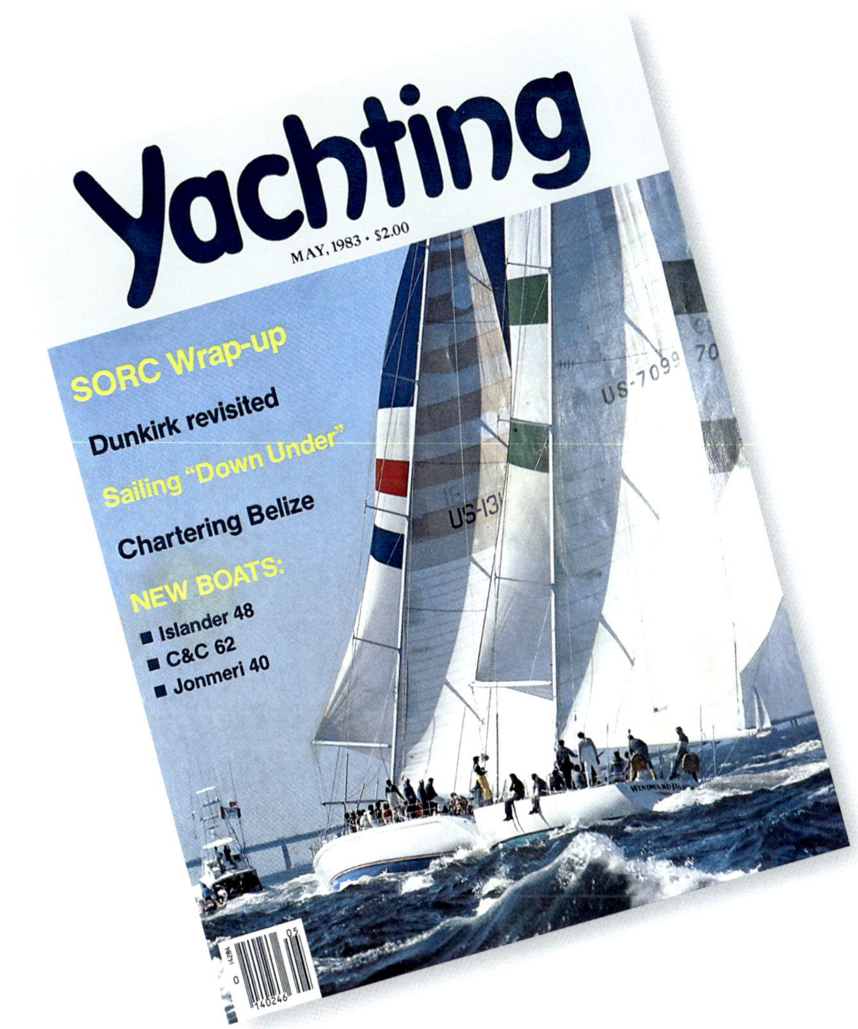

Windward Passage headed north to Newport, Rhode Island, from Florida, then crossed the North Atlantic via Nova Scotia and Scotland to compete in the maxi class at the Royal Norwegian Yacht Club's centennial regatta, celebrating King Olav's eightieth birthday and his personal farewell to competitive sailing.

"That was one of the best trips of my life," says Gargle McClure. He marveled at the wild horses off Sable Island, the cold/fog/bergs/growlers south of Greenland, the shorts-and-T-shirt weather once *Passage* crossed back into the Gulf Stream. This was all new territory for a kid from Southern California. He couldn't get over the idea of twenty-four-hour daylight.

A shipping container full of sails met the crew in Norway where *Passage* lined up for inshore races against *Kialoa IV*, *Nirvana, Midnight Sun, Ondine IV*, and others. The Big Dinghy finished second in the series behind K4, but she shone in the long offshore race that ran from Norway to Sweden, Denmark, and return.

◀ Passage *saying goodbye to* Condor, Nirvana, Kialoa
—©Phil Uhl

▼ *The big boys drying out in Nassau, 1983*
—©Phil Uhl

RVANA

"We got friendly with the future king, Prince Harald and his wife," remembers Sandra Johnson. "I think Bill took him sailing on *Passage*. We were treated like royalty."

She goes on to say, "*Passage* gave me a gift in Norway." Her grandfather had emigrated from Norway to the U.S. to practice veterinary medicine. "When I was a little bitty girl, I used to look at the picture hanging on the wall of his house in Norway. When we followed the boat to Norway, I rented a car with my nephews and found that house. The owners were thrilled to see us, and invited us to stay overnight." It felt like *Windward Passage* had helped her complete an ancestral circle.

On their way to follow the rest of the maxi fleet to more competition in the Mediterranean, *Passage* stopped in Smögen, Sweden, one of the liveliest summer resorts in the country.

"At that time we had a regular crew of six, and no way did the guys want to leave. They had beautiful women on the boat every night of the week," says McClure. "When Rumsey and I tried to leave Smögen, we almost had a mutiny. I thought they were going to throw us overboard."

Eventually, *Passage* sailed for Cowes, in the U.K., before meeting the other maxis for racing at Palma de Mallorca in the Balearic Islands.

"I remember Gargle used to give these teary-eyed speeches about 'the old girl' to get us psyched up before each race," says Dave Birchenough.

But despite McClure's pep talks, Jim Kilroy took the series. *Kialoa IV* won again at the premier maxi series off Porto Cervo, Sardinia. At both events the Big Dinghy finished in the middle of the fleet of eight. But the women who gathered aboard or mingled with the *Passage* crew in the waterfront bars of Mallorca and Sardinia didn't care if she had won. When Bill and

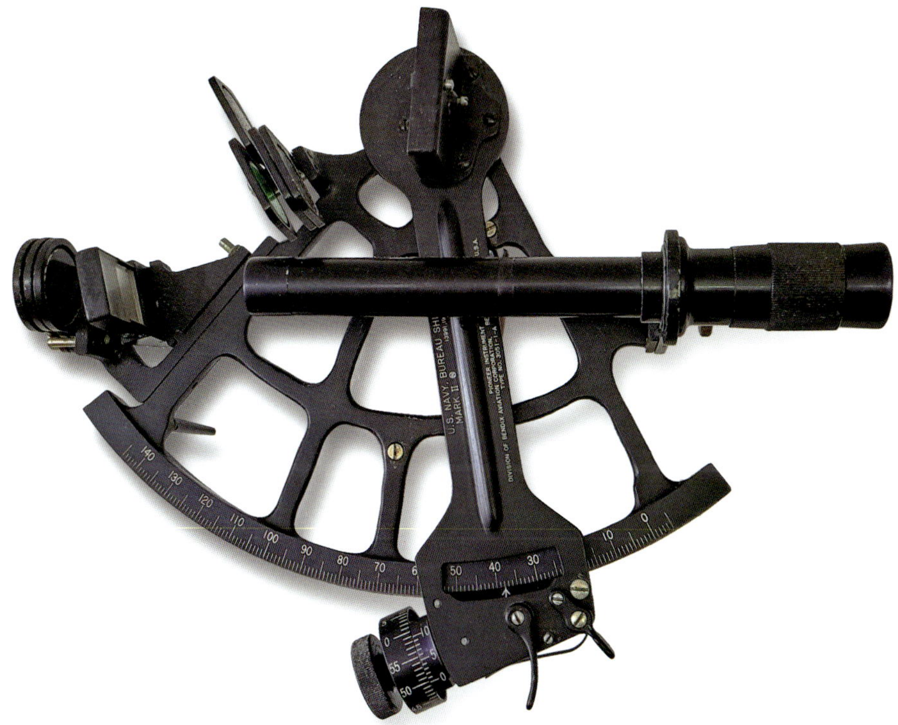

▲ Passage*'s sextant, used well into the 1990s —image courtesy of Carson Jefferson*

◀ *Drying out, Nassau, Bahamas, 1983 SORC —©Phil Uhl*

▼ Nirvana, Kialoa, Passage, *1983 SORC —©Phil Uhl*

7099

KIALOA

51
55
THUNDE
Charisma V
SAINT JOHN

Sandra Johnson flew in for the races, long and lavish dinner parties ensued for the crew and friends. By this point in her career, *Windward Passage* was a legend in Europe where racing yachts were as familiar and glamorous as *futbol* clubs like Real Madrid and FC Barcelona with its midfielder Diego Maradona. The *Passage* sailors were considered rock stars . . . and the guys were happy.

During a stint as waterfront jewelry on the quay at St-Tropez after the Sardinia racing, *Windward Passage* hosted French actress Brigitte Bardot aboard. The guys were *really* happy.

St. Petersburg Yacht Club, 1983 SORC—©Phil Uhl

20

SAVED

After St-Tropez *Passage* started for America again. For Gargle McClure this was a different kind of a sail. There was no demanding timetable, no *Kialoa*s to battle. No owner was following the boat's every move using the global position locator transponder (AIS) that oceangoing ships and yachts carry today. This was a trade wind run—Spain/Canaries/Antigua in fine weather.

McClure was in love. He had met a local Tampa girl, Cindy Howard, who was working her way through college bartending at the Steak & Ale, and he invited her to sail with him on *Passage* from Spain to the Caribbean. John Rumsey invited his girlfriend Laura, too. It was Cindy's second delivery trip on the Big Dinghy with Gargle, and the trip proved to be a romantic turning point. Gargle discovered Cindy was the love of his life. She enjoyed seafaring to the point where she earned her USCG 100-ton master's license just like McClure. Fourteen years after this transatlantic sail in *Passage*, they married. They are still together, still drawn to the water. But for them, life is about fishing these days, not maxis.

In 1984 Courtney Ross worked his magic tuning up *Windward Passage* for yet another SORC. This was at least her eleventh series in sixteen continuous years of racing. The yachting community stood in wonder as, against all odds, *Passage* gave K4 a run for her money in the shorter races. But Jim Kilroy kept taking the top honors.

Then came the Miami–Nassau Race where *Passage* had first dazzled the world with her record-setting run back in 1968. Here she did it one more time. It would be the last Miami–Nassau Race of her grand prix career.

Courtney Ross remembers that for the Nassau Cup race that year Bill Johnson had him charter a 125-foot Burger motoryacht, the *Arawa*, for his business associates, crewmembers, wives, and girlfriends to view the race.

"It was a class act," remembers Ross.

John "Gargle" McClure
—©Phil Uhl

281

So the crew knew something was afoot when the owner Bill Johnson did not sail the race, follow the race with a luxury yacht as a tender, or show up for the post-race banquet poolside at the Gray Cliffs Hotel in Nassau.

According to McClure, "Rumsey told everyone that Johnson was done campaigning the old girl and her future was uncertain."

"Bill was my friend," says Courtney Ross. "But he could just switch the entire direction of his life in a minute."

"My husband had a five-year plan to make *Windward Passage* a star," says Sandra Johnson. "He was moving on. His new big thing was Tennessee Walking Horses. He bought a thousand-acre farm to breed champions."

It was a rowdy bunch that night, remembers McClure. "We had quite a few of the crew off *Courageous* who had recently defended the *America*'s Cup with Ted Turner."

Someone, reputedly Peter Bowker, decided the mood of the evening needed a little lightening up, so he skipped a plate across the surface of the swimming pool.

"Things went downhill from there," laughs Courtney Ross.

Food started flying. This crew wanted to go out with a bang, not a whimper.

"One of the best food fights of my career," remembers Dave Birchenough.

"The end of an era," recalls McClure with a hitch in his voice as if to imply, "The old girl deserved better."

◀ Passage *leading* Ondine IV *and* Midnight Sun *in Nassau*
—©*Phil Uhl*

This could have been the *finale* for *Windward Passage* as a grand prix competitor. But it wasn't. It was only a change of course.

In the fall of 1985 Rod and Kathy Muir of Australia bought *Windward Passage.*

"I think they saved her life," says Gargle McClure who was now her professional skipper.

A New Zealander by birth, Rod Muir had grown up in Tasmania and is widely credited with bringing FM stereo radio to Australia. After being a rock 'n' roll DJ on California radio stations, he moved back to Australia and built a network of FM stations across the country. He also promoted pop music with rock concerts that drew superstar musicians, especially from the U.S. and the U.K.

The Muirs had started sailing in the late 1970s, and Rod had begun racing every chance he could. Kathy joined in the adventure, saying, "You could either be a sailing widow or you could go along for the ride." They purchased their first racing yacht in 1983. Now their enthusiasm for racing under sail led them on a search for a new boat and global competition, possibly in the U.K.'s Admiral's Cup.

"It's a bit of a curious story how Rod ended up with *Windward Passage*," remembers Tom Stephenson. "It all had to do with a sticker." At the time he was designer Doug Peterson's representative in Australia and an accomplished ocean racer whose opinion Rod Muir valued.

As Stephenson tells the story, he and the Muirs flew to France to look at Admiral's Cup boats. Stephenson suggested they should stop in England and take a ferry to the Isle of Wight and visit Cowes where the regatta was held.

"On the ferry I noticed a sticker on the outside of the pilothouse door that read, '*Windward Passage*, Atlanta, 1983.' I had always fancied *Passage*, so I offered the skipper five quid for the sticker."

When the deal was done, Stephenson returned to the Muirs.

"What's *Windward Passage*?" asked Rod Muir seeing the sticker.

"It's the greatest racing yacht of all time," Stephenson told him. Then he added that he had heard she was for sale in America.

"Rod wanted to see her. Our plans changed almost instantly. Next thing I knew we were on a flight to Florida. Courtney Ross met us at the airport."

"I remember they flew into town [Tampa/St. Petersburg]," says Courtney Ross. "They only had an hour or two for me to take them over and show them the boat."

Windward Passage was languishing at the docks of the St. Petersburg Yacht Club.

"It was love at first sight," remembers Muir. The sleek hull, flush deck, and powerful rig called to the him and his wife.

Stephenson told Rod that if he wanted to get into maxi racing, here was the greatest of them all and, because of her age, she could be had for a fraction of the cost of a new boat. The new Peterson keel and rudder, as well as the new rig Courtney Ross had given her, made her still "very competitive."

"There are some times you just have to go with emotions," says Muir. He didn't need to have the boat surveyed. "Doug Peterson had had a lot of work done on her, and I trusted Doug."

"I gave Rod two pieces of advice," remembers Stephenson. "One, I told him he should buy the boat. And, two, I told him he had to hire Gargle for a year to show us how to run her."

"They bought *Passage*," remembers Courtney Ross about the Muirs' brief visit to Florida. "Done deal." Rod Muir was forty-three. Kathy was twenty-seven. Suddenly they owned an ocean-racing legend half a world away from their home in Australia.

As soon as hurricane season began to ebb in Florida, Gargle McClure and Greg Tuxworth, working as co-captains, pulled together a crew. Tuxworth and the crew sailed *Windward Passage* down to Panama, through the Canal, and across the South Pacific to meet McClure in Sydney.

Maybe this time Down Under, Bellin-Bellin, the wind god of Australia's Kulin and Wurundjeri Indigenous people, would smile more kindly on the old girl.

Passage *"visiting" the States—image courtesy of Onne van der Wal*

21

DAZZLING

No sooner did *Passage* get to Australia than the Muirs entered her in the 1985 Sydney Hobart on Boxing Day. "We didn't do too much to get her ready," remembers Gargle McClure. "We just started racing the old girl."

"She got off to a great start and was leading the race," says Tom Stephenson, "but then the mainsail blew to bits in the Bass Strait. It took us another day to get a new one on in the gale. It was too late to make a good show of it."

But Rod Muir was undaunted. With assistance from Stephenson and McClure, he entered *Windward Passage* in Australia's major east coast races during the first half of 1986. She made a clean sweep of things. *Passage* was first to finish in the Sydney to Mooloolaba race. In the Brisbane to Gladstone race she came first again with a record time. Then she won the Gladstone to Hamilton race, and dominated the Hamilton Race Week series in the Whitsunday Islands.

As if *Passage* herself was not enough to add star quality to Race Week, Rod Muir invited guitarist Mark Knopfler, who had been touring in Australia with Dire Straits, to race aboard. Rod's sailing and rock 'n' roll passions intersected more than once this year. In addition to sailing with Knopfler, he composed, with Australian rocker Richard Clapton, a guitar-pulsing ballad called "The Transpac Slide" in the vein of Yacht Rock classics like "Southern Cross" and "Down Under." "The mighty *Windward Passage*" makes a lyrical appearance in the song and has cameos in the video. Meanwhile Muir's crew nicknamed him "Mad Max" after actor Mel Gibson's high-energy Australian action hero.

"After winning almost every regatta in Eastern Australia, we took the boat to the 1986 Kenwood Cup [formerly the Pan Am Clipper Cup] in Hawaii," says Gargle McClure.

◀ Passage *arriving in Sydney Harbour. Customs boat is on the left to greet them, while Rod and Kathy Muir are in the Riva to the right.*

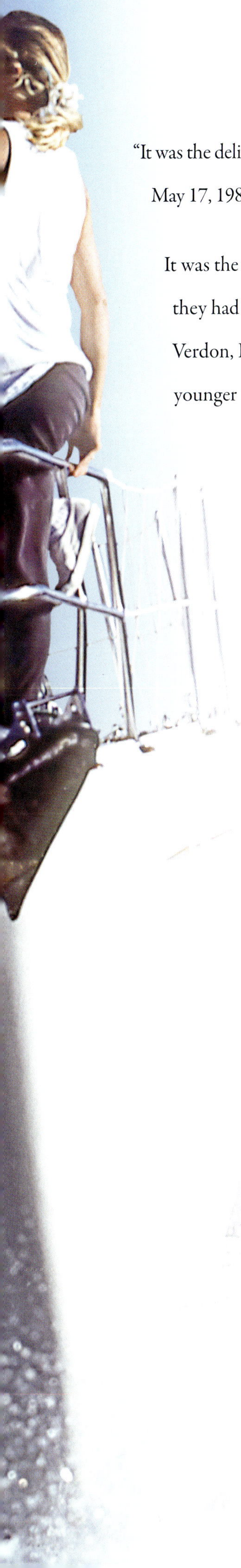

"It was the delivery of a lifetime," says his wife, Cindy. "We left Sydney on May 17, 1986, headed for New Zealand's North Island."

It was the first leg of their nearly 6,000-mile run to Hawaii, and they had two other young couples aboard—Peter and Gabby Verdon, Ian Exton and his girlfriend Angela. They also had two younger sailors with them for extra muscle, Robbie Naismith and Matthew Mason.

"We definitely were taking it easy on the old girl," says Gargle. "We had shipped all the racing sails to Hawaii in a container and were using old Dacron sails for this trip. Most of the time we had two reefs tucked in the main."

The Southern Ocean was behaving as they ran their easting down on their 1,400-mile ride to New Zealand. They had a downwind sail in moderate winds until they closed with the coast at Three Kings Islands on their way to the Bay of Islands. There's a bank out there, and the waves can get tremendous.

"This 30-footer started building behind us," remembers McClure. "I couldn't help myself. I was a surf rat from Southern California, and *Passage* was just a big surfboard."

"Don't you dare," shouted Cindy when she saw the daredevil in his eyes.

▲ *Captain Carson Jefferson kept these two obsolete man-overboard rescue "horseshoes" as souvenirs of his ten years as skipper aboard* Windward Passage.

◄ Passage *on Narragansett Bay, Rhode Island —image courtesy of Onne Van der Wal*

But it was too late. With Gargle at the helm, *Passage* dropped in on the roller and started down its face at 20 knots.

"It had to be one of the biggest thrills I ever had in the old girl," laughs McClure. "When we hit the bottom of the trough, we filled the cockpit with water. I got a scolding for that one."

But the trip was more chill than thrill. They stayed at anchor for four days at Opua in the Bay of Islands sunning, swimming, fishing, and socializing with new friends ashore.

"It looked like Tahiti, all palm trees and white sand," says Cindy.

After provisioning in Auckland, the crew shoved off on the second leg of their delivery, 1,800 miles from Auckland to Rarotonga in the Cook Islands. It was a close-reach all the way, with *Windward Passage* gliding along at 9 knots with no stress or strain. Not a squall in sight.

"We were dragging lures all the time," says Cindy. "There was hardly a time when we didn't have fresh wahoo or some other fish."

"Imagine Rarotonga before the cruise ships," she says. "It was a tropical paradise. We snorkeled, rented mopeds, shopped for coconuts, and hit the bars."

It was hard for any of the crew to believe they were actually getting paid for this.

Passage was about twelve days en route north from Rarotonga to Hilo, Hawaii, across the equator.

"Crossing the Line was a big deal," says Cindy. "Neptune and his minions appeared to initiate the pollywogs."

There was, indeed, alcohol involved as Gargle emerged from the dark regions of *Windward Passage* with a pineapple duct-taped to the top of

Crossing the equator on June 19, 1986, was serious business for sailing professionals. Left to right: Peter Verdon, Ian Exton at the helm, His Majesty Gargle McClure with the trident. At this point Gargle's cabbage-leaf breasts and shaving-cream beard had gone "by the board."

his head, a beard made of shaving cream, and cabbage leaves for breasts. Somewhere he found an actual trident and waved it wildly while making his very best gargling roars.

"Coming into Hilo to meet the Muirs [who had flown in], I heard the 500-pound-test line with the lure we were towing start to hum. I looked back and I saw this 1,200-pound black marlin out of the water trying to shake the lure. He was tail-walking in one direction and *Passage* was charging off at 8 knots in the other. 'Duck,' I shouted."

Crossing the equator on June 19, 1986

Everybody hit the deck just before the line snapped and whipped over *Windward Passage* like a lightning strike.

After *Passage* arrived in Hilo, the Muirs came aboard to sail *Passage* to Big Bob's Lahaina Yacht Club and a banquet. When the boat pressed on to Honolulu to prepare for the Kenwood Cup, Gargle and Cindy found a quiet place on the rail of the old girl to be alone and take stock of themselves, each other, the seafaring life, their past, and their future.

"It was strange," says Gargle. "I wondered if the real world was still going to be there anymore when we got ashore."

"We just got lost in time," says Cindy.

In the 1986 Kenwood Cup, Rod Muir and *Windward Passage* vied for line honors with the 83-foot Gary Mull–designed *Sorcery*. The Molokai Race was close, but "Big Red" *Sorcery* won by 12 minutes. The competition was even closer in the Around the State Race. *Passage* traded the lead back and forth with *Sorcery* seven or eight times.

"We tried to break her. We tried to break her. We tried to break that old girl," remembers McClure. "But she wouldn't break. Running down the Molokai Channel you could hear the wire after guys loading up and then whoosh. She exhaled and took off, surfing, with a roostertail. There's never been a boat like her." After 790 miles Rod Muir and his boat crossed the line "just over a minute behind *Sorcery*." At this point *Windward Passage* had been a top-of-the-line competitor in the world's major ocean races for eighteen years. Maybe she needed a change of pace.

Gargle McClure did. Following the Kenwood Cup, Gargle left the old girl. He had given her the better part of eleven years, but now there was another love in his life.

"It was time to settle down with Cindy and think about earning some money for retirement," says McClure. At age thirty-one, he moved on to run other yachts (including *Windward Passage II*) for a while, then embarked on a totally new kind of seafaring. Eventually, he became the tugboat skipper with Weeks Marine who had the responsibility of towing the "Miracle on the Hudson" airliner to safety in New York Harbor.

Gargle and Cindy McClure

22

A Last Hurrah?

Bruce Vasconcellos took on the role as professional skipper aboard *Passage* and brought her back to Sydney for the Muirs. Carson Jefferson joined the crew then, too.

"Rod really wanted to win Sydney Hobart," he remembers, "so he prepared *Passage* for the 1986 race."

After all her recent victories in Australia and her impressive showing against *Sorcery* in the Kenwood Cup, the Muirs as well as *Passage*'s crew, her fans, and her adversaries were expecting big things from the boat on her charge to Tasmania.

The boat's bio in the 1986 brochure for the race speaks straight to her legendary status before the race:

> WINDWARD PASSAGE
> If there were a hall of fame for yachts, *Windward Passage* would be the showpiece. This grand old lady of ocean racing turned eighteen this year and is still giving modern, high-tech yachts fright. Rod Muir bought her last year and knows what makes her tick. She has formidable opposition this year, but she will show her nice-looking transom to quite a few.

The Muirs thought it was an extremely good omen that the legendary navigator Peter Bowker had signed on to race the old girl one more time. He flew into Sydney all the way from Florida. He was fifty-nine at the time and he had raced on *Passage* from her very earliest days in the late 1960s.

"He showed up with a duffel bag and a Hefty trash bag for his foulies," remembers Carson Jefferson. "Hilarious. A world-class navigator, and he carries his gear in a garbage bag."

It was Bowker's last race on *Windward Passage*, but for her crews, he will always be a part of the boat.

◀ *Rod Muir*

WINDWARD PASSAGE
CYCA
SYDNEY
7099
WYC

"He was a helluva navigator and friend, to us all," says Mark Johnson. Not only could Bowker navigate *Passage* through a hurricane to Bermuda, he could recite doggerel, entertain his bored shipmates by reading aloud from *Stuart Little*, or revive a somber gathering with a food fight. The man spread an infectious gusto and singular way of dealing with what Shakespeare called "the slings and arrows of outrageous fortune."

John Rumsey remembers a moment on a delivery run from Hawaii to Australia when the crew ran short of compass oil when changing the position of the Flinders bar in the compass after crossing the equator. Bowker's solution? Top off the compass with Rex Banks's vodka. Problem solved, mates.

Then there was the time on a long passage from Hawaii to Australia, Bowker convinced a young and naïve Gargle McClure that he needed to write some postcards "to mail home from the [nonexistent] post office ship located on the International Dateline" in the Pacific.

In the men's room of the old Charthouse Restaurant at Newport Beach, California, where world-class ocean-racing sailors long gathered, there was graffiti on the wall that generations of seafarers have ascribed to Peter Bowker. It says, "Don't step in anything soft."

When the '86 Sydney Hobart kicked off on December 26, Bowker, Vasconcellos, Jefferson, Rod Muir, and Duncan Van Worden (Muir's Australian yacht manager) had their shipmates steering clear of anything soft and ready to rumble. At the start of the race, the newest maxi in the fleet, *Sovereign*, led *Windward Passage* and 185 other yachts south toward the Bass Strait. *Passage* and *Condor* dogged *Sovereign* in freshening breezes but could not catch her until her crew discovered a problem with her mast and withdrew from the race before they lost the rig.

Peter Bowker

1986 Kenwood Cup—image courtesy of Sharon Green/Ultimate Sailing

WINDWARD PASSAGE
SYDNEY

With *Sovereign* out, *Passage* and *Condor* dueled each other across the Bass Strait with small jibs and reefed mainsails in gale-force conditions and huge seas. Four other maxis failed to keep up with the pace.

"The cook was under the weather so Peter Bowker and I took over the galley," remembers Carson Jefferson. "The boat has shallow bilges, and we were up to our ankles in water. It was rough, rough."

Designed by Ron Holland like *Passage*'s nemesis *Kialoa IV*, *Condor* was launched in 1981 at Kiwi Boats, U.K. Registered in Bermuda, she was nearing the end of a spectacular seven-year racing career, which already included wins in the Miami–Montego Bay Race, Fastnet Race, and Sydney Hobart Race.

Coming down the east coast of Tasmania, *Passage* slowly but surely began closing the distance on the much younger and bigger *Condor*. By the time they started up the River Derwent toward the finish, *Passage* was moving fast against her rival. *Condor* fell into a hole of dead air just a couple miles short of the finish, and *Passage* charged ahead with Rod Muir at the helm, smiling and almost tasting a come-from-behind victory. Having grown up in Tasmania, he wanted to look good for the hometown crowd. But in the last minutes, *Condor* caught a gust and dashed ahead. *Passage* came in 19 minutes later, second on elapsed time and first in the Illingsworth Division.

The '86 Sydney Hobart turned out to be *Windward Passage*'s last grand prix race of her competitive career. But Fortune still smiled on the Big Dinghy.

▲ *Image courtesy of Kathy Muir*

◀ Passage *visiting the East Coast of the United States —image courtesy of Onne van der Wal*

▼ *Hard work during the 1986 Kenwood Cup*

WINDWARD PASSAGE

23

New Roles

In 1987 Rod and Kathy Muir decided *Passage* was ready for a serious change. They had already begun building the new, all-carbon *Windward Passage II* (a Frers 80) at McConaghy Boats, and while waiting for the new racing machine to launch, they sent the Big Dinghy to Tim Gurr's Southern Pacific Shipyard in New Zealand.

"I thought it would be a shame to let that grand lady deteriorate after what she and her previous owners had achieved," Muir says. He offered Carson Jefferson the job to see *Passage* through her nearly two-year, $1.5 million restoration.

"He didn't have to ask twice," remembers Jefferson. "It was a great opportunity for both of us, the boat and me . . . . Tim and his crew were amazing boatbuilders."

After *Passage* hauled out at Gurr's yard, Jefferson got his own office at the shipyard and moved into Gurr's house with three other roommates.

Hard work was the rule by day, but the good times rolled after hours.

"There was a while when we got to playing rugby in the living room," says Jefferson. "There was also the time Tim was learning to fly a helicopter . . . indoors." Some nights Carson Jefferson and his roommates ended up ducking under the coffee table while Gurr sent his remote-control helicopter careening around in the house. Jefferson laughs at the memory just as John Rumsey laughed about the crew's hijinks when *Passage* was being built at Grand Bahama twenty years earlier. *Windward Passage* was still inspiring new escapades.

Meanwhile, according to Jefferson, the job just kind of grew.

"Rod and Kathy wanted to make *Passage* into a luxurious cruising yacht to follow *Passage II* around as her tender," recalls Jefferson. "When the boat was hauled and we were starting the rebuild with Tim Gurr, Rod, Kathy,

◀ Passage *on tour in the United States—image courtesy of Onne van der Wal*

Duncan, Tim, and I were below talking about the scope of work and we were wondering what she would look like without the centerline bulkhead. Tim said, 'Hang on a minute,' grabbed a chainsaw, and in a few minutes we had our answer."

At Gurr's yard workers peeled off her deck from the primary winches forward to make gutting the hull and installing a new interior easier. Once the hull was empty, they dried out the wood with heaters, replaced 80 percent of the keelson, laminated new floor timbers, did a lot of refastening of the structural members, and coated the interior with epoxy to prevent rot. To spread out the loads from the keel and rig in the center of the hull, Albert Sedlmayer designed a 25-foot-long aluminum grid and fuel tank that spans the floor timbers and bolts to the keel and chainplates. All the bulkheads were replaced, except three. Gurr took the slight "hook" out of the stem, too.

▲ *The Muirs' two-year rejuvenation of* Passage *began in 1987.*

After the structural beef-up, Muir installed a proper yacht interior that evolved over time with the help of designer Alf Lock, Tim Gurr, Steve Wilson, and the crew of the Southern Pacific Boatyard. To give the interior a "woody" yacht finish, the crew laminated a layer of spruce veneer over exposed interior planking. Where the old engineroom had been in the middle of the boat, carpenters built a stateroom and modern galley. They also added a large, comfortable saloon with white leather upholstery and three other staterooms.

"The boat was dark below when we got her," says Kathy Muir.

She's being kind. As beautiful as *Windward Passage* looked on the outside, her interior was a totally different story. Anyone who was ever below decks during *Passage*'s racing days knows the boat had only the most basic interior carpentry to support a racing crew while keeping weight down.

▲ *Speak no evil, see no evil, hear no evil—gee, did they get that right?*

◀ *Gargle McClure and Carson Jefferson aboard WP2* (Windward Passage II)

In 1987 the Southern Pacific Shipyard in New Zealand gave Windward Passage *the last keel Henry Scheel designed before he died. It reduced the draft from 13 feet to 10 feet for cruising into shallower harbors, and served as a fuel tank.*

The total fuel capacity on first filling was now 896 US gallons between three tanks and the day tank, providing around 825 US gallons of usable fuel stored as follows:

Forward keel tank–382 US gallons
Aft keel tank–371 US gallons
Keelson tank–118 US gallons
Engineroom day tank–25 US gallons

Now the boat had 2,244 nautical miles range at 8.5 knots with the generator running.

—source: Carson Jefferson

The renovations at the Gurr yard were substantial and meticulous.

One of her crew said the interior of the boat was like living inside a hollow tree. Some of the berths were known as "The Swamp."

"We wanted to lighten up the feel inside and make her as gorgeous on the inside as she was on the outside," says Kathy Muir, "so we went with all that lovely white leather. It was a risk, but it looked amazing." Subsequent owners have kept the motif, replacing the leather as needed.

Gurr's shipwrights electrified the big winches on the boat. They also rebuilt the Perkins T6.3554 power plant and moved the engineroom well aft. To complete the project, the yard gave *Passage* a Scheel keel. It was the last keel Henry Scheel designed before he died. It reduced the draft from 13 to 10 feet for cruising into shallow harbors and also served as a fuel tank, carrying 896 gallons of diesel.

"We found a few cracked deckbeams, but the cold-molded hull was in great shape, even after all those years of racing and hard deliveries," says Jefferson. "The boat has a strong heart."

It may have been admiration for *Passage*'s original construction and design that prompted Tim Gurr to attempt a call to the U.K.

"He wanted to talk to Gurney, and somehow he got a number for him," remembers Jefferson. "We called. It turned out to be a pub somewhere in the wilds of Scotland. They said Gurney wasn't there . . . but this was where he actually got his phone messages and his mail."

When *Passage* started her new life as a luxury cruising yacht, Rod Muir's wife Kathy wanted to have some fun with their "grand lady."

"Because she had electric winches now, Rod and I sometimes sailed her, just the two of us. We would take her out past Sydney Heads and about 30 kilometers up the coast to an anchorage at Pittwater." Rod could get out his audio speakers there and blast "Stairway to Heaven" while Kathy whipped up spaghetti Bolognese.

But Kathy didn't just want to cook and cruise. She wanted to skipper *Passage* and race her with a crew of women, including Olympian Nicky Bethwaite, helmswoman Vanessa Dudley, and multihull ocean racer and co-skipper, Cathy Hawkins.

"I spent most of my sailing career racing trimarans shorthanded," remembers Hawkins, author of the memoir *Return in the Wake*. "Coincidentally, Kathy and I were childhood neighbors in the beachside Sydney suburb of Clontarf. I caught up with Kathy and Rod in Hawaii during the '86 Kenwood Cup. They invited me and my trimaran co-skipper, racing *Bullfrog Sunblock*, to sail with them in a few races on *Passage*. It was so different for me. All those people working together."

As it turned out, meeting Hawkins gave the Muirs an idea for an all-female maxi racing crew. It bloomed for Kathy Muir after *Passage* came back to Sydney following her rebuild in New Zealand.

"Kathy asked me to pull together a crew of experienced women sailors," says Hawkins. "There were twenty-three of us, and we practiced for the race three or four afternoons a week and on weekends with Australia's Olympic, *America*'s Cup, and Admiral Cup's coach, Mike Fletcher. It took eight of us to lift the spinnaker pole, so everybody had to work together. These were extremely capable sailors with no big egos, and, we built a team we were proud of."

22 crew — and they're all women

ALL-WOMEN crews are a rarity in offshore yacht racing, particularly for for a maxi yacht.

Kathy Muir has taken on the task of gathering 22 other experienced women sailors to sail husband Rod's original Windward Passage in the Sydney to Newcastle ocean race next weekend.

As for Rod, the former FM radio entrepeneur, he is sailing his new maxi, Windward Passage II, in the same race with an ALL-MALE crew.

Picture shows Kathy Muir (right) with crew boss Cathy Hawkins and others crew members including Susan Allsop, Susie Bell, Debra Bowes, Adrienne Cahalan, Jule Canfield, Karyn Davis, Michelle Davis, Vanessa Dudley, Jenny Ellers, Christine Evans, Susie Green, Nicola Green, Antonia Hawkins, Patria Heathwood, Andrea Holt, Susie Kidd, Pip Kyle, Judy Micklewright, Trish Murphy, Jodie Poe and Toni Wilkinson.

Left to right: Deborah Bowes, Christine Evans. The sense of teamwork and intensity radiate from this photo of the two women on the coffee-grinders when Passage *fielded the first all-female maxi crew for the 1989 Sydney–Newcastle Race. She was twenty-one years old and won her class. —image courtesy of Christian Février*

In 1988, as part Australia's bicentennial celebrations, the Cruising Yacht Club of Australia had initiated 110-mile overnight race from Sydney north to Newcastle along the east coast of Australia. For the second running of the event in 1989, the Muirs entered both *Passage* and *WPII*. Kathy Muir was skippering *Passage* with her all-women crew. Rod had the helm of *WP II*.

Sailing in mild east-nor'easterly winds, Rod Muir led his new Frers maxi to a line-honors victory in a time of 6 hours, 58 minutes, 52 seconds. Kathy and *Passage* finished about an hour behind *Windward Passage II* after a boat-for-boat duel up the coast against the 60-footer *Rager*, beating her across the finish line by seconds. It was a big day for the Muirs. *Passage* and "P2" had won their respective divisions, and the women in the grand lady had won the race on corrected time.

And, it was one more jewel in the tiara of the Muirs' grand lady. As far as anyone can tell, her race to Newcastle carried the first all-women racing crew in a maxi. Rod and Kathy Muir hosted the awards ceremony and post-race banquet at their Windward Passage Tavern. It had a bar built around the mold used to construct the carbon hull of *Windward Passage II*. There were resounding cheers for Kathy Muir, her crew, and her superbly restored sloop. When the assembled company raised their glass to *Windward Passage*, someone said, "Long live the queen."

She was twenty-one years old. By Jim Kilroy's standards, she had already survived four or five lifetimes as a racing yacht.

Left to right: Nicky Bethwaite, Andrea Holt, Cathy Hawkins, Toni Wilkinson. The all-female crew aboard Windward Passage *trims the spinnaker during a breezy run.—image courtesy of Christian Février*

The First All-Women Maxi Crew

Kathy Muir—*skipper*
Cathy Hawkins—*sailing master & helm*
Adrienne Cahalan—*trimmer*
Julie Canfield (now Hodder)—*navigator*
Nicky Bethwaite—*helm & trimmer*
Vanessa Dudley—*helm & trimmer*
Suzie Allsop (now Allsop-Jones)—*bow*
Karyn Davis (now Gojnich)—*trimmer*
Christine Evans—*grinder*
Susie Kidd—*mast*
Judy Micklewright—*trimmer*
Andrea Holt (now Gus)—*mast*
Jodie Poe—*grinder*
Toni Wilkinson—*second bow*
Trish Murphy—*grinder*
Deborah Bowes—*grinder*
Suzanne Green (now Sherwood)—*mast/bow*
Antonia Hawkins (now Patterson)—*hydraulics*
Michelle Davis (now McGrath)—*grinder*
Petrea Heathwood (now McCarthy)—*cockpit*
Suzie Bell (now Grimes)—*pit*
Kip Kyle—*second bow*
Jenny Ellers

24

Above & Beyond

It was not *all* bikini day-sails, postcard anchorages, cocktail parties, and gourmet meals as Carson Jefferson shepherded the yacht up and down the Windward and Leeward Islands chains. But *Windward Passage* was definitely enjoying the good life. The Muirs and charter guests flew in and out, meeting the boat at island paradises like the Grenadines. The boat also hopped up the east coast of the U.S. to Newport, Rhode Island, for summer cruising.

"One of my favorite memories was stopping in New York," says Kathy Muir. "We were in a little boat basin [North Cove Marina] in the shadow of the World Trade twin towers. *Stars and Stripes* was tied up next to us with Dennis Conner aboard, and we took him sailing. That was one of the amazing things about the boat, people were just drawn to her. Everyone wanted her at their dock."

In Norfolk, Virginia, *Passage* joined a race sponsored by *Cruising World* magazine from Norfolk to the Bitter End Yacht Club resort in the British Virgin Islands. Most of the crew were paying for the experience, not trying to build their résumés as professional sailors, and *Passage* did not place in the money. Eventually, the boat sailed back to Fort Lauderdale.

"With *Passage* so far from Australia, Rod and Kathy decided they wanted me to take her to San Diego and put her up for sale," remembers Jefferson.

But like *Passage*'s previous owners, the Muirs found letting go of their grand lady was not easy or final.

"I have boxes of photos and things from those days," says Kathy, "and every day I still wear a necklace with the *Windward Passage* whale on it."

A new decade was dawning. It was the start of the 1990s, and there were big changes afoot, not just for *Windward Passage*, but in the world,

◀ Passage *visits the Big Apple*

America, and the sport of ocean racing. The Soviet Union was crumbling. The internet was exploding. Wilson Phillips ruled pop radio with "Hold On." Michael Jordan dominated the basketball court. Legions of TV viewers became obsessed with the sitcom *Friends.* J. K. Rowling published *Harry Potter and the Philosopher's Stone.*

In the arena of international maxi racing a new crop of maxis by designer Bruce Farr burst on the scene. *Steinlager II*, sponsored by the New Zealand brewery of the same name, won all six legs of the Whitbread Round the World Race and the Fastnet Race. At the maxi championship races off Porto Cervo, Sardinia, another new Farr design, *Longobarda*, was the boat to beat. The latest iterations of *Passage*'s old rivals *Kialoa* and *Ondine* could do no better than the middle of the fleet. With the rapid acceleration of technology applied to yacht design and construction during the era, few people would remember the names of the current stars of the maxi fleet in five years.

It was against this backdrop, with *Passage* laboring toward San Diego to be sold, that she seemed to throw a tantrum of sorts.

Carson Jefferson remembers that he and his delivery crew in *Passage* were about 250 miles from Panama on their way to California. "It was the middle of the night and *bang*. The rig let go. We had to sail her through the Canal and up to San Diego with 20 feet of mast and a jury rig."

Jefferson got some used sails from a Canal pilot, took them to a Panamanian flag maker, and had them recut "so that we would have something to steady the boat on the way up the coast."

When the old girl arrived in San Diego looking forlorn with her jury rig, the port was gearing up to host its second *America*'s Cup match with *America3*, built to the new International *America*'s Cup Class (IACC) rules and raced by a syndicate headed by industrialist Bill Koch.

Kathy Muir's whale necklace

Passage *playing tourist in Boston next to* Stars and Stripes

Windward Passage no longer lived in this adrenalin-fueled world. She was above and beyond it. But whenever her name was mentioned on waterfronts around the world, the stories flowed. A legion of fans kept track of the Muirs' grand lady and hoped for chance just to see her under sail.

"Where ever she went, she opened doors and turned heads," remembers Carson Jefferson.

One of those turned heads was Kevin Jaffé's. He was from Newport Beach, California, an accomplished Star Class racer, and one of the owners of the Behr Paint company. He had also been waiting in the wings for *Windward Passage* and dreaming of her for a very long time:

> My love affair journey with "WP" started in 1971, when I saw her for the first time in Newport Beach. My initial reaction—"What is this?" Her extreme low freeboard, flush deck, enormous beam, and very large, raked transom differentiated her look and style from anything I had ever seen in the sailing world.
>
> My only critique was the ketch rig proportionally and aesthetically looked undersized for such a powerful, massive hull. Laughing to myself, I thought, "If I owned her, she would be converted to a sloop," which ultimately happened. As I walked away from *Passage* the "wow" factor made that brief encounter memorable for a lifetime.
>
> Seventeen years later, in September 1988, I was in San Diego watching the *America*'s Cup with my good friend, Pat Farrah, who had recently purchased the racing sloop *Ragtime.* Pat was one of the three founders of Home Depot and knew no boundaries when it came to having fun. Upon my arrival Pat said *Windward Passage* had arrived from Hawaii several days ago and Rod Muir, the owner, had invited us to go see her.

Passage *with Carson Jefferson at the helm arriving in Newport Beach in 1991 for her sale to Kevin Jaffé*

Kevin Jaffé (left) together with Pat Farrah, sailing off Anguilla. Farrah at the time owned arch-competitor Ragtime, *and advocated for Kevin buying a wooden boat and for buying* Passage *in particular.*

"Perfect will be just fine."

WINDWARD PASSAGE
NEWPORT BEACH

I was overwhelmed with excitement and within 15 minutes Pat and I were standing alongside "WP" inhaling every detail. The most visual was the height of the mast, which I guessed at 105 feet off the deck using the estimated distance between the four spreaders for my calculation. This number was later confirmed spot on. My 1971 vision for a large sloop rig was more than realized but seemed somewhat intimidating for cruising short-handed, which was the new mission for "WP."

Within a few minutes Rod Muir came on deck and gave us a warm welcome and invited us to go below for a drink. Entering through the forward companionway, I was immediately in awe as I stood in such a voluminous main saloon painted all white, trimmed in varnished teak—a timeless look with beautiful simplicity bordering on minimalism without compromising seagoing functionality. The entire interior was consistent with this clean design look and the overall footprint was exceptional for cruising. I loved it.

After our quick tour, Rod opened a bottle of champagne and gave us an overview of his ownership and the complete rebuild at Tim Gurr's yard in Auckland, New Zealand, to transition "WP" from a remarkable, legendary race boat to a world-class, high-performance cruising yacht. During that discussion, I made the mental decision to buy "WP" when and if she became available. The following day I called my longtime yacht broker, Jim Elliott, and told him my intentions.

In May of 1990, Jim called and said "WP" was officially on the market and located in Fort Lauderdale. I flew to Florida and met Captain Carson Jefferson for the first time. After a couple of hours together, I felt he would be a great fit and would understand my obsession for chasing perfection. His firsthand knowledge of the rebuild proved invaluable in many ways, but most importantly, gave me the confidence the structural integrity of the hull had been totally restored.

My feelings about the mast and the rigging were the polar opposite. Carson thought it was from the Bill Johnson era,

Teresa "Tee" Jaffé up the mast for a bird's-eye view of the Panama Canal

Kevin and Teresa Jaffé in Costa Rica, 1993

which would make it ten years old with a history of more than 100,000 miles of deliveries and hard ocean racing. Looking up the sail track, I could see significant and excessive pre-bend with almost no load on the hydraulic backstay. I told Carson if I bought "WP," a new mast, rigging, and boom would be at the top of the refit list.

He smiled and said, "I like it."

The biggest feature that came to light on my visit was the Henry Scheel keel built and installed during the New Zealand refit in 1987–88. Carson said it accomplished two very important objectives for long-distance cruising. First, It reduced the draft to 10 feet. Secondly, it put two additional fuel tanks in the top end of the keel. This increased total tankage gave *Passage* a range of 2,244 nautical miles at 8.5 knots. Both features further convinced me "WP" would fit my mission of extended cruising in the Caribbean and South Pacific.

The parting surprise on my visit was Carson saying he thought there was a chance "WP" could return to Southern California in early 1991 where her legendary history was far better known, and the market would be more receptive. The risk of not making an offer now versus waiting eight to nine months for "WP" to maybe return to the West Coast was a real roll of the dice.

But I got lucky by waiting. After almost nine months of silence by both parties, I received a call in early March from Jim Elliott.

"Kevin," he said, "I have bad news for you, 'WP' lost her mast 250 miles from the Panama Canal on February 23rd."

According to Jim, no one was hurt and there was no serious damage to the hull. Knowing the mast would reduce the selling price, but Rod would recover the loss through insurance, I foresaw a potential "win-win" for both the buyer and the seller.

Petey became an integral crewmember throughout the Jaffé cruise.

It wasn't all tropical breezes for Kevin and Teresa.

My next call from Jim Elliott was very uplifting. He announced "WP" had arrived in San Diego on April 29, 1991, and was docked at the Shelter Island Marina. The very next day, Jim and I drove to San Diego, knowing I could not sit on the sidelines any longer if I wanted *Windward Passage*.

Seeing "WP" with only 20 feet of broken mast and looking rather rough and tired after her journey did not deter my desire or intentions to move forward. Considering the very long (3,976 nautical miles) and challenging delivery from Tortola, BVI to San Diego, Carson was in good spirits and appeared happy to see me, especially after I told him as soon as we could contact Rod in Australia an offer would be made.

On the way back to Newport Beach, I told Jim, since he had the central listing (which meant he was representing both parties), I would like to have my own man who was not a yacht broker negotiate the price directly with Rod with no loss of any commission to Jim or his company Ardell.

Before Jim agreed, he only asked one question, "Who is your man?"

"Pat Farrah," I said, "but I have not asked him."

Jim immediately volunteered all Rod's contact information in Australia for me to give to Pat if he was willing to make the call. The next day I called Pat. With his classic exuberance he couldn't wait to call Rod and do the deal. Within two hours of the call, we had a verbal price agreement. Knowing the refit would exceed the purchase price by three times, I still felt it was a fair transaction in US dollars. Thank you, Pat Farrah, and Rod Muir!

"WP" left San Diego and arrived in Newport Beach on June 12, 1991, to be hauled out at the Lido Shipyard for survey. Knowing the extent of the rebuild completed in 1988 and Carson's knowledge of all the maintenance for the past four years, I was confident there would be no issues, but the insurance company wanted their own baseline, and they got it—"no recommendations other than a new mast."

The legal paperwork side of the transaction took a month due to issues of buying a foreign-flagged vessel in U.S. waters with the boat's origin in the Bahamas then being reflagged into the U.S. Ardell Yacht & Ship Brokers more than earned their commission navigating California and Federal maritime laws and procedures.

On July 12, 1991, Kevin Jaffé was, in his words, "given the privilege of being the fourth owner of 'WP.'" It was twenty years after seeing her for the first time in Newport Beach. "My vision and mission for 'WP' never wavered over those two decades," he says. "Finally, the time had arrived to turn dreams into reality."

Nambé serving platter acquired by Teresa Jaffé in 1992 for Passage

25

Guardian Angels

As soon as the purchase was complete, Kevin Jaffé sent *Passage* and Carson Jefferson to the Marina Shipyard in Long Beach, California, with a lengthy list of changes and improvements to be made.

At one point Jefferson asked what level of polish Jaffé wanted on the stainless-steel hardware.

"Perfect will be just fine," said the new owner.

Carson Jefferson picks up the narrative from here:

> Once she was hauled, *everything* was taken off the deck. We rented two 40-foot containers, set them up as workshops, and catalogued all the deck gear as it went in. Kevin usually drove up a few times per week, and we would go through the hardware and decide what to do with each piece. Literally *every* piece of stainless was delivered to Kim Harding, owner of S/S Metal Fabricators, who did whatever it took to reach a #10 mirror finish (before meeting Kevin, Kim's highest polish level was a #5 polish!). I know people talk about "deck jewelry," but we (I only take credit for delivering the hardware to Kim) created a new standard. If Kim couldn't get anything to the level Kevin wanted, he would make a new one.
>
> All the winches, coffee grinders, sheet cars, snatch blocks, etc. were completely rebuilt, and new bases ordered for most of the winches. A new pulpit, pushpit, and radar arch were also fabricated by S/S Metal Fabricators. All new Lewmar deck hatches were ordered.

Kevin decided to have Dennis Choate at Dencho Marine build a new rudder. Kim Harding built a new rudder bearing, which we had not replaced during the New Zealand refit as the alignment was critical and the under-deck support for it also housed linkage for the coffee grinders, with another critical alignment.

◀ *Kevin Jaffé*

Gus Larson made new teak pads for under the stanchions and pad-eyes. Being the varnisher, I [Carson] had tried to talk the Muirs out of using the pads because they were a real maintenance pain-in-the-ass to tape and varnish. Rod's answer was quick and to the point: "Every captain has bitched and moaned about them, but stay they will." I didn't approach the subject with Kevin. They are part of the reason I've had one knee replacement, and a surgery date to replace the other!

We had a great crew working on all the deck gear. Aussie Steve Baker, winches/deck gear; Gus Larson, shipwright; Bob Hall, winches/deck gear/finish; Molly Oldham, winches/deck gear/finish; John Oldham (no relation to Molly), varnish; Bob Armstrong, electrical/hardware; Kyle Tremlet, paint/finish. Roger Eeds and his crew of Joe Connors, Martin Hickey, Jim Wharton, and Mark Templin, all good blokes, prepped and painted the hull and deck. Alex Sandas, a master with a brush, was repainting the entire interior with Awlgrip. I watched him paint one of the guest showers without losing a wet edge or bumping into it. Amazing, and he's 6 feet 5 inches!

We ordered a new aluminum mast and Park Avenue boom, along with Navtec rod rigging from Ron Love at Sparcraft. Kevin wanted all the rod rigging polished to the same #10 mirror finish as the rest of the deck gear. Kevin also ordered a new carbon fiber spinnaker pole to finally replace the old aluminum pole that took several people to lift and was more than a bit dangerous. North Sails got the order for a new set of sails.

Passage looked beautiful when she left the yard and headed home to Newport Beach to finish things up and step the mast. John Craig from San Diego joined the crew to deal with all the electronics and new wiring for the mast. Roger Lowery from Glacier Refrigeration worked on the refrigeration and air conditioning. Peter Garbani of Vantage Marine (and the first professional captain on *Windward Passage*) built a new watermaker for us. We also restored the interior. The boat

> was sprayed eleven times before the exterior paint job was acceptable to Kevin. He spared no expense when it came to *Passage*. He was very good to her. He would put a board meeting at Behr on hold to take a call from me about the boat. That's how committed he was.

By 1992 Kevin Jaffé pronounced *Windward Passage* ready to voyage with himself, his wife Teresa (as chef), their black feline Petey, Carson Jefferson, and a deckhand aboard. *Passage* did some local cruising to Catalina Island that summer, and once again, she turned heads.

Kevin Jaffé remembers one such moment before shoving off for the tropics:

> After the "WP" refit, the Newport Harbor Yacht Club wanted to host a celebration by having both *Windward Passage* and *Ticonderoga* come to the main dock for viewing followed by dinner and a historical presentation by myself and Bob Voit, the owner of *Ticonderoga*. The idea that "WP" and "Big Ti" would finally cross paths (believed to be the first time) and share center stage under the ownership of two Newport Harbor Yacht Club members had all the ingredients for a magical evening of nostalgia, storytelling, and yachting camaraderie. The challenge? With only three weeks' notice, how to tell the "WP" story in the allotted 20 minutes? Teresa volunteered to do a video and worked day and night putting it together. Sourcing material starting with the build on Grand Bahama Island took extraordinary persistence, but she pulled it off with just hours to spare.
>
> The atmosphere dockside was like a spirited college alumni reunion. While everyone came to see these two magnificent sailing yachts, there was a special joy and energy among all the guests seeing each other and knowing "WP" and "Big Ti" played a role in their friendships and life journeys. The evening was truly memorable, and Teresa's video made my presentation come alive. Bob Voit jokingly said afterwards, "Your video completely upstaged my presentation."

Even in "cruising mode" with a modest jib, Passage *loves to charge to weather. —image courtesy of Kevin and Teresa Jaffé*

> I laughed it off but thought to myself that *Windward Passage* has been upstaging the yachting world since Bob Johnson and Alan Gurney designed and built her in 1967–68.

Following her red-carpet moment in Newport Harbor, *Windward Passage* left on December 26, 1992, for Cabo San Lucas, Puerto Vallarta, and then La Paz for a few months of cruising in the Sea of Cortez. In late May 1993 she departed La Paz and headed back to Newport Beach for the summer before hurricane season started in the tropical Eastern Pacific.

Carson Jefferson remembers that by the fall the Jaffés were getting excited about the upcoming Caribbean cruise. "Everything was in good shape on *Passage*. and on December 27, 1993, we left for Costa Rica. We did some great cruising there and spent some time in the Panamanian Islands on the Pacific side before heading down to the Canal."

Transiting the Panama Canal was an unforgettable moment. Kevin Jaffé says:

> While "WP" had logged an amazing twelve trips through the Canal, Teresa and I were experiencing our first. Teresa was born and raised in Panama before moving to Long Beach, California, at age fifteen. However, she never had the opportunity to transit the most iconic canal in the world. Teresa, known as Tee to her friends and crew, told Carson and me she wanted to take her camera, video equipment, water, snacks, and a VHF radio and sit on the first set of spreaders to maximize the view and fully capture all the workings of the Canal.
>
> Fortunately, we had an excellent bosun's chair with large canvas side panels and plenty of pockets to hold gear. We put extra safety lines around her to ensure if she fainted, she would not fall out. The heat and humidity are physically draining in Panama so I was convinced Tee would only last an hour before the "bring me down" request. To my amazement, Tee's stamina and endurance lasted eight hours, with one ten-

> minute break. She is what she calls "a true Panamaniac." She crossed her beloved country from the Pacific to the Atlantic on the spreaders of *Windward Passage* and photographically documented every mile. In addition, "WP" brought her home to see family she had not seen in over fifteen years.
>
> "WP" made her thirteenth and fourteenth crossings of the Canal under my ten-year ownership. I would be very surprised if any privately owned, noncommercial sailing vessel has achieved this many transits.

According to Carson, the crew spent "a marvelous few weeks in the San Blas Islands." The Jaffés and their guests flew into and out of Porvenir Island in the San Blas group, always "an interesting and white-knuckle landing and take-off," recalls Carson.

From there *Passage* left for Grenada, with an unexpected layover of close to three weeks in Cartagena, Colombia, due to very strong trade winds and large seas. She arrived in Grenada in late April 1994, to continue her cruising with the Jaffés. It was time for her annual haulout, so she headed to Peter Peakes's boatyard in Trinidad to haul and paint the bottom.

Windward Passage found herself firmly in the spotlight at Trinidad, says Kevin Jaffé:

> When we arrived at Peakes's yard, there were about two hundred people, a mobile TV truck, and two police cars. Carson was at the helm while we were docking, so I immediately assumed the spokesman position and quickly found out they wanted to do a three-minute story for the local six o'clock TV news. Further questioning as to why the police were there, I learned the six o'clock news the night before had announced "WP" would arrive today and they wanted to make sure there would be no security issues. Obviously, I was very relieved but surprised that this tiny island nation 7 miles off the coast of Venezuela would create so much arrival fanfare.

Kevin Jaffé included a star in his house flag to represent his days racing in the Star Class.

> No matter where we went with "WP," there was always a huge inquisitive appetite for information—but the six o'clock TV news raised the media information bar to new heights. Once again, "WP" was the legendary rock star.

After the haulout, the cruising continued northbound through the islands of the Caribbean. Finally, *Passage* settled in Dutch St. Maarten at Port De Plaisance Marina and Resort. By all accounts it was a magical time. But in early September 1995, *Windward Passage* and Carson Jefferson were in for the fight of their lives. The captain remembers:

> Hurricane season was upon us. Kevin and Teresa had gone home, and I was alone on the boat. There was a large tropical storm in the Atlantic that was forecast to further develop into a named storm and most likely a hurricane. As it developed, it was named Luís and was quick to become a major hurricane with all the right conditions to increase in intensity. I spoke with Kevin in great detail about what would be our best plan of action. We had previously decided if we stayed in the Leeward Islands and a hurricane approached, I would take the most favorable route to put us in the SW quadrant of the hurricane . . . as long as there was a relatively safe route to sail. The boat was fast, and I felt her speed would get us out of harm's way.
>
> It was a nerve-wracking few days, watching Hurricane Luís increase both in size and intensity. Word was definitely out and everyone was listening to every weather update. The forecasters could not predict the path it would take through the island chain, but the meteorologists knew it was a very serious storm that was going to inflict massive damage, whichever path it took. It wasn't until the day before it hit St. Maarten that the path became evident enough to risk heading south which would put the hurricane to the NE of us. I was

frequently talking to both Kevin and my brother, Hugo Leckey (who taught me how to sail). Hugo was spending a lot of time on the internet and filling me in on all the forecast updates.

We made a plan that started with getting *Passage* through the drawbridge and out into Simpson Bay so we wouldn't get slowed down by the bridge schedule and all the other yachts that decided to leave. My girlfriend and the dockmaster of the marina, Angela Eade, was going to come with me once the marina's hurricane plan had been implemented. Rounding out the crew was my West Indian friend and varnisher extraordinaire, Norris David (whom everyone just called David) and Angela's two cats, Nikki and Moggi. I was going nuts waiting for Angela to finish prepping the marina and was sick to my stomach with nervousness. I decided to strap on a dive tank and clean the already clean bottom, thinking perhaps an extra ¼ knot may, indeed, help.

The marina was finally as secure as it was going to get, so off we went. At first there was no wind at all, just a very alarming and eerie sky. As we were passing the island of Saba the wind started to pick up. We were tuning into the local AM radio stations as we went past each island, and all the talk was of this monster hurricane heading right for us. We hoisted our storm stays'l on the inner forestay, and as the east, northeast wind increased we were doing 15 knots in 60 knots of wind. It was relatively sheltered in the lee of the islands, but quite bumpy between them. The cats were the only ones having any fun. Moggi's spot was under the gimballing stove and as you walked through the galley a paw would reach out and swat you!

We ran downwind until the wind eased up and we knew the storm was far enough north of us so we could stop and anchor in Bequia. The single-sideband weather reports were not good from our friends at St. Maarten. We knew we had made the correct decision, and from what we were hearing, a lot of yachts stayed and trusted the lagoon's "Hurricane Hole" reputation. They should have followed us south.

◀ *Carson Jefferson*

Angela needed to get back to the marina and her home, so after two days, on September 7th, we headed north. Our only communication was the single-sideband radio. Friends were asking for us to stop down-island and get as many staples as possible. Everything from flour to cigarettes and rum. We stopped in both St. Vincent and again in Guadeloupe for supplies. It wasn't safe to travel at night as we were passing everything from floating roofs from houses and swamped boats, to large free-floating navigation buoys. We anchored in Simpson Bay at St. Maarten the evening of September 9th, sharing it with only a Dutch warship anchored next to us.

In the morning we could see the massive devastation. There was hardly a blade of green grass to be seen on the hills. The lagoon was full of masts sticking up from sunken yachts, and the beaches were littered with boats piled on top of one another. There were yachts strewn across the airport runway, preventing any flights in to bring aid. Angela's marina office had been sequestered by the Dutch military, and they were using it as their command post. The resort casino had been converted to an emergency operating theater. They told us there were two refrigerated containers full of unidentified bodies. The talk was that over a thousand yachts had sunk or were on the rocks. Officials on the island recorded 150-knot winds. Approximately twenty thousand people on St. Maarten and neighboring islands were now homeless.

We couldn't navigate inside the lagoon, so we had to stay at anchor outside in the bay. Kevin was very concerned about looting as so many people were left without anything. We made sure to have someone on board at all times and kept a high profile on deck, lots of lights all night. It was very hot and humid with not a breath of wind—very uncomfortable on shore. People were in a daze. It was all very sad.

Then, three days after we anchored in Simpson Bay, there was chatter about another hurricane forming. The island's recovery from Luís was barely underway, and it was the last thing everyone's frayed nerves and foggy minds needed. But it certainly couldn't be ignored.

I had become friends with the Dutch military guys, so I was getting all their information on this new storm that had been named Marilyn. As it developed, it became evident I would have to leave again. The warship was going to head due east into the Atlantic. Marilyn was forecast to go between Antigua and Guadeloupe . . . so going east seemed like the best possible route to put some distance between us and the hurricane. On September 14th we departed the lagoon, just five days after returning. Angela was busy dealing with the devastation at the marina. All of my other mates were in a daze after losing their boats and pretty much everything they owned, and were just trying to sort their lives out. So it was just Norris David and I who followed the Dutch warship east into the Atlantic.

We were beating to windward, and it wasn't very comfortable. I went below after about six hours to roust David so I could take a break. I found him in his bunk with his Bible and a photo of his family clutched to his chest. I knew I was in for a very long and tiring watch with no relief in the foreseeable future. On the way through the galley, I made a pot of coffee, which was the first of many on that journey. When Hurricane Marilyn went through the islands it was a Category 1 hurricane with a relatively tight diameter, so we really didn't have a ton of wind above 40 knots where we were.

After a day we were able to jibe over and turn back towards land. I knew a spot on the north side of Anguilla that would be relatively calm and we could anchor and rest until we figured out what to do next. After jibing, things started to calm down. I had to rest, so I went down and woke David up, telling him he *had* to come up and give me a break. He came up, and I hit the rack and fell instantly into a deep sleep.

Well, after a few hours he came down and woke me . . . or so he thought. But I never really fully woke up and drifted back into my deep sleep. What I didn't know until later was that he had gone straight back to his bunk and *Passage* was heading west towards Anguilla under autopilot with no one on watch.

I remember well to this day something waking me up with a startle. I leapt out of the rack and went topside to find no one on watch and the boat only 10 nautical miles off a reef! I got her back on course to the anchorage and once we were safely anchored, I told David, "We're going to have a strong Bloody Mary, a nice meal, and sleep until we wake up. Then we'll figure out where the hell to go next."

It's hard to put into words the feeling I had, and still get, knowing I was very close to having lost *Windward Passage*. I think about it to this day and am pretty damn positive either the boat, myself, or the combination had a guardian angel or lucky star that woke me up that day.

Eventually, Kevin Jaffé and Carson decided to move the boat over to Tortola from St. Maarten and see how they liked basing her there. It was going to be a very long time before things bounced back to normal on St. Maarten. Within a year, Carson Jefferson left *Windward Passage* in Tortola. He had sailed 80,000 miles in her over nearly ten years. Like Gargle McClure before him, he needed a break from ship-keeping, but before he left, he wrote an extensive maintenance and operation manual for Kevin Jaffé and the captains and owners to come.

"I have a lot of my heart in that yacht," he says. "I really loved her."

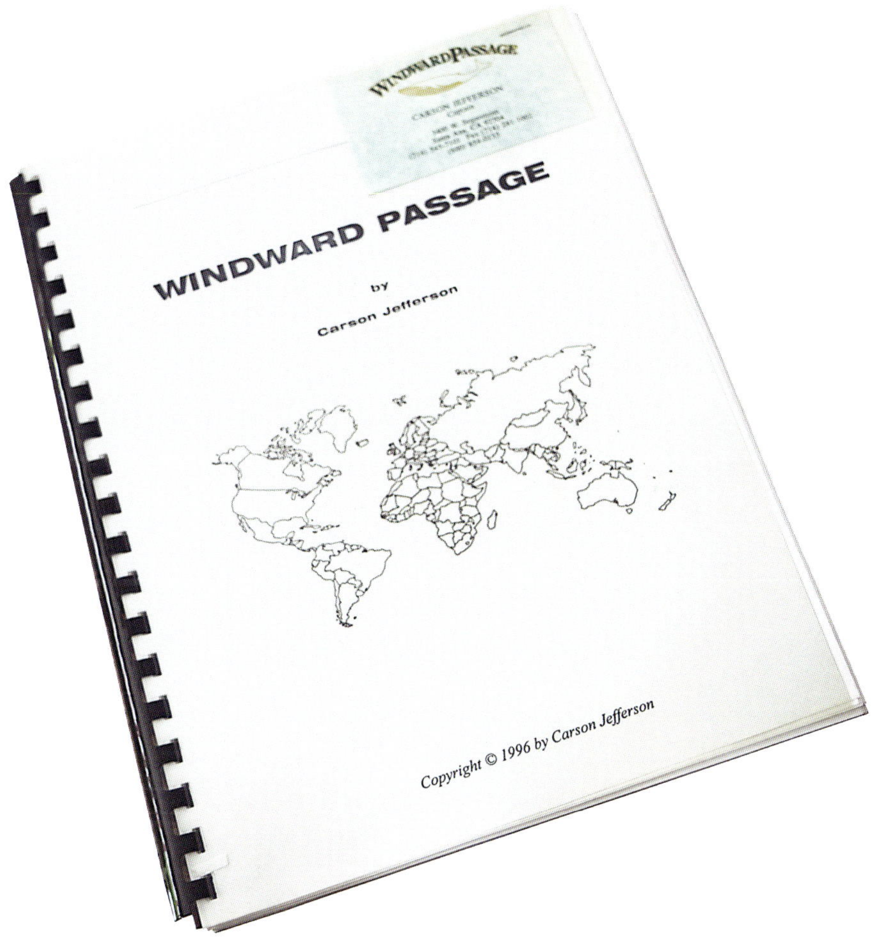

The ship's manual originally authored by Captain Carson Jefferson, expanded and updated by Captain David "Halfdeck" Johnson

26

The Grand Tour

In 1995 Captain Mike Hein and his wife Annie, as chef, took over as the full-time crew for the Jaffés aboard *Passage* at Tortola in the British Virgin Islands. Back in 1992 Mike had been racing aboard *America3* with Bill Koch and Buddy Melges, defending the *America*'s Cup in San Diego, when he met Kevin Jaffé at the Opening Day Race of the Newport Harbor Yacht Club. Kevin liked the fit and finish of the yacht Mike was running at the time. After Carson Jefferson left *Passage*, Jaffé offered Hein the captain's job on the grand lady.

It seemed like the opportunity of a lifetime to the Heins who, in their early thirties, were building their résumés as professional yacht crew. The Jaffés had plans to take *Windward Passage* on an extended cruise of the South Pacific islands and on to New Zealand or Australia. So the Heins sold their house and cars in San Diego and joined "WP" in the BVIs.

From there, the Jaffés and Heins sailed *Passage* to Bermuda and onward to the Palmer Johnson yard in Savannah, Georgia, for a new Northern Lights generator and selective paint work. After loading provisions and parts aboard, WP took off for the Cayman Islands, rounding Cuba to the west. She sailed on to Roatan, Honduras, and then to Panama.

"*Passage* was made of timber, and the best sea boat I've ever sailed," remembers Hein.

Many of the crew were divers, so they made time in their travels to dive the reefs in Honduras, a Darwin-like cove in the Galápagos, and the coral gardens of the Marquesas and Rangiroa.

The Jaffés met *Passage* at various ports along the way, then joined the boat for good as she cruised through French Polynesia, from the Marquesas through the Tuamotu Archipelago and the Society Islands. Life slowed to a fantasy of light-air sailing, swimming in secluded tropical coves, fishing,

◀ Passage *in the San Blas Islands —image courtesy of Kevin and Teresa Jaffé*

turning heads in anchorages, and long evenings dining on local vegetables as well as fresh-caught mahi-mahi that Annie grilled on the after deck.

When asked about their cruising and what was their favorite anchorage, Kevin and Teresa Jaffé never fail to answer simultaneously, "Toau." It's a small atoll in the Tuamotu Archipelago in French Polynesia, which was discovered by Captain Cook in 1774. Kevin paints the picture:

> After our arrival, I just sat in the cockpit overtaken by the spectacular beauty of this magnificent atoll, feeling like no one had ever been here before. The pristine environment was a display of Mother Nature that I had never witnessed. In our short five days at Toau, there were no other boats or people, and everything looked untouched by mankind. Manta rays were splashing and playing. Fish were swimming between our legs, and the sunrises and sunsets started and ended the days with a peaceful aura of pure visual serenity. I distinctly remember a longtime crewmember Adam Belshe saying, "You had better enjoy this now because if you come back in five years, you will be disappointed." We have returned twice and, unfortunately, Toau is slowly being transformed.

Sometimes there were mishaps in Paradise. At one point four of the crew surfaced after a dive in the Galápagos to find their tender nowhere in sight. They had no alternative but to start swimming a mile back to *Passage*. It was a long way and getting dark, so Mike Hein took his safety whistle and kept blowing out the Morse Code SOS distress signal. It wasn't long before

▶ *Toau in the Tuamotus, Christmas Day, 1997*
—image courtesy of Kevin and Teresa Jaffé

◀ *Christmas Day, 1994*
—image courtesy of Kevin and Teresa Jaffé

a hard-bottomed inflatable came to their rescue. It was world-champion pro-surfer Kelly Slater and friends, who had been shooting a surfing video nearby. Once again fortune smiled on *Windward Passage.*

"We had wonderful, silent sails at night with the generator off," remembers Hein. "One night we found ourselves gliding through a huge fleet of fishing *pongas* that had no running lights. We were missing them by only two or three yards." At such a moment Carson Jefferson might have wondered if *Windward Passage*'s guardian angel was hovering near again.

But then the South Pacific junket came to an abrupt halt. After swinging to an anchor for six weeks at Bora Bora, the crew learned the Jaffés' plans for the boat had changed. She was no longer headed Down Under or continuing on for another year of meandering among the islands of the South Pacific. Jaffé's business in California required more of his attention so he wanted to sail his boat back home to Newport Beach, via Hawaii. At this point *Passage* was only about halfway across the Pacific. The Jaffés' dreams of cruising the globe would have to wait.

New marching orders were familiar territory for *Windward Passage.* Those who had known her since 1968 said she had made this trip back east across the Pacific so many times, every wave probably knew her name. They guessed Big Bob's island girl had sailed a million miles.

Left to right: Gordo Johnson, Rex Banks, and Kevin Jaffé
—image courtesy of Kevin Jaffé

The Jaffés' Cruising Life aboard *Passage*

Mexico
Cabo San Lucas, Sea of Cortez, La Paz, Puerto Vallarta, Acapulco

Costa Rica
Flamingo Bay, Tamarindo, Puntarenas – Gulf of Nicoya, Marina Ballena, Papagayo

Panama & the Panama Canal
Panama City, Taboga Island, Contadora Island, Colon, Portobelo, San Blas Islands

Caribbean Sea Islands
Anguilla, Antigua, Barbuda, Cayman Islands, Grenada, Mustique, Saba, St. Bart's, St. Lucia, St. Maarten, Trinidad, U.S. Virgin Islands (St. John's)

British Virgin Islands
Tortola, Virgin Gorda, Norman Island, Peter Island, Jost Van Dyke

Bermuda

Roatan, Honduras

Galápagos Islands, Ecuador

Marquesas Islands
Nuku Hiva, Ua Pou, Fatu Hiva

Tuamotu Archipelago
Toau, Rangiroa, Fakarava

Society Islands
Tahiti, Moorea, Huahini, Bora Bora, Raiatea

After all this, WP sailed from Raiatea to Honolulu, then home to Newport Beach, all while dodging Hurricane Guillermo (1997).

TICONDE
Tales Of An Encha
Jack A. Some

27

A Touch of Class

In 1997 the Heins moved on to run other yachts. The Jaffés, along with the remaining and recruited crew, sailed *Passage* from Raiatea to Hawaii, then on to Newport Harbor. David "Halfdeck" Johnson then came aboard as the professional skipper for Kevin. A former rep for Awlgrip and a painter, Halfdeck was a Newport Beach local, as well as a widely traveled and seasoned ocean racer. His first mission was to revarnish the interior. He spent six months cleaning, refurbishing, and painting the engineroom, exterior, and deck. The deck is painted a custom color, "Windward Passage Green."

At the same time, *Passage* gained a new admirer, Clifford Ronnenberg, an Orange County entrepreneur. He had developed a nightly ritual of going down to Newport Harbor in the evenings to walk along the water's edge to clear his mind and admire the boats. The sea had always been in his blood. His grandfather had been a Danish sea captain and harbor pilot. His father was a dedicated dinghy racer who built three wooden Snipes, and also owned both a Kettenberg PC and Lapworth 36. Some of Ronnenberg's fondest memories are of the hours spent with his father working on Snipes and sailing in the PC and L-36.

As he walked along the harbor's edge, Ronnenberg promised himself that one day he would own a boat. He always appreciated the sleek lines of racing yachts. They reminded him of airplanes. As a young boy, he had been enthralled with aviation. He enjoyed the slow, careful process of building gliders and engine-powered free-flying models with balsa framing and paper skin. "I built ship models as well. I always admired the classic fishing schooners. As a boy, I made a model of *Bluenose*," he says.

Cliff Ronnenberg is a tall, fit man with a shock of white hair. His is polished and debonair, and is often seen in a starched white shirt and business suit. Today he continues to work full time. He owns and operates

◀ *The main saloon, significantly upgraded under the careful eye of Kevin Jaffé, continues to receive thoughtful updates.*

a large environmental services company that is in the vanguard of its field. Besides his strong interest in technology and the environment, Ronnenberg has a deep awareness of cultural history and strong sense of nostalgia running through him. This extends to seafarers and their boats.

"My business demanded so much of me for many years, I had no time for sailing," he says. Then finally, at age sixty, with thirty-three years of business success, he was finally able to make more time for other things. He bought the 70-foot aluminum sloop *Alina,* built by Jongert in the Netherlands. But as much as he liked *Alina,* the boat that truly tugged on his heartstrings was the wooden sloop tied up a few slips away, *Windward Passage.* Perhaps because it reminded him of sailing memories with his father, or because she is made from wood. Maybe it's the sloop's pristine condition or the "perfect curves of her hull." When Ronnenberg looked at *Passage,* he imagined her glory days. He pictured Bob Johnson at the helm, and helmsmen like Rumsey and Weisman steering on the edge through the Molokai Channel, or Kathy Muir and Cathy Hawkins breaking barriers with their first all-female maxi crew, or the irrepressible Gargle McClure rallying his shipmates before yet another duel with *Kialoa.*

In 2002, the dream of owning *Windward Passage* became a reality. Thinking back on that time, he adds, "Kevin is a perfectionist, and the boat was perfect. He was also exceptional in making the owner's transition both comfortable and enjoyable. I saw that my mission was to keep *Windward Passage* perfect . . . and to do what I could to make her stronger and lighter for whoever comes to care for her after me."

The romance that began with *Passage* in 2002 has now stretched into its third decade.

John Oldham has worked on Passage *for thirty-one years, going back to when the Jaffés aquired her. He continues to be responsible for much of her impeccable brightwork. Seen here with Dave Johnson,* Passage*'s current captain.*

28

The Royal Treatment

MY HUSBAND IS A WONDERFUL STEWARD aand caretaker of everything that he owns," says Janet Ronnenberg. "It is his ambition to care for *Windward Passage,* just as the owners before him have done."

The yacht has been maintained in Bristol condition over the years. There have been regular cosmetic treatments and refits, as well upgraded and reconditioned hardware, sails, and rigging. In 2007, Ronnenberg and Halfdeck Johnson discussed improving performance and lightening the boat. Ronnenberg decided to give *Passage* a state-of-the-art keel, rudder, and rigging, if he could do it "without changing her pedigree." He enlisted Newport Beach naval architect Alan Andrews, known for designing some of the world's most famous contemporary ocean racers, for the project. Together Ronnenberg, Johnson, Westerly Marine, and Andrews came up with a plan, as Andrews said, "to turbo-charge" *Windward Passage.*

Their plan was to make her lighter and faster, thereby extending her life by unloading a great deal of weight. "This was a cool project for a number of reasons," says Andrews. He had been following *Passage*'s career since the summer of 1976, when he worked in Doug Peterson's design office and Peterson made the first modifications on the maxi's keel.

"Some boats are winners because their design meshes with a rating rule. Some are winners because they are great boats," says Andrews. "*Windward Passage* is the latter. She's a great boat. She was a step up from anything else when she was built, and she has been continuously upgraded. She has had very caring owners. Cliff Ronnenberg wanted to make her faster, lighter, and more weatherly. We could do that."

So . . . like Fritz Johnson, Courtney Ross, Tim Gurr, and Carson Jefferson before him, Johnson plunged into overseeing a major modernization.

◀ *Clifford and Janet Ronnenberg*

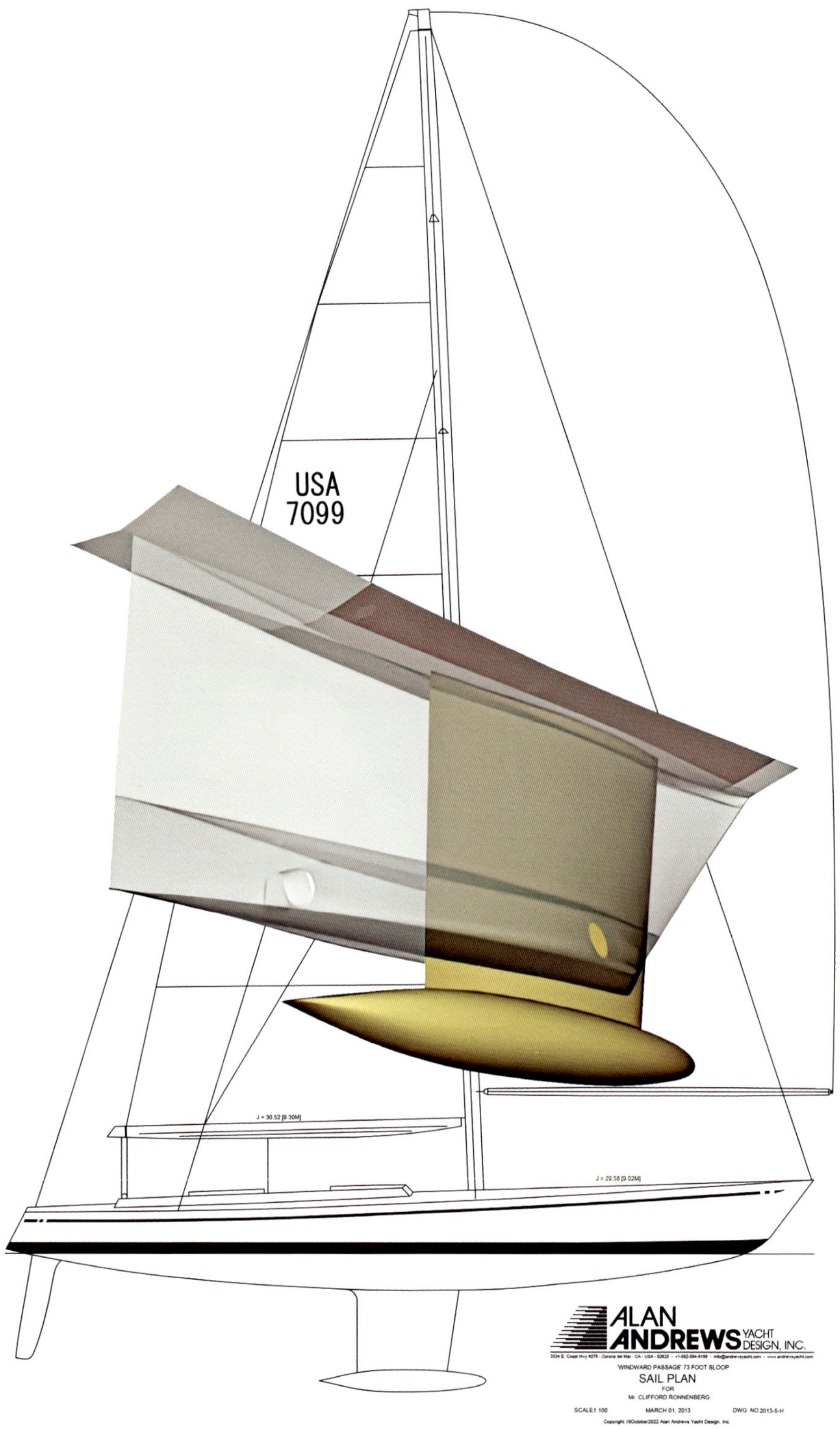

Alan Andrews redesign showing both old and new keels

The project started on July 11, 2007. The rig had to be unstepped and stored, and the rudder and keel removed for transportation to Santa Ana. A permit was pulled to use the dockage at "The Rhine," the very tip of Newport Bay, first thing in the morning at high tide. The spars were removed and loaded on a cage on top of a semi-trailer and driven to Westerly Marine for storage. The Westerly crew arrived to start on the keel, and Halfdeck Johnson and his crew removed the rudder. If all went according to plan, the yacht would be loaded onto the trailer Thursday and depart at 12:00 A.M. on Friday morning. Thursday was a very busy day, loading a 73-foot-long and almost-20-foot-wide yacht aboard a semi-trailer. At midnight sharp, the parade of trucks set off on the 10-mile trip to Westerly Marine in Santa Ana.

It took the shipwrights at Westerly Marine six months to prep and fit the hull with an Andrews-designed keel, which was made in Mexico with an ingenious titanium kelp cutter on the leading edge. The new keel added 2 feet to the draft and with a much lower center of gravity, allowing *Passage* to shed over four tons of unnecessary weight while maintaining the same sail-carrying ability. With its thinner profile and shorter chord, the new keel reduced keel volume and drag by about 40 percent. The change moved the boat's center of ballast forward, correcting stern-down trim, and brought her up on her original lines.

Andrews explains:

> We kept righting moment the same but reduced weight by about 9,000 pounds, rather than increase RM (righting moment) significantly. RM determines sail-carrying ability and hence the loads on shrouds, chainplates, and even winches and sheets. Those all worked well, and had for decades, and we couldn't risk overloading them.

The keel change and rig change brought *Passage* back very close to the racing trim she'd had as a stripped-out maxi-sloop, but with the cruising comforts still in place and without twenty-five guys on the rail. We were able to shed a lot of unnecessary weight while maintaining strength and reliability added with the internal frame in the New Zealand refit.

Keel volume was reduced tremendously so that extra volume didn't have to be pushed through the water, absorbing energy.

Center of ballast wasn't moved all that far forward, but caused a big trim change. It allowed 800 pounds of chain to be removed from the bow and still not have the previous stern-down trim. The keel LCG shift also helped reduce the stern-dragging effect created when the engine was moved aft in New Zealand (compared to the mid-boat engine in the original racing configuration).

In her senior years Passage *prefers even deck shoes be left behind on the dock.*

There was a significant drag reduction by the boat rising out of the water, both wavemaking drag (often called "residuary resistance") and wetted-surface drag.

I designed a new rudder blade to fit on the existing rudderstock. This appears to be the third blade on this titanium stock—first the Peterson blade, then the changes in New Zealand, and now the current update. Using the same stock allowed the bearings to remain in the same locations and reuse the refurbished parts.

Meanwhile, Halfdeck's crew reduced weight in the hull by removing the washer/dryer, massive hot-water heaters, and obsolete spare parts and tools. To show his appreciation for all the hard work, Cliff Ronnenberg and Halfdeck hosted Friday afternoon BBQs at Westerly Marine.

After the Westerly crew had added the new rudder fabricated by Dencho Marine, *Passage* made another midnight sojourn through the streets for her re-launch in Newport Harbor. This time, with the new keel attached, men had to ride on deck with staffs to lift power lines out of the way.

In 2015, Cliff Ronnenberg commissioned Hall Spars to build a 110-foot carbon fiber mast, with carbon rod rigging and custom titanium turnbuckles and hardware for *Passage*. At the time, Hall Spars was the pre-eminent carbon fiber spar fabricator in the U.S., with a list of celebrated customers ranging from three *America*'s Cup campaigns to Roy Disney's canting-keel *Pyewacket*. Perhaps Hall Spars is best known for the masts they built for the J/Boats, custom masts taller than 200 feet for megayachts, as well as parts for the Space X Falcon 9 rocket.

2019 Newport Harbor Yacht Club
Opening Day Race Crew

Cliff Ronnenberg—*owner/skipper*
David "Halfdeck" Johnson—*captain*
Brad Avery
Paul Blank
Argyle Cambell
John Cotton
Bruce D'Eliscu
Marshall "Duffy" Duffield
Sean Farrell
"Fizz" Foster
Gordo Johnson
Dougall Johnson
John "LJ" Edgcomb
Piere "Pepe" Loubet
"Big" Mike Marshall
John Marshall
"Dollar" Bill Menninger
John "JP" Peschelt
Tyler Wolf

The new 104-foot carbon fiber mast with four sets of spreaders and carbon rod rigging for Windward Passage *added about 10 feet of height to the rig, resulting in 10 percent more sail area.*

The carbon fiber boom, built by Omohundro Co. in Minden, Nevada, in 2001, has two reefpoints, a tapered wing on each side with deadeye holes for the lazyjacks—adjusted through an access port on the the boom near the gooseneck. The outhaul car and track were later removed, and the wings modified slightly to accommodate a sliding strop for a loose footed mainsail, saving weight and becoming more efficient.

"A happy day." Passage *is about to be splashed with her new Alan Andrews rudder and keel.*

"We are building spars the same way Boeing is building aircraft," says Ben Hall. His artisans formed the mast by wrapping the "pre-preg" carbon fiber cloth around an aluminum mandrel on a "spinning machine" that looks like a giant lathe. After curing the spar overnight in a 153-foot autoclave at 250 degrees, the mandrel was extracted and the mast let cure further. Eventually they faired and painted the spar white.

"It was a dream," recalls Hall. "It was a clean, simple, beautiful mast, and once the truck got the mast and rigging to Newport Harbor Shipyard, everything fit perfectly." After that, Hall's project manager, Henry Maxwell, and his crew had the mast rigged and in the boat in three days.

"The carbon fiber rigging weighs 80 percent less than the old rod rigging weighed," says Hall, "and it is 50 percent stronger." The aluminum mast he replaced weighed about 2,800 pounds without standing rigging or halyards. The bare Hall mast weighs 780 pounds. It added approximately 10 feet of height to the rig, and 10 percent more sail area.

With her new keel and mast, *Windward Passage* was now 18,000 pounds lighter and sportier than ever. To complete her performance up-grades, she got 3Di-molded, composite sails from North Sails in 2015.

"If only Big Bob could see her now," says Dotty Johnson.

Keeping *Passage* pristine is a constant ambition. Several times a week she receives a soft-water rinse of de-ionized water so that the boat does not spot. Additionally, the metal polishing and wood varnishing is tended to daily. Caring for *Windward Passage* is a full-time job. "Janet and I appreciate the beauty, glamour, speed, and maneuverability of *Passage*, and the care that Halfdeck and the crew give her," reflects Ronnenberg. "We have enjoyed so many wonderful moments and look forward to many more years of great memories."

Cliff and Janet standing next to the new carbon rod rigging and custom titanium turnbuckles

WINDWARD PASSAGE
NEWPORT BEACH

OPENING DAY 2019
N
USA 7099

29

The Diva Reigns

SHE'S LIKE A CHAMPION THOROUGHBRED that has run her races and deserves to rest on her laurels," say Cliff Ronnenberg, about *Windward Passage*.

When she's day-racing or just romping along the Southern California coast, the spectator fleet hovers close. And when the wind pipes up suddenly, as it does sometimes when *Passage* has been ghosting home into Newport Harbor under sail, you are in for a treat. There's no holding the old girl back. In a matter of seconds, she can put her rail down and start charging to windward at 9.5 knots in less than 11 knots of breeze. If you are lucky enough to be aboard at such a moment, you can feel your blood hum. You can almost hear the boat singing. And you will sense something in your bones that must be a bit like what Big Bob, Mark and Fritz Johnson, Peter Bowker, John Rumsey, Gary Weisman, and Gargle McClure felt flying down the Molokai Channel toward Honolulu all those years ago. A bit, too, like Kathy Muir, Cathy Hawkins, and their all-women crew felt chasing the sunset to Newcastle, Australia, in their grand lady.

And then you will want to shout like Big Bob, "What a boat!"

It's a singular ecstasy. Dotty Johnson, Bill Johnson, Kevin Jaffé, Rod Muir, and Cliff Ronnenberg would call it "perfection."

At quieter times, when *Windward Passage* tucks into an anchorage at Santa Catalina Island, the sloop inevitably draws admirers. They take photos, marvel at her sleek elegance and perfect condition, and imagine the stories she could tell, as so many admirers have done since she first came on the scene. Brigitte Bardot and Prince Harald of Norway are just a few of the famous names that have been aboard and had their own stories to tell.

"Some of my favorite memories of the boat," reminisces Janet Ronnenberg, "include warm summer nights anchored in Moonstone Cove over at

▲ *Mark and Dotty Johnson revisit an old love.*

◀ *Janet and Cliff Ronnenberg*

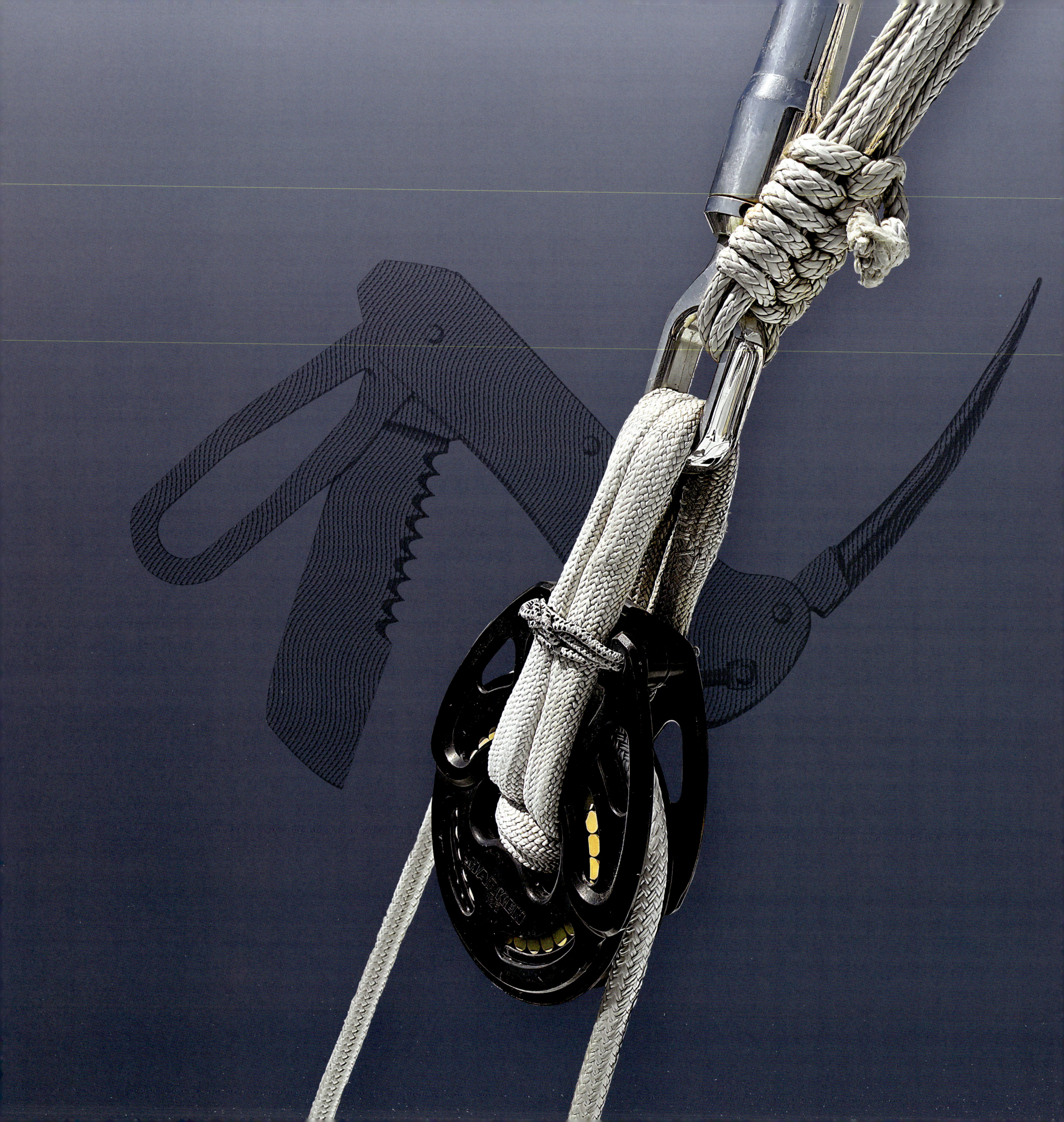

Catalina Island, or out on a beautiful, windy day, sailing down the coast with good friends or family. We feel very blessed that we have enjoyed so many wonderful moments over the years, including the Newport Harbor Yacht Club Opening Day Races. So few people have shared the unique privilege of moments like these."

If Bob Johnson, Alan Gurney, and Chappy were to join any of these festivities, they would certainly raise a glass to toast *Windward Passage,* and her great fortune. Extraordinary owners, captains, and crews have enjoyed and loved this sailing legend. She was built by men with a dream where the pink coral shores of Grand Bahama meet the pale-blue tropical waters, and like a true diva, she defies her age.

Charmaine and David with son Cai and daughter Elle. Five-year-old Cai Ronnenberg II is the fifth generation of Ronnenbergs to be a sailor.

Marlinespike seamanship will always be in Passage's *DNA.*

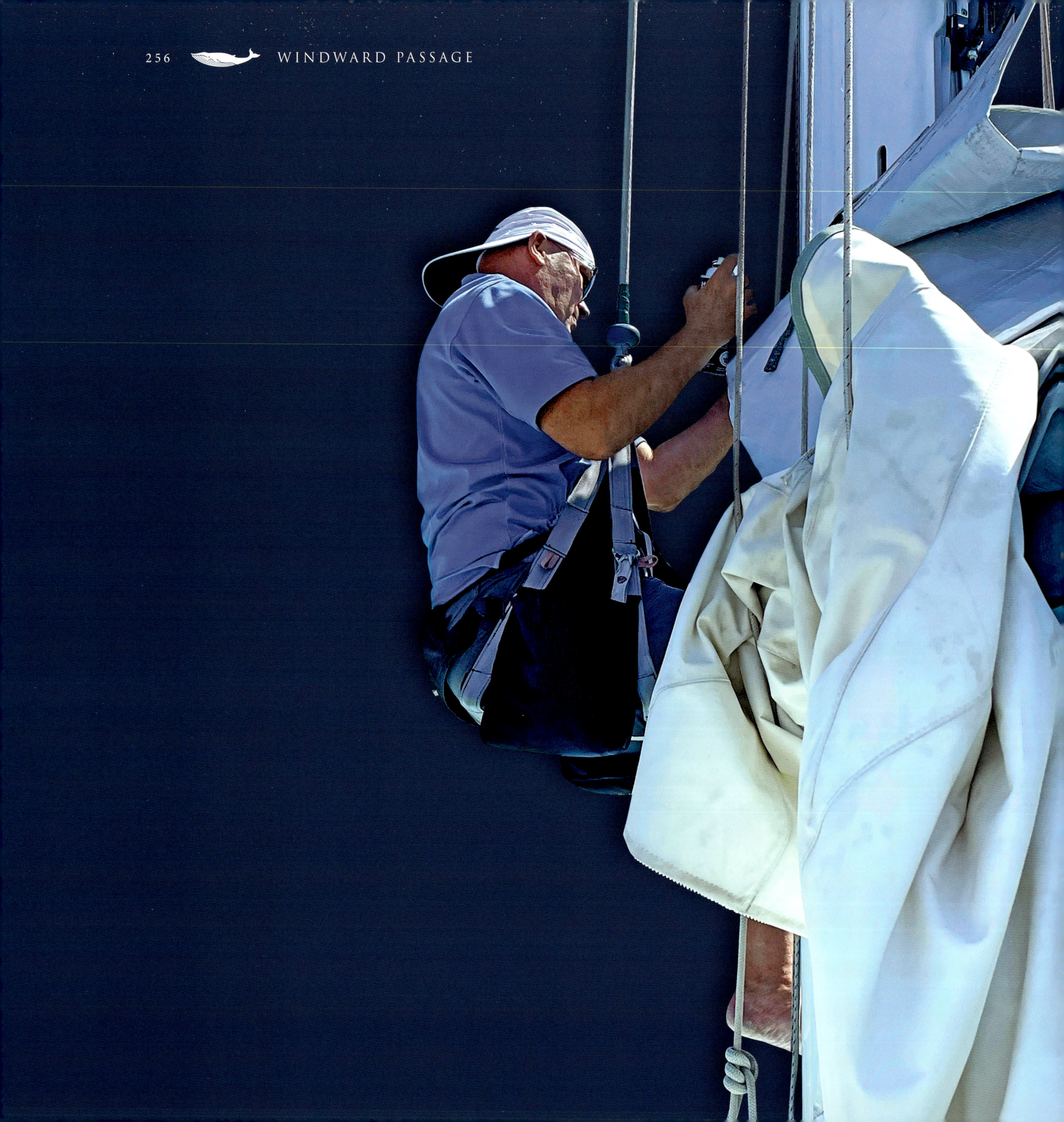

30

ABOVE-DECK IMAGES

Friedrich Nietzsche famously said, "The devil is in the details." That has never been truer than on a high-performance racing yacht. And there Passage *has a decided advantage over many of her peers: longevity and passionately caring owners and captains, all of whom have done whatever it takes to refine, modify, renew, and update the complex gear that is this boat.*

Deck configuration, April 2022

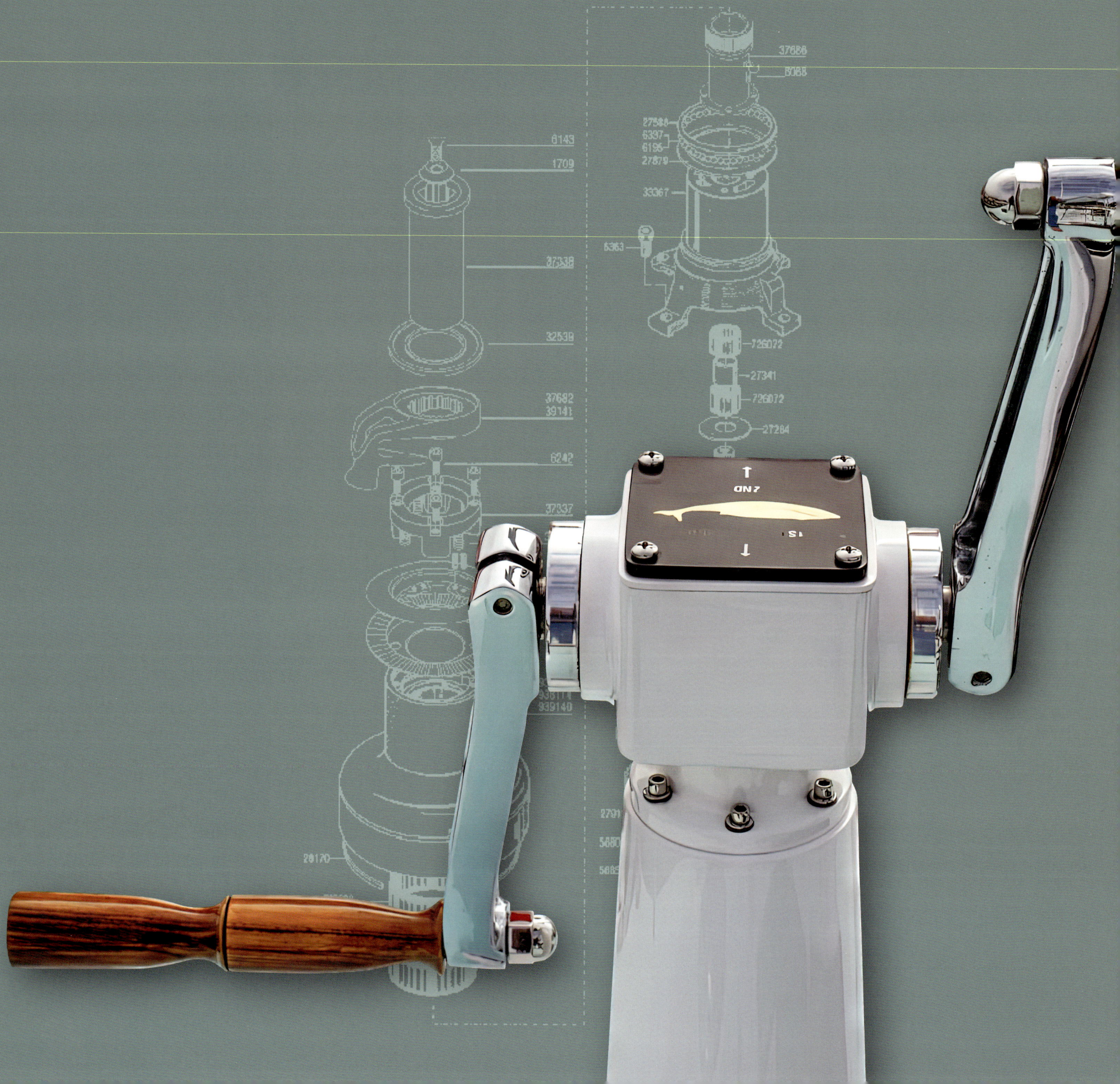

In 1987 the winches were all sent to Barlow Marine Ltd. in Australia where they were completely rebuilt. Electric drives and disconnects for the primary and mainsheet winches were designed by Bill Ottemann of IMI Barient, Inc. A new electric Barient 737 was added aft of the mast to actas a slave winch, which in essence, made all the winches at the mast electric.

It was decided to go with electric winches, rather than hydraulic for weight and space. The requirements of the hydraulic power pack, which would have to be located in the new engineroom, were considerable. Given the amount of equipment already in an area that would greatly affect the trim of the yacht, it was decided to install electric winches to distribute the weight more evenly throughout the yacht.

The primary and mainsheet winch motors are 24-volt DC, 190-amp-hour motors. The control boxes for the electric winches, which contain control fuses, relays, and solenoid switches, are located in the following locations:

Primary winches—under the lazarette shelving below the winches.

Mainsheet winch—behind the Nav-Graphic.

Utility winch aft of the mast—just under the winch in the fiberglass casing aft of the television.

Main halyard winch—in the starboard guest cabin, just under the winch in the leather-bound cover box.

For the first time in her long-life the yacht had an anchor windlass, manufactured by Muir Engineering in Tasmania, Australia.

In the 1991 refit, new polished stainless steel winch bases replaced the o1d aluminum ones. Self-tailers were fitted to the primary winches and the secondaries were replaced with new System 10, three-speed self-tailers.

Few of the winches that remain on deck today are original. They've had new bases, drums, and parts installed through the years and still are working well.

—from the ship's manual

Playing with a full deck

▲ *There are numerous small custom-made drain screens throughout the two cockpit wells.*

▼ *Jewelry*

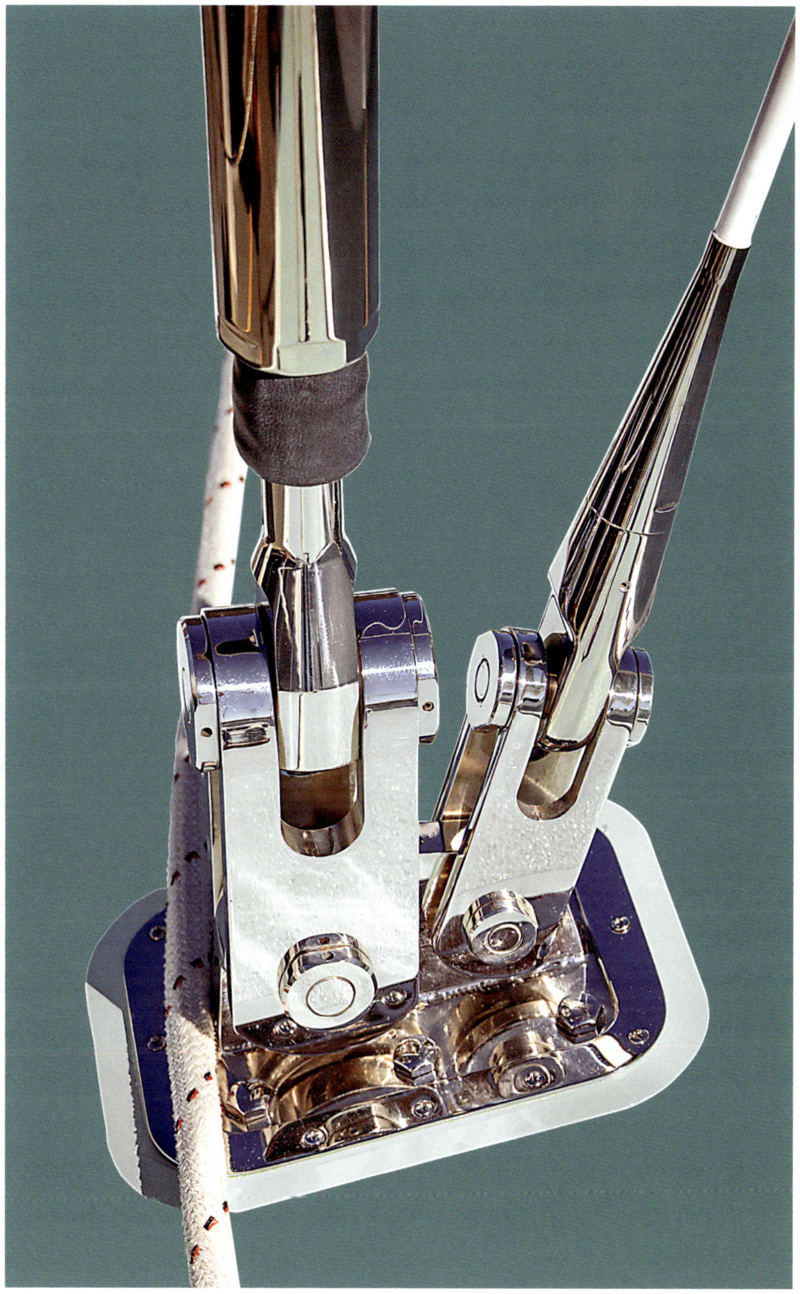

▲ *One of the things that Dave "Halfdeck" Johnson has done under his stewardship of* Passage *is to mitigate the amount of blood shed by the crew on the boat's "Awlgrip Windward Passage Green" (yes, an actual color).*

He has systematically replaced all the cotter pins in the standing rigging with new crew-friendly nuts with set-screws.

◄ *Yet one more labor of love is* Passage*'s beautiful cockpit table. Look closely: can you find the iconic whale here? The whale was meticulously inlaid in oak by Greg Palmer.*

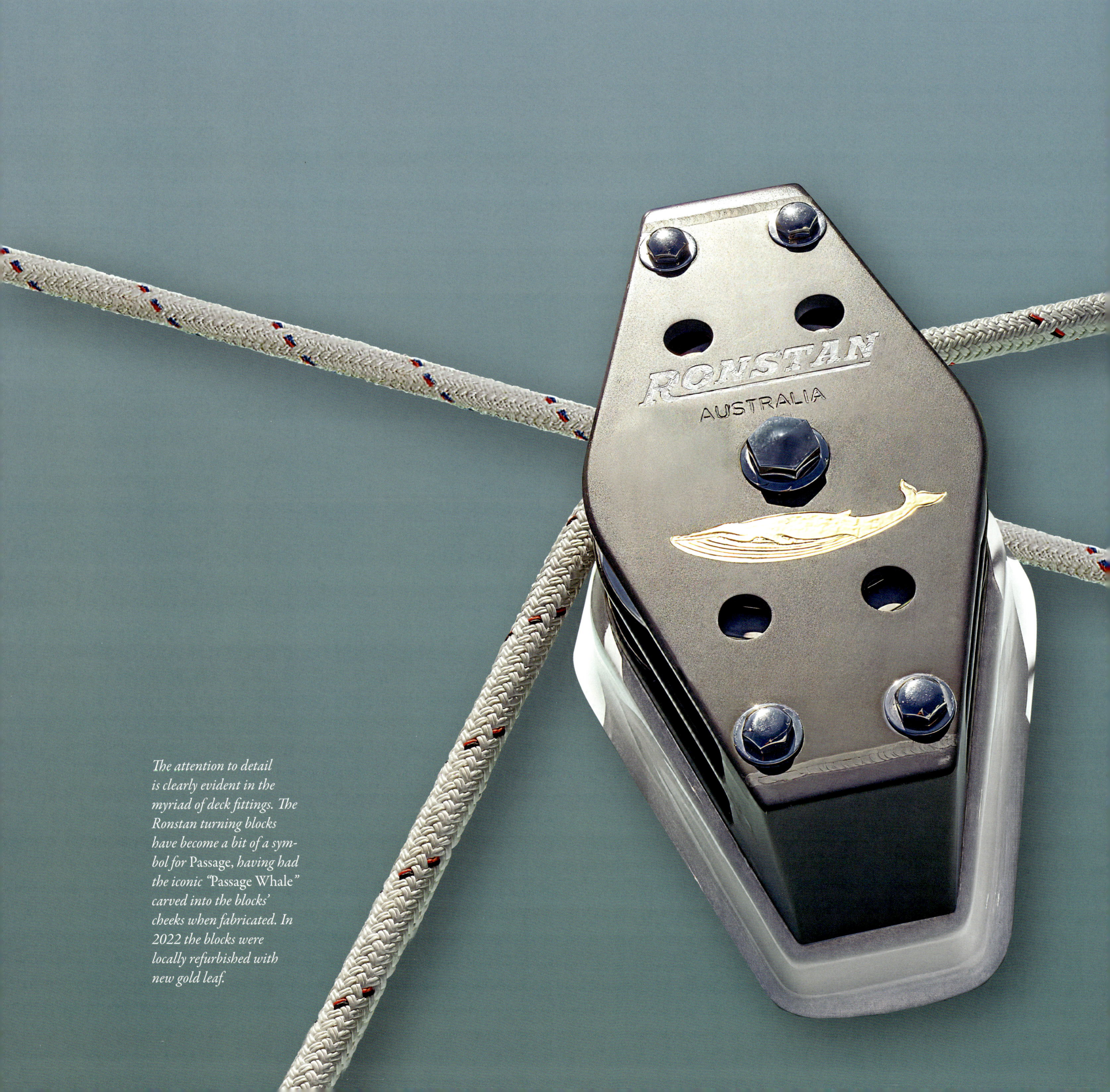

The attention to detail is clearly evident in the myriad of deck fittings. The Ronstan turning blocks have become a bit of a symbol for Passage, *having had the iconic "*Passage *Whale" carved into the blocks' cheeks when fabricated. In 2022 the blocks were locally refurbished with new gold leaf.*

2ND
3RD
1ST

Mainsheet winch

Total attention to detail is evident everywhere on-deck.

◀ *The infamous Barient grinders, originally five but now just two*

HERRESHOFF

31

BELOW-DECK IMAGES

Steve Jost's contemporary images of Passage's *interior begin with the starboard side of the main saloon.*

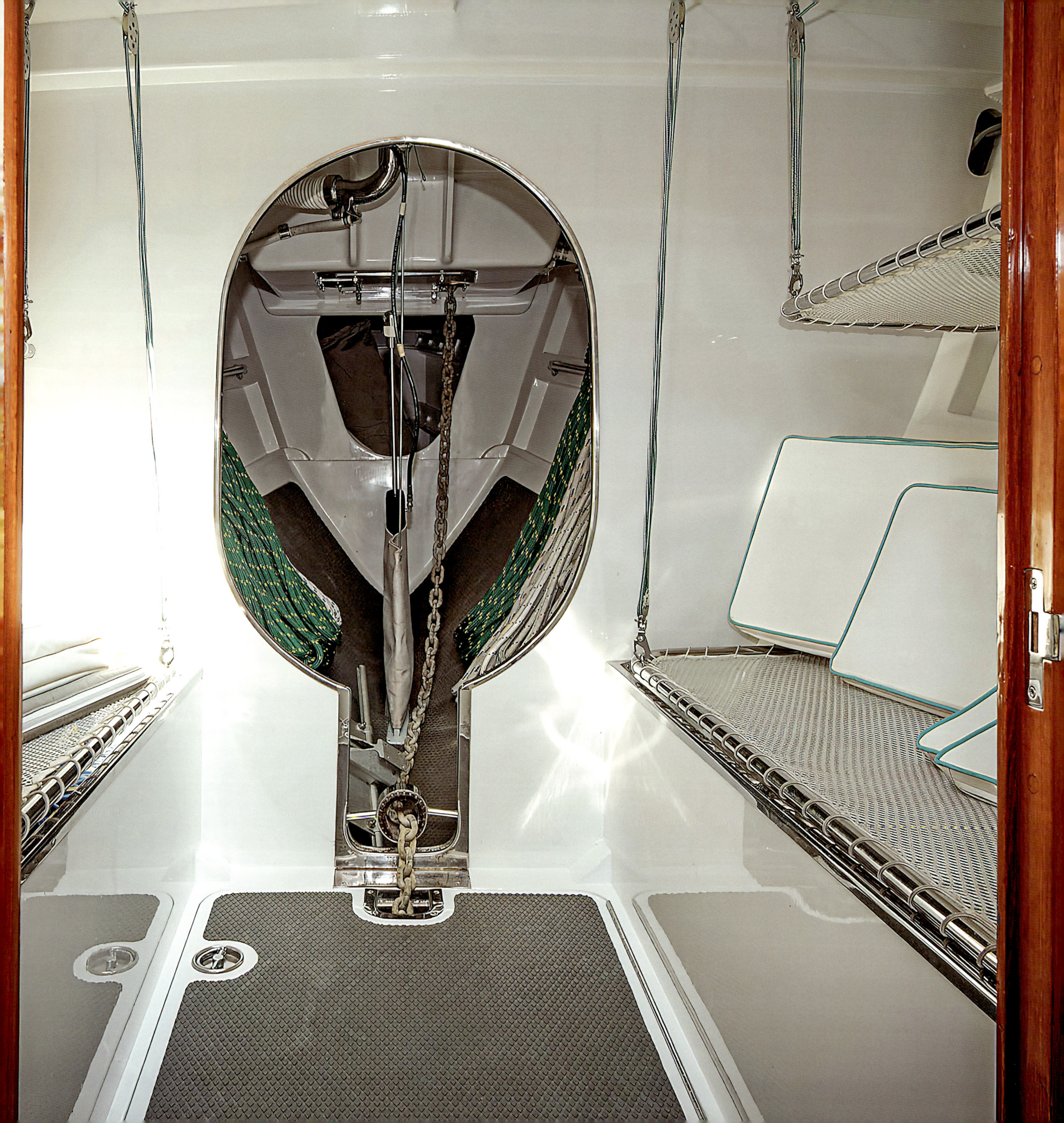

Fitted with four pipe berths, Passage *has crew's quarters aft of the chain locker and rope locker in the bow of the boat. If you were aboard her in the 1970s and early 1980s, you will not recognize this space.*

The port-side view of the main saloon shows off the varnished teak used for the furniture, tables, and trim throughout Windward Passage. *These details were added during the refit in the late 1980s at Southern Pacific Shipyard in New Zealand. The exposed cold-molded veneer on the inside of the hull is Sitka spruce. The deckbeams are fir.*

Guest head to port just forward of the saloon.

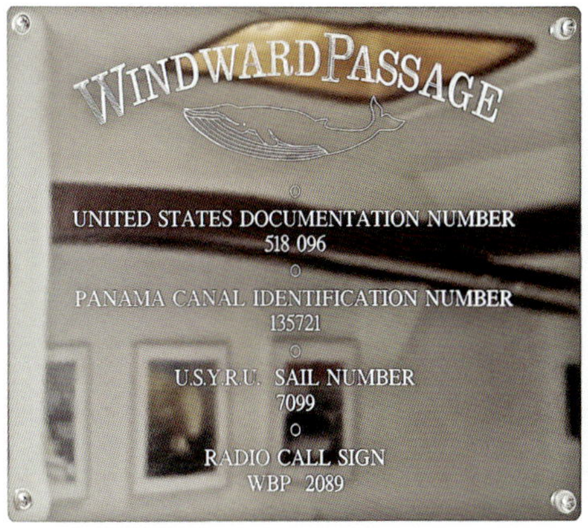

◀ *The nav station is exactly where it has always been: belowdecks on the port side next to the aft companionway. Forward of it on the port side is the galley.*

▲ *Starboard is the owner's suite with a small sitting area and a head.*

The cabin sole on Passage *is made of 5⁄16-inch teak-and-holly veneer over an ultralight combination of foam and fiberglass, giving the sole strength and rigidity while significantly reducing weight over the original. This is one more way the boat has been continuously upgraded over the years by thoughtful owners and captains.*

▲ *Main saloon table set for a special dinner.*

◀ *View of the nav station looking aft from the galley.*

The owner's stateroom is located aft and is accessed from a passageway through the galley and nav station or from above decks through a companionway hatch and stairs.

Adjacent to the cabin is the owner's head and shower.

Passage has two saloons: one that functions as the boat's main cabin; and a second, smaller area, pictured here, that is adjacent to the owner's cabin and the aft companionway hatch.

HARD ON THE WIND
SAILING
RECORD FLEET FORM GUIDE
Upwind tactics
Sea

Starboard guest stateroom and head

The half hull models on the forward bulkhead of the main saloon illustrate the evolution of her keel designs. They show both the Henry Scheel keel installed at the Gurr yard in New Zealand and the Alan Andrews keel installed at the Westerly yard in Santa Ana, California. Both projects also saw new rudder designs as well.

Passage *has two guest cabins and a second head forward of the main saloon.*

RADAR DETECTOR
POWER
RANGE
AUDIO
LEVEL
SEA WATER TEMP
DEPTH
International Offshore
17.0
DEPTH Surface
BACKSTAY
VERTICAL
SEA
TS450
OFF
BOTH
RECEIVE ONLY
READY
SEA HF SSB
ANTENNA CONTROL
TS450
COURSEMASTER 300
17.9
WIND ANGLE Apparent
WBP 2089
Nobeltec
User's Guide
Logitech

The Sea SSB and VHF radios, Kenwood ham radio, Furuno color radar, Suntuu Magnetic Compass, and the CARD radar alarm were new in 1991.

The Furuno weather fax, Coursemaster autopilot, Digicourse fluxgate compass, and Datamarine fathometer were installed in 1988.

Ockam wind and speed instruments were new in 1985. The CPU was replaced in 1988.

All electronics except the SSB and ham radios are grounded to a Dynaplate located under the cabin sole in the navigation station.

There is an antenna control panel that switches between the SSB and ham/weather fax receivers. The purpose of this "magic black box" is to prevent RF damage to the unit not in use.

—from the ship's manual

Passage*'s original dividers still see occasional use.*

There are both port and starboard guest stateroom amidships, both able to sleep two people. They have a shared head.

(facing page) While it may not look like it, this cabin on the starboard side just aft of the mast is Passage's *"attic." There is a work surface, tool chest, and numerous bins and drawers to hold the odds and ends that every sailing yacht both needs and acquires over the years.*

The wheel system consists of a pedestal and steering wheel (custom made by S/S Metal Fabricators) attached to a shaft with a chain sprocket. About 8 feet of chain sits over the sprocket. Attached to the chain via two Sta-Lok terminals, are two lengths of 5/16 inch stainless steel 7x19 wire that run to the quadrant through a series of sheaves.

The cables cross under the aft cockpit floor and are tensioned at the quadrant. All the sheaves in the system have greased nipples.

There is a spare set of cables on board that should always be aboard for any long-range trips.

The chain should be greased occasionally and is accessed by removing the compass binnacle on top of the pedestal.

There are two Spectra stops on the quadrant to keep the rudder from turning too far. A shaft brake is located on the starboard side of the pedestal and can be turned to secure the rudder while at anchor or dockside.

—from the ship's manual

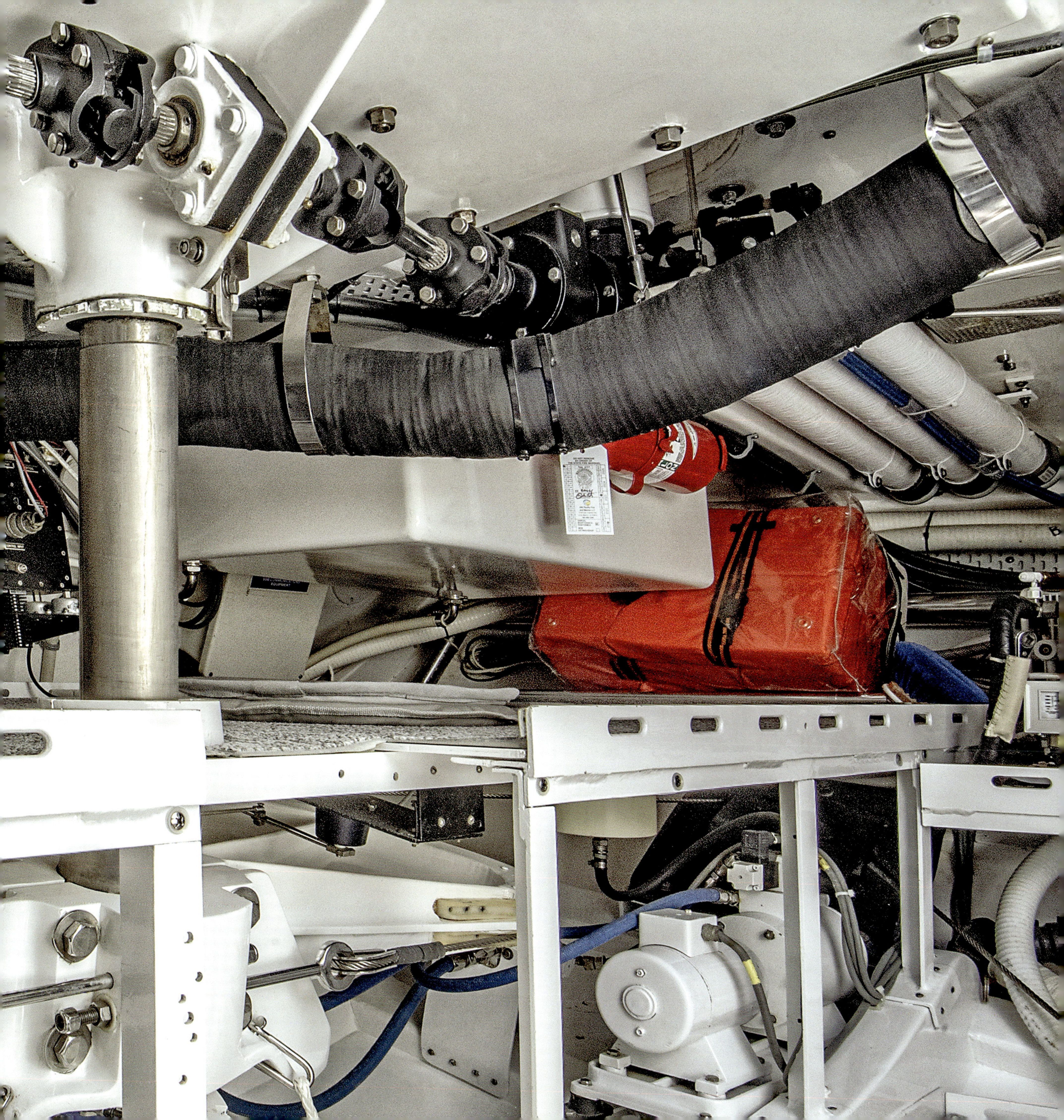

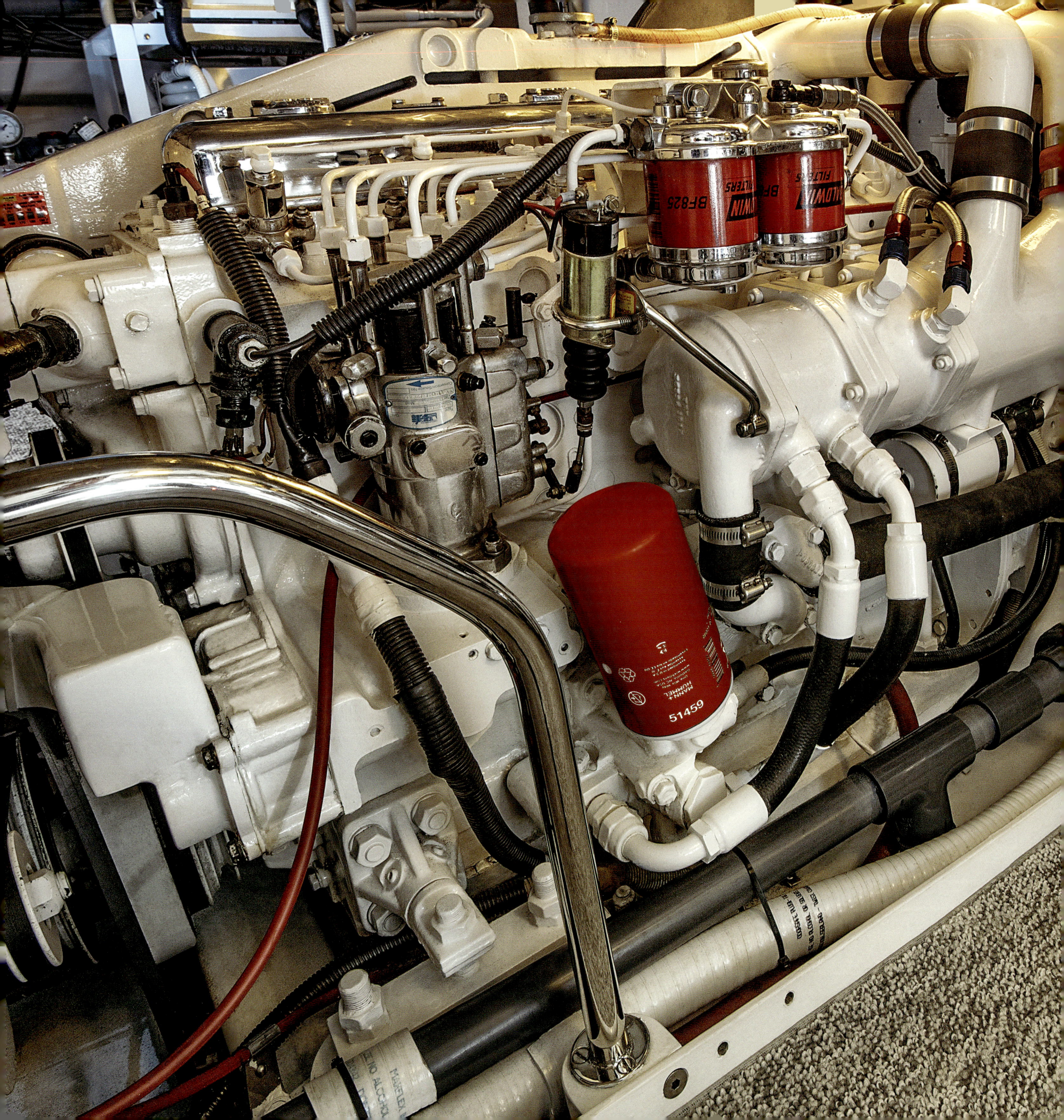
BF825
51459

Propulsion

The Perkins T6.3544(M) is a high-performance 5.8-liter (354 cubic inch) turbocharged intercooled six-cylinder diesel. "Turbocharged intercooled" means that the four-stroke cycle is pressure-charged with air that has been cooled in a heat exchanger, located on the starboard side of the engine, increasing power output and reducing exhaust temperatures.

230-Volt AC Power

This 60 Hz insulated return system provides power supply for AC, lighting, watermaker, air conditioning and heating, galley, battery charging, and entertainment systems.

120-Volt AC Power

This is provided by the 12 kW 1 Phase Northern Lights AC generator or from the shore power connection. The shore-power connection is fed via a "Multi-Tap" primary isolation transformer with a galvanic isolator allowing for various shore-power voltages as an input.

12-Volt DC System

There are two 12-volt 8D no-maintenance gel-cell batteries, located in a vented box on the port side of the main engine, that service the 12-volt needs of the yacht.

24-Volt DC System

Supply is provided from two 550 amp-hour battery banks located in the saloon under the stereo cabinet and under the starboard stateroom bunk. The battery banks are switched to enable either or both banks to be "on duty" or to isolate the batteries completely.

Air Conditioning

A Cruisair reverse-cycle air conditioning system runs on 230-volt/60Hz either off the generator or shore power. It may also be run on 200V/50Hz. The system consists of one 20,000 BTU/hr and two 12,000 BTU/hr Type F condensing units.

Water

A Vantage Marine reverse-osmosis water maker produces about 40 gallons per hour of fresh water while away from the dock.

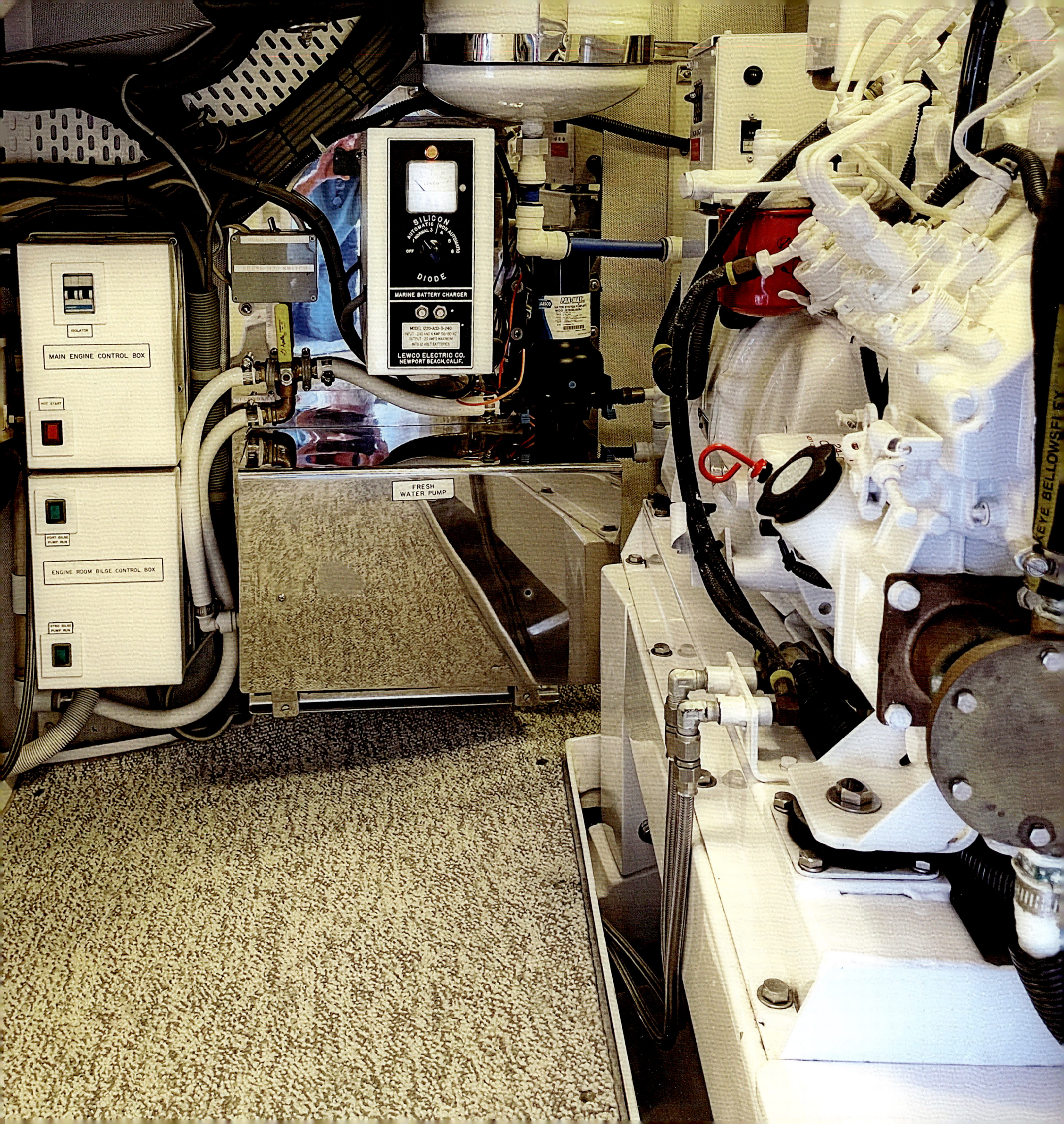
MAIN ENGINE CONTROL BOX
ENGINE ROOM BILGE CONTROL BOX
SILICON
DIODE
MARINE BATTERY CHARGER
LEWCO ELECTRIC CO.
NEWPORT BEACH, CALIF.
FRESH
WATER PUMP

PERKINS T6.3544(M)

At about 9,000 hours of operating time, the Perkins motor underwent a major overhaul in 1987/88. It was completely stripped and rebuilt, right down to grinding the crankshaft. The work was done in New Zealand by the BMW Racing Team mechanics, blue-printed, and has performed very well since. Upon completion, the engine was dyno-tested with the following results:

Horsepower developed	174.20
RPM at which HP developed	2400
Duration of test	4 hours
Water temperature	165°F
Oil pressure	65 PSI

In 1991, with 3,000 hours of operation since the major overhaul, the motor went through a minor overhaul. The injectors and injection pump were serviced. New valves, valve-guides, and valve-stem seals were installed. The head was surfaced.

A new hour meter was installed in 2020 and as of December 2020, the combined hours are 2,453 or around 5.423 hours since the major overhaul in New Zealand.

Normal oil pressure with a cold engine is 60 PSI, hot about 55 PSI, and idling about 35 PSI.

The exhaust temperature should be somewhere in the range of 520 to 750 degrees Fahrenheit. Over 1,000 degrees Fahrenheit is bad, and at 1,300 to 1,350 degrees the pistons will break down.

The transmission is a Borg Warner Velvet Drive 73C with 1:1 reduction in forward and reverse, and was replaced in 2005.

The V-drive is a Walter RV-48 with a 3.12:1 ratio. This means that for every 3.12 turns of the shaft coming out of the engine, the propeller will make one revolution. The V-drive was replaced in the 1987/88 refit.

At 1,750 RPMs, in moderate sea conditions, the engine uses about two gallons of diesel fuel per hour. The fuel curve rises rapidly from there.

The exhaust system made from hand-laid fiberglass and heat-resistant isothetic resin is corrosion resistant and has never been a problem.

A "hot start" for the Perkins is provided in the engineroom. This bypasses the instrumentation in the navigation station.

—from the ship's manual by Captains Carson Jefferson and David "Halfdeck" Johnson

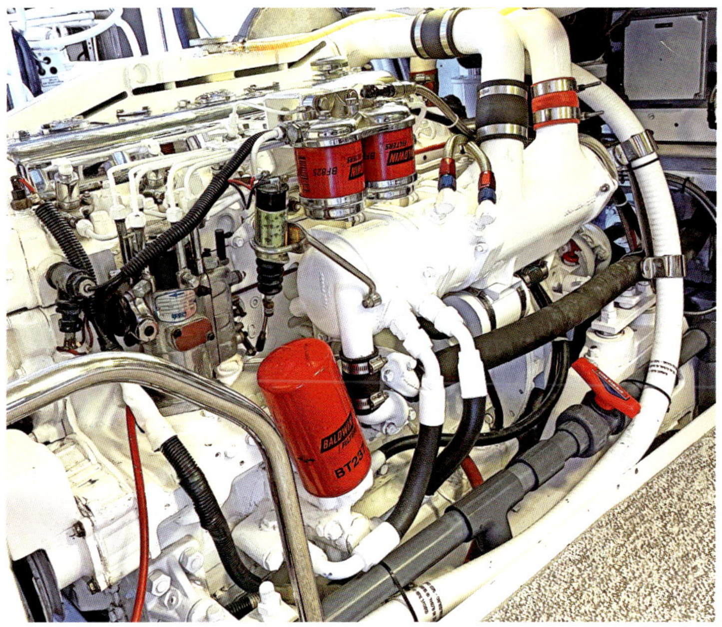

32

Images Under Sail

For the August 20, 2022, sail and photo shoot, Captain "Halfdeck" Johnson hand-picked his crew of nineteen for the setting and the dousing of the 5,300-square-foot kite.

WINDWARD PASSAGE
NEWPORT BEACH

WINDWARD PASSAGE
NEWPORT BEACH

USA
7099
WINDWARD PASSAGE
NEWPORT BEACH

Janet and Cliff Ronnenberg at the helm

USA
7099

USA
7099

Assembling a crew is not an easy task. Once the date was set, this crew of nineteen came from both coasts to be a part of this small bit of yachting history. We are grateful for their expertise, contributing mightly to the creation of this book.

LIFESLING 2

Crew for August 20, 2022

David "Halfdeck" Johnson—*captain*
Pierre "Pepe" Loubet
Dougall Johnson
Brad Wheeler
Britton Hammond
Dave Culver
Ron Geisman
Randy Peffer
Peter "The Breeder" McDonald
Deon McDonald
Karen Grewar
Greg "Gramps" Palmer
Noah Peffer
Randy Moreno
David "Roo" Stevenson
Patrick Leber
Erik Kristiansen
Bob Steel
Tyler Wolke

Medallions courtesy of Patsy Bolling/John Rumsey and Carson Jefferson

Passage by the Numbers

LOA:	73' 0"
Beam:	19' 7"
LWL:	65' 0"
Draft:	12' 0"
Mast Height:	103' 0"
Home Port:	Newport Beach, CA
Designer:	Alan Gurney
Rig:	Sloop
Gross Displacement:	79,500 lbs.
Sail Number:	US 7,099
Sail Area:	7,870 sq. ft.
Engine Model:	Perkins T6.3554
Total Engine Horsepower:	195
Builder Name:	Robert Johnson
Location Built:	Freeport, Grand Bahama Island
Year Built:	1967/1968
Owner Name:	Clifford Ronnenberg
Yacht Club:	Newport Harbor Yacht Club

SOURCES & GRATITUDE

ROBERT F. JOHNSON, THE MAN WHO IMAGINED, built, and raced the yacht the world knows as *Windward Passage*, stands front and center as the inspiration for this book as well as for the yacht herself. He, designer Alan Gurney, and builder Carl Chapman gave birth to a legend that has brought together an exceptional cast of characters whose stories fill these pages.

Bob Johnson's oldest son Mark and his wife Dotty have been enthusiastic supporters of this project, giving freely of their time to share memories and historical memorabilia. They were with *Windward Passage* from her inception in the Bahamas. They campaigned the boat through the first half of the 1970s, following Big Bob's death, and led the way to some of her greatest records like the 1971 Miami–Montego Bay race and the 1971 Transpac "triple crown." Mark's younger brother Fritz "Fritter" Johnson shared the role of skipper starting in 1974 and shepherded *Passage* through years of no-holds-barred racing, particularly in the Southern Ocean, until the Johnson family sold the boat in 1981. He, too, has generously shared his memories and stories.

An invaluable contributor to this book has been David "Halfdeck" Johnson, who has been skipper on *Windward Passage* since 1997. Finally, this book could not have been made without the vision, guidance, and support of Clifford Ronnenberg, owner of *Windward Passage* over the past twenty-three years.

Some of our best sources have been long-term members of the *Windward Passage* crew. They were not only aboard for the racing. They sailed *Passage* hundreds of thousands of miles, delivering her to the start of ocean races in virtually every watery corner of the globe from 1968 to 1986. John "Rumdum" Rumsey, sailmaker and helmsman, gave of his time to unfold recollections and supply us with contacts and photos. John "Gargle"

McClure's enthusiasm for this book project has been more than immensely helpful; it has been inspiring. During their careers in *Windward Passage* both Rumsey and McClure rose through the ranks to be the professional captains aboard. Their longevity with the boat over the course of three different owners gave us a coherent timeline of events as well as vivid anecdotes. Gargle's wife, Cindy Howard McClure, not only witnessed what she calls the "Glory Years" from shore, but joined in on offshore delivery sails and has shared those memories and photos. Both Rumsey and the McClures helped us piece together the history and anecdotes of the four years the late Bill Johnson owned the boat in the early 1980s. Bill's wife Sandra graciously offered her memories and shared her scrapbook with us as well.

Shipwright, sailor, and yacht broker Courtney Ross recounted his experience of taking *Windward Passage* through a major refurbishing in Clearwater, Florida. Courtney raced on *Passage* frequently in the early '80s and had rich collections of stories and images from his scrapbook to add to the legend. Tom Stephenson in Australia shared his story of introducing the boat's third owners, Rod and Kathy Muir, to *Passage* and taking her Down Under.

After turning her loose on the maxi circuit in the mid-1980s, the Muirs saved the boat's life with a major structural restoration in New Zealand that saw *Passage* evolve into a glamorous cruising yacht. They have been generous in contributing their memories and photographs to these pages. Cathy Hawkins, one of Australia's pre-eminent female sailors, shared with us her memories, memorabilia, and photos of racing *Windward Passage* with the first all-female maxi crew.

Kevin Jaffé was the yacht's fourth owner. He and his wife Teresa shepherded the boat through another major restoration in the early 1990s

and took her on a world cruise of the tropics. The Jaffés' restoration of *Passage* and their cruises in her to places like the islands of the Caribbean and the South Pacific are the stuff of dreams.

Several luminary yacht designers weighed in with their thoughts and memories of *Windward Passage*. Thanks to Ron Holland, Bill Lee, and Alan Andrews.

Over her fifty-five years *Passage* has had a legion of crewmembers who cycled on and off the boat for various races, deliveries, and cruises. Some of these men like Greg Palmer, Peter McDonald, and Bobby Steel sailed aboard her during her glory days and have returned to crew aboard her for our contemporary photo shoots. Bobby went above and beyond to share his recollections and connect us to his former shipmates and a network of maxi sailors from "back in the day." Many other sailors (hundreds) were Corinthians who signed aboard *Passage* for a chance to sail a legend. Quite a few of these shipmates have shared their memories with each other and us on the Facebook page "Friends of *Windward Passage*," ably managed by Bill Brewer.

Shipwright Alistair "Tosh" McIntosh spoke about his memories of building the Big Dinghy and shared his photos from the early days with us. Sailor and shipwright Wayne Ettel's video "The Building of *Windward Passage*" tells Tosh's story and includes great graphics, some of which appear in this book. Bill Bowers remembered the never-ending Transatlantic Race crossing. Bill Leary offered his story of a hellacious delivery aboard the yacht from Australia to Hong Kong. Mike Farley bore witness to the night Fritz Johnson got shot after a race in Hawaii.

A special shout-out goes to photographers Phil Uhl, Sharon Green, Onne van der Wal, and Christian Février who contributed striking images to this book. They are four of the most published yachting photographers of the last fifty years. Phil has not only contributed stellar vintage photos to this book of *Windward Passage*, but also images of her rivals. Having been an observer of *Passage* and the maxi-boat scene since its inception in the late 1960s, Phil has been a wealth of knowledge about the chronology of events as well as the colorful cast of characters who sailed in the Glory Days. He has also collaborated with us by offering astute observations and counsel about design elements of the book.

Before becoming president of North Sails, Gary Weisman was a stalwart member of the North Sails band of professional sailors/sailmakers and one of the grand prix race circuit's most respected "drivers." He has vivid memories of the '82 Pan Am Clipper Cup in *Passage* and shares them in this volume.

In addition to John Rumsey and Gargle McClure, many of *Windward Passage*'s other professional skippers have offered their memories and helped us clarify her racing record, her far-ranging delivery trips, and her pleasure cruises. These captains include Peter Garbani, Paul Buttrose, Dave Birchenough, Rob Vaughan, and Mike Hein. More than once these men choked up as the memories came flooding back. Good on you, mates.

Among these professionals, Captain Carson Jefferson stands out. He sailed 80,000 miles aboard *Passage* over a ten-year period in the 1980s and '90s and was instrumental, along with New Zealand shipwright Tim Gurr, in the transformation of *Windward Passage* from grand prix racing machine to a glamorous world-cruising yacht. Carson shared both his stories and his photographs with us for this book. He also dedicated scores of hours helping us to vet a plethora of details in the text. Bravo, Carson!

Alas, we lost Captain Rex Banks and Captain Greg Tuxworth before the creation of this book. Legendary crewmen like Chip Cleary, Don Vaughn,

Vaughn, Arnie Schmelling, Gary Miltemore, Kirk Elliott, Con Findlay, Sandy McKenzie, Tosh McIntosh, Peter Bowker, and Gordo Johnson are gone, too. Although Chip Cleary and Big Bob have passed, we are fortunate to have their narratives of two legendary Transpac Races, preserved in yearbooks of the Lahaina Yacht Club. Owner Bill Johnson, as well as rivals Jim Kilroy, Ken DeMeuse, and Huey Long, have sailed their last races, as have *Windward Passage*'s designer Alan Gurney and naval architect Doug Peterson who updated her rig and underbody more than once. They are sorely missed by their friends and shipmates and have an enduring presence in this volume as well as in the quiet, shadowy places aboard *Windward Passage*.

Many of the crew and their friends have shared photos and memorabilia with us, as well as memories, for this book. We have tried to acknowledge you all here, in the text, and in photo captions. But with such a vast number of professional captains, crew, shipwrights, technicians, and supporters associated with *Windward Passage* over fifty-five years, it is inevitable we will have left out the names, deeds, and kindnesses of relevant, accomplished, and spirited men and women who helped to build the legend of *Windward Passage*. The thought of such oversights nags at us.

The best we can hope for in this regard is that the yacht in her pristine condition (after all the races, all the deliveries, all the cruising, all these decades), and the Facebook page where her friends gather and reminisce, stand as symbols of what so many have given to each other, the yacht, and her everlasting legend.

INDEX

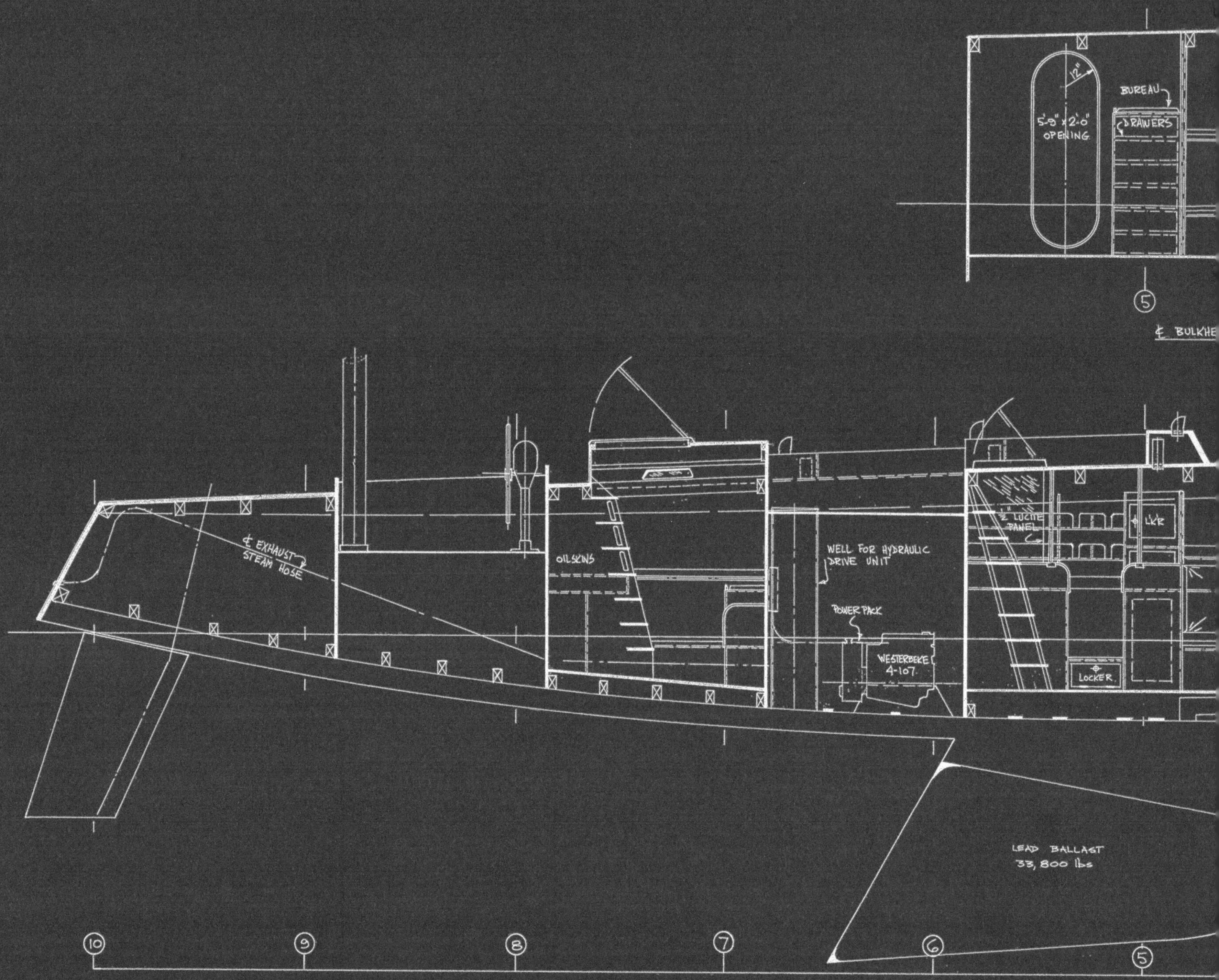

BUREAU
DRAWERS
5'-9" x 2'-0" OPENING
12"
5
℄ EXHAUST STEAM HOSE
OILSKINS
WELL FOR HYDRAULIC DRIVE UNIT
POWER PACK
WESTERBEKE 4-107
℄ LUCITE PANEL
LKR
LOCKER
LEAD BALLAST
33,800 lbs
10
9
8
7
6
5